Goerge T. Denison

Modern Cavalry

Its Organisation, Armament, and Employment in War

Goerge T. Denison

Modern Cavalry
Its Organisation, Armament, and Employment in War

ISBN/EAN: 9783337109356

Printed in Europe, USA, Canada, Australia, Japan

Cover: Foto ©Andreas Hilbeck / pixelio.de

More available books at **www.hansebooks.com**

MODERN CAVALRY:

ITS

ORGANISATION, ARMAMENT,

AND

EMPLOYMENT IN WAR.

WITH

An Appendix

CONTAINING

LETTERS FROM GENERALS FITZHUGH LEE, STEPHEN D. LEE, AND
T. L. ROSSER, OF THE CONFEDERATE STATES' CAVALRY;
AND COL. JENYNS' SYSTEM OF NON-PIVOT DRILL
IN USE IN THE 13TH HUSSARS.

BY

LIEUT.-COL. GEORGE T. DENISON, Jun.

Commanding the Governor-General's Body Guard, Upper Canada;
Author of 'A Manual of Outpost Duties' &c.

LONDON:

THOMAS BOSWORTH, 215 REGENT STREET.

1868.

PREFACE.

—◆—

THE IMPROVEMENTS which have taken place of late
years in the weapons of modern soldiers have rendered necessary a certain amount of change in the
tactics of the different branches of the service; and
the following pages are written with the view of
advocating certain alterations in the organisation,
armament, and employment of cavalry in modern
warfare.

The arguments adduced are based mainly upon
the teachings of the late wars in America and Germany, where for the first time breech-loading and
repeating rifles were used to any great extent. Of
course many of the principles of cavalry operations
are still the same as they have been for ages; on
these points I have followed the rules laid down in
the best authorities on the subject.

In so doing I have consulted, and have to acknowledge the assistance I have received in consulting,
the following works, viz.: Nolan's 'History and Tactics
of Cavalry'; Beamish's 'Use and Application of

Cavalry in War'; Jervis's 'Manual of Field Operations'; and Dufour's 'Strategy and Tactics.'

The chapter on Outposts and Patrols was published as part of a Manual of Outpost Duties some time since. It was compiled by me from the best authorities on the subject, and is reproduced here with some few alterations and additions.

I have also to express my sincere thanks to Generals Fitzhugh Lee, Stephen D. Lee, and Thomas L. Rosser, of the late Confederate States Army, for the kindness and courtesy with which they complied with my request to give me their views on the questions discussed in this book. Their letters are in full in the Appendix, and will well repay an attentive perusal.

I must also express my grateful acknowledgments to Lieut.-General J. A. Early of the same service, one of the ablest generals of the present day, for many kindnesses and much assistance which I have received from him, as well as for the permission which he accorded me of extracting parts of his manuscript notes of his personal recollections of the war, for insertion in these pages.

Heydon Villa, Toronto :
July, 1868.

CONTENTS.

INTRODUCTION.

PAGE

Few Books on Cavalry—Improvements in Fire-Arms—Changes
necessary—General Stephen D. Lee's Opinion .   . xv

CHAPTER I.

CHARACTERISTICS OF CAVALRY.

Peculiarities of Cavalry—Infantry—Artillery—Qualities of
Officers—Great Energy required—Wartensleben at Wurtz-
burg—Cavalry weak after a Charge—Dependent on its
Horses — Should never surrender — Colonel Hasbrouck
Davis—General Forrest—Anecdote of General Seidlitz—
Cavalry must be intelligent—General Rosser's Opinion .   1

CHAPTER II.

ORGANISATION.

Great Diversity of Opinion on this Point—Changes necessary—
Teaching of War in America, 1861 to 1865—In Germany,
1866—Heavy Cavalry—Light Dragoons or Mounted Rifles—
Speed in Movement necessary—Cavalry should be armed to
fight on all Ground—Origin of Dragoons—Alexander of
Parma—Dragoons at Valencia—General Early's Use of them
at Cedar Creek—Men should be chosen for Cavalry—Must
be good Riders—General Rosser's Opinion—Height and
Weight of men—Hozier's Opinion—Cavalry cannot be im-
provised—Squadron Officer necessary—Emperor Nicholas'
Organisation of Dragoons—General John H. Morgan's
Mounted Rifles—Mosby's Partizans—Marmont's Opinion—

PAGE

Kentucky Mounted Riflemen at Moravian Town, 1813—
Captain Ganzauge's Letter—General Stephen D. Lee's Opinion
—Napoleon's View   9

CHAPTER III.

THE COMPARATIVE MERITS OF THE DIFFERENT ARMS.

Sword — Lance — Carbine—Pistol—SWORD the Weapon of Cavalry for Ages—Abolished in many Instances in Confederate
War for Independence—Sword should be sharp — Revolver
seriously affects power of Sabre—The old Pistol useless—
Revolver most deadly—Colonel Harry Gilmor's 'Four Years
in the Saddle '—Colonel Von Borcke—Major Scott's 'Partizan
Life with Mosby '—15th Hussars at Egmont-op-zee—Defeat
of Captain Blazer's Federal Cavalry—Sling of Sword must be
changed—Mexican Arms—Battle of Presburg 1866—Shiloh,
1862—General S. D. Lee on the Weapons—LANCE—Good
for disciplined Troops—Useless with raw Troops—Nolan's
Views wrong—Albuera—Aliwal—Torres Novas—General
Halleck's Views—Von Borcke—General Lloyd's Cavalry
Fight at Saar, 1866—CARBINE—Spencer the best—Sharp and
Snider next in Efficiency—Sights—Tubes—Cartridges—
Carbine should only be used on Foot—General Lloyd on the
Carbine—General Duke's Opinion of Breechloaders—Cavalry
Fight at Ticshnowitz in 1866—PISTOL—Revolver the best
—Changes advocated in its Construction—Its Deadliness
superior to all other Weapons—Examples—Nolan's Views—
Instances from Major Scott's Book—From Colonel Von
Brocke—Colonel Jenyns, 13th Hussars, at Balaklava   .   29

CHAPTER IV.

ARMS OF CAVALRY AND DRAGOONS.

Cavalry of the Line—Swords—Lances—Revolvers—No Carbines
—Swords around the Waist—Revolver on Waist-Belt—*Light
Dragoons or Mounted Rifles*—Carbine the Weapon —Dismount
to fight—Revolvers—Carbine in Bucket on the Saddle—
Sword attached to Saddle not to Man—Revolvers carried on
Waist-Belt—General S. D. Lee's Opinion—General Fitzhugh
Lee's opinion   72

CHAPTER V.

DRESS OF CAVALRY.

Should be neat—Not too elaborate—Jacket—Overalls—Forage
Cap—Jack-boots—Tunics bad—Busby too heavy—Colonel
Jenyns' Opinion—The Felt Hat—No Valises required on
Service—Luggage a Nuisance—Extract from General Early's
Manuscript Notes—Axes required—Blanket—Hozier on
Prussian Troops, in 1866   78

CHAPTER VI.

THE HORSE AND HIS EQUIPMENT.

Value of Cavalry depends on Condition of Horses—Weight
must be reduced—Saddle—Hussar Saddle—M'Clellan
Saddle—General Rosser's opinion—General Fitzhugh and
Stephen D. Lee's views—Experience in my Command—
Letter from Oliver Cromwell on the subject of Saddles—
Riding—Colonel Brackett's Remarks on English Cavalry—
Criticisms on his views—Colonel Brackett on Care of Horses
—Shoes must be attended to — Colonel MacDougall's
Regulations   91

CHAPTER VII.

FORMATION OF CAVALRY AND ELEMENTARY DRILL.

Tactics continually changing—Roman Formation—Greek For-
mation—French—Gustavus Adolphus' Changes—Single-
rank System—General Rosser and Fitzhugh Lee's Ideas—
Non-pivot System—Colonel Jenyns' System the best—In the
Appendix—Tactics of Dragoons—Sir Henry Havelock's Work
—General Morgan's Tactics   102

CHAPTER VIII.

MORALE.

Moral three to one to the physical—Moral Effect greater now
than formerly—Confidence in their Commander creates it in
the Men—Stonewall Jackson—Winning first Battle improves

PAGE

the Morale—Examples in the War in America—Taking the
Initiative—Napoleon—Stonewall Jackson's Morale—General
Breckinridge—McClellan's strategic Change of Base before
Richmond—Breechloaders not so deadly, but improve the
Morale by giving Confidence—Busaco—Kinglake's Account
of the Advance of the Highland Brigade at the Alma   112

CHAPTER IX.

CAVALRY TACTICS.

Cavalry cannot fight defensively—Mounted Rifles can—Cavalry
must be supported—Balaklava—Must have Reserves—
Ground must be reconnoitred—Must have Intervals—Horse
Artillery should accompany—Chancellorsville—Stuart's
Raid in Pennsylvania—Battle of Hartsville, Kentucky—
Second Battle of Hartsville—Monocacy—Sheridan at Five
Forks—Havelock's Remarks on it—Cavalry Tactics must
be changed 124

CHAPTER X.

CAVALRY AGAINST CAVALRY.

Reserves absolutely necessary—Archduke Charles's Views—
Wurzburg—Three Maxims—General Lloyd—Marston Moor
—Leipsic, 1813 – Surprise must be guarded against—Always
take the Initiative—Flanks must be guarded—Château-
Thierry—Balaklava—Captain Krauchenberg at Gallegos—
Colonel Gilmor—Second Manassas Cavalry Fight—Échelon
Formation—The Rally   143

CHAPTER XI.

CAVALRY AGAINST ARTILLERY.

Unsupported Artillery must succumb to Cavalry—Napoleon's
Views—Cavalry must be supported—Balaklava—Jena—
Echmuhl—Somosierra, in 1808—Tobitschau, in 1866—
Splendid Action of Colonel Bredow and his Regiment of
Cuirassiers—Deductions from this Action—Mounted Rifles
against Artillery   153

CHAPTER XII.

CAVALRY AGAINST INFANTRY.

PAGE

Physical Force of Cavalry greater than moral—Bayonets do not stop Cavalry—Opportunities must be chosen to charge—Much rarer—Morale must be kept up—Waterloo not a fair Example—System of charging Squares at Reviews bad—Colonel MacDougall's Suggestion—Another Plan of Drill—Horse Artillery should accompany Cavalry—The great Condé at Rocroi—Monterey in Spain, in 1809—Salamanca—Albuera—Montebello, 1859—Colonel Morelli—Königgrätz—Langelsalza, 1866—Two Prussian Squares with Needle-guns broken by Hanoverian Cavalry—Tobitschau, 1866—Chances of Cavalry against Infantry calculated—Number of Shots fired—Time to cross intervening Space—Probable Loss—Experiments with Breechloaders at Targets silly—Table of Losses at great Battles for 150 Years—Losses diminish as Arms improve—Instances—General Lomax's Cavalry Fight—Difficulty of bringing down Horse and Man—Warnery—Revolvers should be used in charging—Gustavus Adolphus—Instances 162

CHAPTER XIII.

OUTPOSTS AND PATROLS.

Section 1: Definition—Examples—Portugal, 1808—Gebora, 1811—Colonel Adam at Ordal—Stonewall Jackson—Section 2: Formation of Chain of Outposts—Section 3: Posting Videttes and Sentries and their Duties—Section 4: Patrols and their Duties—Section 5: Duties of Officers on Outpost Duty—Section 6: Relieving Outposts—Section 7: Duties of Picquets 189

CHAPTER XIV.

ADVANCED AND REAR GUARDS.

Advanced and Rear Guards absolutely necessary—Mounted Rifles best for this Duty—General Lloyd's Remarks—Scouting Parties—Battle of Luzzara, 1702—Passing Villages

PAGE

—Night Marches—Hozier on Prussian Marches—Entering
Defiles—Stonewall Jackson, 1862—Guides—Lists kept—
Napoleon's Remarks—General Morgan's System of advanced
Guards—General should be well up in the Advance—
Marshal Marmont at Vauchamps—Königgrätz, 1866—
Sailor's Creeks, Virginia, 1865—Rear Guards—Best Men in
the Retreat—Flankers and Scouting Parties—Examples of
rear Guards 224

CHAPTER XV.

RECONNOITRING.

Absolutely necessary—Maps—Napoleon—Reconnaissances in
force—Must be commanded by an experienced Officer—
Should be composed of Mounted Rifles—Moves vigorously
— Guides—Information — Bridges — Roads — Fords — Villages—Duty of Officers—Stuart's Raids—Secret Reconnaissances — Peculiarities — Instructions for topographical
Sketches—*Ruses*—Anecdotes—Benedek   .   .   . 248

CHAPTER XVI.

INTELLIGENCE.

Means of gaining Intelligence—Intercepted Orders—Letters—
Napoleon's Instructions on this Point—Spies—Friendly
Inhabitants—Double spies—Telegraphs—Signals—Strata-
gems—Bivouac Fires—Couriers—Examples   .   . 267

CHAPTER XVII.

MARCHES—CAMPS—SUPPLIES.

MARCHES: Men and Horses should be trained for marching—
Frequent Halts necessary—Columns should not cross each
other — Stonewall Jackson — Night Marches — Colonel
Brackett's Views—Forced Marches—Examples—Prussian
Marches in 1866—Railways—Examples of their Use—
CAMPS: System in America—Not suited to Europe—Tents—
Huts—Billeting—SUPPLIES: Feeding Infantry—Cavalry—
Requisitions—Foraging—Magazines—Carriage of Supplies. 287

CHAPTER XVIII.

PASSAGE OF DEFILES AND RIVERS.

PAGE

PASSAGE OF DEFILES by Cavalry very different from former Plan—Nolan's Instructions out of Date—Changes—Present System—General Sohr—PASSAGE OF RIVERS : Changes required under the proposed armament of Cavalry—System laid down—Mounted Rifles—Bridges—Swimming Horses . 307

CHAPTER XIX.

SURPRISES AND AMBUSCADES.

Surprises very difficult if Enemy's Outposts are efficient—Ambuscades also if the advanced Guards are vigilant—Care taken in Surprises—Great Secrecy required—Rules—Examples   317

CHAPTER XX.

CONVOYS.

Convoys not so important now—Railways do most of the Work—Convoys sometimes necessary—Escorts—Part Infantry part mounted Rifles—Care as to Line of March—Examples—Tobitschau—Rules for Convoys—Duties of Officers   323

CHAPTER XXI.

FLAGS OF TRUCE.

Officer bearing Flag must be a Man of Intelligence—Trumpeter should also be shrewd and steady—Both should be careful in their Conversation—Flag should not be received except from commanding General — Examples — Colonel Von Borcke's Flag of Truce to M'Clellan, in 1863   .   . 330

APPENDIX.

PAGE

A. COLONEL JENYNS' SYSTEM OF NON-PIVOT DRILL .   341

B. TWO LETTERS FROM GENERAL FITZHUGH LEE   .   .   351

C. LETTER FROM GENERAL STEPHEN D. LEE   .   .   362

D.   ,,   ,,   GENERAL THOMAS L. ROSSER   .   .   366

E.   ,,   ,,   A GENERAL OFFICER C.S.A. ON THE SADDLE
AND REVOLVER   369

INTRODUCTION.

Le perfectionnement des armes à feu a produit une grande sensation dans l'armée.—*Comte de Rochefort.*

THERE is, perhaps, no subject of any importance that has been so little written upon, and concerning which so few books have been published in our language, as the Organisation, Armament, and Employment of Cavalry in War. While innumerable treatises and works on artillery and engineering have been continually issued from our presses, and while, to a smaller degree, a great number of authors have written on subjects connected with the infantry service, the books confined exclusively to the cavalry are very few in number, the only works of any value being Captain Nolan's 'Cavalry, its History and Tactics,' and Colonel Beamish's 'Use and Application of Cavalry in War.'

The extraordinary changes which have taken place of late years in the armament of the other forces, and the wonderful improvements that have been made in projectile weapons have altered the comparative value of the different branches of the army, and have necessitated many variations in the principles of organisation and equipment, as well as in the tactics of the cavalry service, as laid down in the books hitherto published on the subject.

The formation and arming of cavalry at the present day must, necessarily, differ to a certain extent from the system adopted by Frederick the Great, in the wars of his age. At that time, armies fought on level plains, pioneers made parallel roads for the columns, and one might overlook a whole battle-field. The cavalry then had not the advantages of the improved fire-arms of to-day, and had not to fear the deadly effect of the breech-loading rifle. They were, consequently, in most cases, provided with cuirasses to protect them from the fire of small arms, a defence useful in that age, but utterly useless against the arms of our modern infantry.

It is absurd, therefore, to organise cavalry now on the same system as in the 'Seven Years' War,' or even in the wars of the French Revolution and of the reign of Napoleon, for the circumstances under which the system originated have changed, and as the groundwork has gone, the structure based upon it cannot stand.

The principle of this world is progress; it has always progressed (I will not say whether always in the right direction) and will always do so, it is a law of nature. This principle applies more to the art of war than to any other subject. The organisation of the different branches of armies is, therefore, ever changing, ever improving. If one service remains at a stand-still, it loses its place among the others, they pass it, and it depreciates in value. This is the case with the cavalry. While the greatest improvements have been effected in the arms and equipment of the artillery and infantry, cavalry has been allowed to retrocede. It does not now hold the high position it occupied in the days of Turenne, of Marlborough, and of Frederick the Great.

At the present day, the telegraph has replaced the courier or mounted orderly in the transmission of orders, the railway has taken the place of the long tedious convoys of stores and provisions, and serves also to concentrate armies more speedily than by the old system of marches; balloons are used for reconnoitring, the 'Needle-gun,' the 'Chassepot,' and the 'Snider' have replaced the old 'Brown

a

Bess,' and the Armstrong guns and rifled cannon have replaced the smooth bore artillery; and yet, what improvements have been made in the cavalry arms and accoutrements? Comparatively speaking, none. Cavalry in most countries are now armed with almost the same weapons as when Alexander the Great used them against the Persians. They are armed with lances and swords as they were when Richard 'Cœur de Lion,' with his English chivalry, defied the Saracen host at Jaffa, or when Seidlitz and Ziethen at the head of the Prussian cavalry astonished the world by their deeds of arms at Zorndorf, Leuthen, and Rosbach.

It must be admitted that the improvements in fire-arms have wonderfully increased the value and power of the artillery and infantry, and it is manifestly important that an attempt should be made to so apply the advantages and powers of the modern projectile weapons to the arming of the cavalry service, as to improve its efficiency, increase its value, and enable it to compete on more favourable terms with the other arms.

A great war has lately been waged on the continent of America. The natural and physical features of the country, rendered it impossible to employ cavalry in the same manner, and according to the same rules as are followed in the mounted forces of European nations. A new system of tactics suited to the time and applicable to the locality, was instinctively adopted and employed during the war by both parties. Colonel Heros Von Borcke, of General Stuart's staff, says distinctly on this point: 'The nature of the ground in Virginia did not favour the operations of cavalry, and the great improvements in fire-arms in our day had necessitated a very material change in cavalry tactics.'

Lieut.-General Stephen D. Lee, a well-known and distinguished officer of the Confederate States army, in a letter to me with reference to this point says: 'In my opinion the great improvement in fire-arms has made an essential change in the handling and using of cavalry, and the charge against infantry or cavalry as formerly is less frequent and more dangerous. The long range fire-arms now in use are so effective, that battles are decided quickly and at longer range than formerly, and the hand-to-hand conflict is not so frequent. Hostile bodies are compelled to approach each other with more caution, and cavalry offering a good and effective mark must select its opportunity for the charge or it will pay dearly for it.'

If then our service is organised in the best possible method, if the tactics are changed to suit the changed circumstances, there is little doubt that this branch of the service will once again occupy the proud position it formerly held, and become the most powerful, as well as the most useful, portion of armies.

Holding these views, I will endeavour, in the following pages, to show the changes required in the organisation, armament, and tactics of cavalry, under the present condition of military affairs.

MODERN CAVALRY.

CHAPTER I.

CHARACTERISTICS OF CAVALRY.

La Cavalerie paraît, de toutes les armes, la plus difficile à manier.
Jacquinot de Presle.

An ARMY is mainly composed of three different kinds of troops—viz. Cavalry, Artillery, and Infantry.

Each description or arm is entirely distinct in its composition, in its armament, and in its method of fighting, and each has its own peculiar characteristics. For instance, the cavalry perform their duties boldly and impetuously; the gunner in battle quietly and steadily, being guided alone by the art which he practises; while the infantry execute theirs in a regular, composed and collected manner.

It will be perceived, therefore, that the leaders of the different arms of the service require different talents and dispositions. It will also be perceived

that the cavalry leader requires the rarest combina-
tion of talent. He must have the great prudence
which is always required in an officer holding a responsible post; and at the same time he must possess
extraordinary rashness and bravery, and combine the
greatest calmness with the greatest impetuosity.

For with the cavalry the greatest prudence must
be used in the conception of a plan, the greatest
boldness and impetuosity in the execution of it, the
greatest calmness in retreating under disaster, and
the greatest caution in pursuing in the event of
success.

Without a general, therefore, who understands the
characteristics of cavalry, and is suited to lead it to
success, it will never perform deeds worthy to be
recorded in history. But where it has been led by
good generals, it has not been a mere stop-gap in
the line of battle, but an active co-operator in the
victory, overthrowing everything in its impetuous
rush, like the inundation of a mighty river carrying
away and destroying every impediment with its
irresistible force.

All celebrated cavalry officers have been noted for
the energy, the zeal, the impetuosity, I may say, the
fire of their dispositions; and they have excelled
each other only, in possessing to a greater degree
the caution and prudence necessary to a responsible

command. There may have been cavalry officers of reputation who have altogether lacked the caution, Prince Rupert for example, but we will venture to assert that there never was one with the slightest claim to the name who lacked the energy and the impetuosity.

Wartensleben at Wurzburg in 1796 showed the true spirit of a cavalry officer. Archduke Charles, in his 'Principes de la Stratégie,' after stating that Wartensleben was ordered to form up immediately on the right wing of Sztarray, says: 'Struck with the importance of this order, this brave veteran swam across the Main at the head of his cavalry (24 squadrons) and marched through Bibergau, while his infantry passed over the bridge.'

It is necessary that cavalry should always have reserves at hand, when an attack is made to support the attacking force, and it is a peculiar characteristic of this arm that success will always lean to the side which brings up the last reserves.

Cavalry is never weaker or easier overcome than immediately after a success. The men and horses are blown, the lines disordered, confusion reigns paramount, orders are not heard or attended to, and a fresh force falling upon it in that state will invariably put it to rout.

Cavalry are the eyes and ears of an army; they

form an impenetrable curtain around it, which pro-
tects it from surprise, conceals its movements, and
gives warning of the designs of the enemy. This is
one of its most important uses, and in this way it is
invaluable to a force engaged in hostilities. It is
also the most useful force for foraging and reconnoitring, and is specially adapted for these services.
It is always dependent upon the condition of its
horses. If they are not in an efficient state, if their
shoes are not carefully looked to and sore backs
guarded against, they are soon destroyed, and the
force becomes worthless.

Cavalry should never surrender—this is one of the
best established maxims of the arm, at any rate in
a country at all open. It must always attempt to
cut its way through, or, if that is impossible, by
scattering to elude pursuit. Herein it differs from
the other forces. A good example of the benefit of
this principle occurred when Stonewall Jackson was
besieging Harper's Ferry in Virginia, in September
1862. Colonel Hasbrouck Davis, who commanded
the Northern cavalry in that place, made his way
out by an unguarded road the night before the
surrender with his whole mounted force; and during
the night this corps under its bold leader accidentally
came in contact with General Longstreet's ordnance
trains, capturing and destroying a great number of

the waggons, and stampeding the whole of the teams. At the capture of Fort Donelson in Kentucky, in 1862, General Forrest cut his way through the beleaguering lines, and brought off his entire regiment.

An anecdote of General Seidlitz, Frederick the Great's celebrated cavalry leader, the most distinguished cavalry officer of ancient or modern times, will not be out of place here as an illustration of this principle, as well as of the spirit which should animate an officer of this arm of the service. It is translated from Comte de Rochefort's 'Idées pratiques sur la Cavalerie.' 'Seidlitz, to whom Frederick owed the greater part of his success, was so skilful, so vigorous a horseman, that he could not conceive how an officer of cavalry could be made prisoner if his horse was not killed.

'Once he expressed this opinion while escorting the king when he was captain of the guard. Frederick, whom nothing escaped, was struck with his remarks, and decided to put him to the proof. The opportunity soon presented itself.

'The escort was obliged to pass over a bridge; the king stopped in the middle of it, and turning towards Seidlitz, who was surrounded in front and rear, said to him :—

'You pretend, Monsieur Seidlitz, that an officer

of cavalry ought never to be made prisoner; certainly
it is the idea of a brave man, nevertheless there are
occasions where one could surrender without dis-
honour. Suppose, for instance, that we were enemies,
you would not attempt to pass by force. What
would you do, then?'

Seidlitz, prompt as thought, drove in his spurs,
and threw himself with his horse into the torrent,
and without suffering any injury, returned to the
rear of the retinue near the king, whom he saluted,
saying: ' Sire, behold my reply.'

Frederick on one occasion found fault with
Seidlitz on account of the number of deaths caused
by accidents in drilling over rough ground with his
regiment. Seidlitz coolly answered : ' If you make
such a fuss about a few broken necks, your Majesty
will never have the bold horsemen you require for
the field.'

Cavalry is a very difficult arm to handle in the
field ; it easily gets out of hand and becomes dispersed.

It cannot be employed mounted except in situations
where the ground is favourable.

It has no fire, and therefore is not suitable for
defence, and can only resist an attack by making an
anticipatory onset.

Its reputation is not affected by a repulse. For

cavalry that has been overthrown and driven off the field in confusion, has often rallied and reappeared, confident and victorious. This is caused by the rapidity of its movement.

Cavalry is as necessary to cover the retreat of a beaten army, as to pursue an enemy when victorious. In fact a defeated army without cavalry to cover its retreat is liable to be annihilated, especially if the victors pursue with a strong proportion of that force; as, for example, the pursuit of the Prussian army after Jena in 1806, or the pursuit of the French army after Waterloo, when the French cavalry had been shattered by many charges against an army in position. On the other hand, the Austrian cavalry, in 1866 at Königgrätz, so effectually covered the retreat of the broken infantry, that the latter suffered little or nothing in retreating.

The charge of cavalry must be rapid and unexpected, and must be made with confidence, and pushed 'home.' There should be no doubt when the order to charge is once given—then caution should give way to impetuosity.

Cavalry proper once dismounted are no longer formidable. Napoleon had about 10,000 dismounted men at Moscow in 1812. They were formed into companies, battalions, and regiments, and were armed like the infantry, but after the first three days' retreat, the men, discouraged at being on foot, dispersed, and the whole organisation was destroyed. In fact, so important are the horses, that the effective strength of cavalry is never reckoned by the number of men, but by the number of horses.

Cavalry men require to be more intelligent and better drilled than in the other forces. On outpost duty, patrolling and reconnoitring, the men are obliged to use their own judgment. This does not occur to anything like the same extent in the infantry or artillery. On this point I quote from a letter received by me from Major-General Thomas L. Rosser, one of the most distinguished of the cavalry leaders of the Confederate States of America. He says:—

'Cavalry which is not *thoroughly drilled*, and *ably officered* is worthless under any circumstances. These requisites are necessary in every arm, but more so in cavalry than any other, for in battle a cavalry soldier has his frightened horse to manage, and at the same time to use his weapon at close quarters upon his adversary, whilst infantry and artillery are employed more or less at long range.'

CHAPTER II.

ORGANISATION.

La Cavalerie n'est pas si facile à improviser que l'infanterie.

General Foy.

THE organisation of cavalry is a subject concerning which there has always been a great diversity of opinion. The different writers on cavalry matters, and the various commanders who have been intrusted with the organisation of this arm, have generally advocated and adopted different systems, to suit the method of warfare of their times or the arms and tactics of their opponents.

It is proposed in this work to propound a system of organisation and equipment for cavalry, modified to suit the altered state of the armament of the other branches of the service, and based upon the results of the war in America from 1861 to 1865, and the war in Germany in 1866. As has been before stated, the improvements in the weapons of the other arms necessitates a totally different method of em-

ploying mounted men, so as to apply the improved
weapons to that service and give to it the full
advantages of them.   I shall therefore give my views
plainly and frankly, and endeavour to show good
reasons based upon facts for the propositions I ad-
duce.   Many may differ with me, but we must
remember that we are in a state of transition in the
tactical management of all three arms, and that
whoever brings forward views carefully considered
may add some little information or give some useful
hint on the subject on which he is writing.

In the first place, then, cavalry should be divided
into two distinct species.

Heavy cavalry or cavalry of the line.

Light dragoons or mounted rifles.

Speed in movement is one of the greatest elements
of success in war.   So much was the great Napoleon
imbued with this idea, that he expressed the opinion
that an army of 10,000 men which could average
twenty miles a day, would produce as great an effect
on the success of a campaign as one of 20,000
which marched only ten miles a day.   If this is
true, and it undoubtedly is the correct principle, if
by placing 10,000 men upon horses we enable them
to move at twice the rate of speed at which they
could march on foot, their value ought to be increased two-fold, and they ought to be equal to

20,000 men. But we have seen that cavalry cannot defend a position, cannot even act effectively on the defensive, that they cannot act on every description of ground or attack entrenched positions; therefore in most instances these circumstances would detract from the value of the 10,000 men, and counterbalance the effect of the extra speed. But if these men, on arriving at the point where they are required, can dismount and fight on foot as infantry, they can then be used on any kind of ground, and cannot fear the danger of being cut off in case of being obliged to retreat. This fact led to the formation of dragoons.

Prince Alexander of Parma, when in 1552 he wished to surprise the Duke of Alençon, mounted several companies of infantry on pack horses, and thus hastened towards the enemy. This was the first instance of the employment of that force, and shortly afterwards it became customary to mount large bodies of infantry in order to move them quickly upon the decisive points, until at length dragoons came to form a portion of every army. Now that firearms are so much more deadly than heretofore, so much the greater advantage will be derived from the employment of mounted men trained to fight on foot with these new weapons.

Numberless examples can be adduced to show the wonderful advantages to be derived from the use of a force of this nature, able to act on any kind of ground, able to ride round and beyond the enemy's infantry, to cut it off in the retreat, to destroy its communications, seize its trains, and burn the bridges in its rear.

These light dragoons or mounted rifles should also have the duty of watching over the safety of the army, and are expected to perform outpost duty, to reconnoitre, to harass the march of the enemy, and to pursue him when beaten.

Many instances have occurred where officers have mounted infantry behind cavalry, in order hurriedly to seize positions or make attacks, or the more effectively to pursue a retreating enemy.

After the battle of Valencia in 1811, Suchet sent three parties of French cavalry, each man having an infantry man behind him on his horse, in order to overtake some of the remnants of Blake's army. In consequence of the speed of the pursuit, the parties were not able to rally, and shortly afterwards Blake surrendered.

Lieut.-Colonel Simcoe, of the Queen's Rangers, in the American Revolution of 1776, sometimes gave his cavalry muskets when he wished hurriedly to surprise a post he could not attack mounted.

In 1864, in the Shenandoah Valley, just before the battle of Cedar Creek, General Early, commanding the

Confederate army in that part of Virginia, detached General Rosser with a brigade of infantry mounted behind the same number of cavalry, to attempt the surprise and capture of a camp of a brigade of the Northern cavalry who were separated from the main army. It was effected in the night, the camp surprised, and the whole force captured, although it was not so large as had been anticipated, the greater portion of the enemy having changed their position the evening before, a strong picket only being left behind.

The services performed by the dragoons or mounted rifles were very valuable all through the Confederate war for independence. And without doubt this force was far more available and useful, as well as suitable to the natural features of the country, than regular cavalry would have been.

Another great advantage in mounted rifles is that they do not require the same amount of training and instruction as the regular cavalry, and very often the recruits are more adapted to the service, as well naturally as by habit, than to the cavalry of the line. If armies are raised hurriedly, or new levies are called out, the mounted force should be composed of riflemen or dragoons. Men in civil life learn nothing of the use of the sabre, but most men know a little about the use of fire-arms, and at any rate the same time is not required to create the same skill in the use of the rifle, and under any circumstances it is not so important.

Men should not be enrolled at once into the cavalry or dragoons. The recruits for an army should be brought together into large camps of instruction, and there drilled and exercised, in order to learn somewhat of their abilities, both physically and mentally. In Prussia every young man is obliged to serve between the ages of twenty to twenty-five for a certain period of time. They do not choose which force they will enter, but a board of officers from each branch of the service determines into what part of the army the recruit shall be en-rolled. This is the proper system; it is useless to put men into any service unless they are better qualified for that than for any other.

Again, men should be chosen, if possible, who are good riders. It takes so long a time to teach a man to ride, and to get him so perfectly accustomed to his horse as to have a thorough mastery over him, that it is well, if possible, to obtain men who have been accustomed to horses from their childhood, for it is a strange yet true fact, that men who have never learned to ride in their youth have seldom become good horsemen in after years. Speaking on this subject, Count Bismark, in his 'Lectures on Cavalry,' gives a somewhat amusing, yet nevertheless a very correct view. He says : ' What, for instance, is to be expected from a stocking manufacturer, or linen weaver, who considers the horse as a wild beast ? It is well known that such men never have confidence in their horses, but look upon them as their greatest enemies, against whom for the future they struggle for their lives. They never learn to ride, never can preserve their balance, but hang on the horse like a senseless lump, which, in order to preserve its equilibrium, unnecessarily wastes a great part of its strength, and on this account is soon exhausted.

' Therefore we find some horses in a squadron who, at the slowest pace, sweat and tire themselves exceedingly. The horse becomes at last refractory against the ignorant and heavy hand of its rider ; he hangs upon the bridle, overcome by the pain of his mouth, goes crooked, jumps, &c. The rider, whose fear and anxiety increases, clings still closer, and tires himself by sticking with his knees and heels, in order to prevent himself from falling. Thus the quietest horse becomes at last passionate, and will endeavour either to get rid of his burthen, or to run away.

' Such an ignorant rider often brings an entire squadron into disorder, which in a charge must be productive of fatal consequences, added to which, a man who cannot manage his horse will be unable to do any injury to the enemy.'

General Rosser, from whose letter to me I have before quoted, in reference to the cavalry soldier, says: ' No soldier should be taken into the cavalry service *directly*, but into a general camp of instruction, and there exercised in the use of the various arms, until his capacity for each be determined, intellectually and physically. Then no one should be taken into the cavalry who is not possessed of at least ordinary intelligence, a strong constitution, and of more than ordinary muscular power, for in battles, his muscle and the weight of his horse are to determine results. Hence he should be a good rider, and possess a strong arm.

' My experience has been that the majority of men are defective as soldiers in the feet, and if this is the only difficulty, they answer just as good a purpose for cavalry service with this defect as without it.'

This opinion of an experienced soldier in America is fully borne out by the results of the last war in Germany. It has been held that the men in the cavalry should be light small men, especially for the light cavalry, and many writers have lately strongly argued this view. Nolan particularly advocates small men. He says five feet four inches is a good height, and the weight on the horse's back is light-

ened. In this there is no doubt he was wrong. Low
stature does not necessarily carry with it light weight,
nor tall stature heavy weight. A good example came
under my own experience while on service during
the Fenian raid on Fort Erie in 1866. My height
was 5 feet 11¼ inches, and my weight about 148 lbs. ;
my trumpeter was 5 feet 3½ inches in height, while
his weight was 205 lbs. It is to be hoped that the
reader will not make any invidious comparisons
between me and my trumpeter, and Don Quixote
and Sancho Panza.

The advantage of the length of limb of a tall man,
if the weight is not great, is of much importance in
a cavalry soldier. If he rides well his seat is more
secure, while the leverage of a long arm makes the
sword a more deadly weapon in his hands.

Hozier, in his History of the 'Seven Weeks War'
of 1866, gives many instances where the tall strong
men of the Prussian cavalry overpowered the lighter
Austrian troops, and in one place he remarks : 'The
experience of this campaign has taught, that needle
guns and rifled artillery have no more driven cavalry,
and even very heavy cavalry, from the field of battle
than they have from the theatre of war. But it has
been found that in the shock of closing squadrons,
small men and light horses must go down before the
powerful onset of stouter assailants.'

After the men have been first tested in a camp of instruction, the men best suited for the mounted forces should be chosen and drilled together for a time, and the most active and powerful swordsmen and the best riders should be placed in the cavalry of the line, and the remainder organised into dragoon regiments or mounted rifles.   The proportion of the two services combined, with reference to the whole army, should be as one to five.   Gustavus Adolphus had 13,000 foot to 8,850 horse, more than one-third.

This proportion, however, I consider too great, especially if the armies are large.   Napoleon held that cavalry should be one-fourth of the army, but in mountainous countries, one-fifth.

Cavalry cannot be organised or drilled quickly—it takes time, and should be carefully attended to in peace.   Volunteer cavalry should always be dragoons or, what is the same thing, mounted rifles, as they have not time to reach the perfection in drill required for the other branch of the service.

In the Confederate war for independence, both parties found the difficulty of organising or drilling cavalry hurriedly, and however incredible it may appear, it is nevertheless a fact, that when the Federal forces under command of General McDowell marched to Manassas in 1861, to fight the battle of Bull's Run, there were, in an army of some 40,000 men, exactly seven companies of cavalry, hardly one small regiment! and that on the other side the proportion was not much greater. Later in the war, the Northern States, at one time supported as many as 80,000 mounted men, almost all mounted riflemen.

In the early part of the war great difficulty was experienced in drilling.

In his life of Stonewall Jackson, Dabney says on this subject: ' Colonel Ashby had little genius for organisation and discipline, tasks which at best are arduous in a force continually scattered upon outposts, and harassed by hardships, and which were impracticable for a commander seconded by few competent officers, and compelled to launch his raw levies at once into the employments of veteran troopers.'

When the men are chosen and assigned to the different services, they should be divided into regiments of four squadrons of about one hundred and twenty men each, and each squadron should have a separate officer to command it, one who is known as its chief to attend to its internal management in barrack and in the camp, and to lead it in the field. The troop officers should be likewise attached to their troops. The system of the English army, where the senior officer of the two troops commands the squadron is a mistake, and adopted to save the expense of the extra officer; but there is no doubt

that it is false economy, and that the same amount
of money might be saved in a much better way.

The cavalry proper, or cavalry of the line, should
be organised and armed for the charge alone; they
should never be used as dragoons.   Comte de Rochefort, in his ' Idées pratiques sur la Cavalerie,' holds
this view, and General Rosser, in the letter before
quoted, says: ' It (the cavalry) is worthless except in
the charge, and should never be used for any other
purpose.   The cavalry soldier should never be dismounted to fight, if you expect him to ride over
masses of infantry, but be educated to the belief that
*nothing can withstand a well-executed charge of
cavalry*, and should feel perfectly " at home " on
horseback.   All picketing should be done by mounted
rifles, and all escorts and guards for trains and the like
should be composed of the same.   *And the cavalry
always kept in mass, and used in the charge alone.*'

To show the necessity of having the two methods
of using mounted men, I quote again from General
Rosser's letter: ' During the late war, I rode into
the strongly fortified post of New Creek and captured
the garrison with cavalry, and with the loss of only
two men, but when I undertook the same thing at
Beverly, I saw I would not succeed on horseback,
and dismounted in 200 yards of the camp, and attacked it as infantry, and thus easily accomplished

on foot, that which I undoubtedly would have failed in on horseback.'

The Emperor Nicholas of Russia was much struck with the value of dragoons to fight dismounted, and in 1833 organised a complete corps, consisting of eight regiments of ten squadrons each, eight squadrons being armed with muskets and bayonets, and destined to fight on foot, the two others being armed with lances and composing the cavalry proper of the corps.

The eight squadrons formed when dismounted a battalion of eight companies, and the centre man of each three held the horses of the other two. All the squadrons of lancers united together, and made two regiments of cavalry of eight squadrons each. This corps had also a pontoon train and artillery, and presented when in line eight battalions, sixteen squadrons, thirty-two cannon, and sixteen pontoons. It required 15,000 horses. This force was disbanded before it was ever tested in actual service. The great fault with it lay in the armament: long muskets and bayonets are not the most convenient weapons to carry or to use on horseback, and it can easily be imagined that the greatest difficulty and confusion would occur in a mounted force so clumsily armed.

In the Confederate war for independence, this

.dea was carried out, though not to the same extent.
The mounted rifles fought on foot, some being held
in hand to charge if the opportunity offered, while
a few pieces of artillery always accompanied the
mounted men in all their operations.   In Kentucky,
General Morgan's command had attached to them
two small mountain howitzers, which were easily
transported, could be kept along with the main body
in the most hurried marches, and enabled them to
succeed against stockades and intrenchments when
without them they would most assuredly have failed.
His men became very much attached to these pieces,
and christened them the ' Bull pups,' and always
cheered them loudly when they came into action.

General John H. Morgan applied this principle of
mounted rifles to its fullest extent.   General Basil
W. Duke, in his ' History of Morgan's Cavalry,' says :
' Whatever merit may be allowed or denied General
Morgan, he is beyond all question entitled to the
credit of having discovered uses for cavalry, or
rather mounted infantry, to which that arm was
never applied before.   While other cavalry officers
were adhering to the traditions of former wars and
the systems of the schools, however inapplicable to
the demands of their day, and the nature of the
struggle, he originated and perfected not only a
system of tactics, a method of fighting and handling

men in the presence of the enemy, but also a strategy as effective as it was novel.

'Totally ignorant of the art of war as learned from the books and in the academies—an imitator is nothing ; self-taught in all that he knew and did, his success was not more marked than his genius.

'The creator and organiser of his own little army, with a force which at no time reached 4,000, he *killed and wounded* nearly as many of the enemy, and captured more than 15,000. The author of the far-reaching "raid," so different from the mere cavalry dash, he accomplished, with his handful of men, results which would otherwise have required armies and the costly preparations of regular and extensive campaigns.'

Colonel John S. Mosby, the celebrated Confederate partisan leader, was one of the most efficient partisan officers the war produced, and the career of his command shows what can be effected by a mounted force so armed and equipped as to adapt itself to every description of ground. Major John Scott, one of his officers, and a gallant soldier, has written an account of the operations of Mosby's command, and in his dedication thus speaks of him :
'With a command of his own creation, at no time numbering more than a few hundred kindred spirits,

he planted himself in a district abandoned to the occupation of the enemy, and besides capturing a multitude of prisoners, destroying many millions of public property, kept in a defensive attitude, according to their own admission, 35,000 of their troops, which would otherwise have been employed on the active theatre of war. But this was not all. More than once, with his band of followers he compelled the invading armies to relinquish actual and projected lines of communication, to fall back from advanced positions, and, if we may credit the assertion of the Federal Secretary of War, occasioned the loss by the enemy of an important battle.'

This certainly is most valuable testimony in favour of this species of service, and it is borne out by the facts.

Marshal Marmont, in his 'Esprit des Institutions Militaires,' says : ' In the beginning dragoons were only mounted infantry; they should always have preserved that character. With this condition dragoons may in a thousand circumstances render immense service—in detachments, for surprises, in retrograde movements, and principally in pursuit. . . . Nothing is more useful than the establishment of dragoons, but they must not be perverted.'

At the battle of Moravian Town, in Western Canada, on October 5, 1813, where our troops were beaten, the defeat was caused by a charge of Colonel Johnson's regiment of Kentucky mounted riflemen. By this charge our infantry were entirely broken up and many captured. Johnson then turned to his left, and attempted to charge a large force of Indians who were stationed in the edge of a growth of timber, but he found the ground was swampy, and his horses began to sink. Seeing this, he ordered his men to dismount and make the attack on foot. Tecumseth and his braves were defeated, Tecumseth being killed. We cannot imagine a more striking example of the advantage of having mounted riflemen, equipped to fight on foot in case of necessity; this regiment having fought in two capacities in about as many minutes.

I shall quote here an extract from a letter published in Nolan's book, written by Captain Ganzauge, of the Prussian Lancers of the Guard, showing that this system of fighting was also in use among the Cossacks in the war of 1813 and 1814, and was of advantage to them in their operations. He says : 'During great part of the last war against the French, I was attached to the Cossacks of the Don. These men were at that time but little accustomed to the use of firearms. Whilst advancing into Western Europe, the advantages of firearms became apparent, more particularly when acting in inter-

sected and difficult ground, and the Cossacks managed to arm themselves with French infantry
muskets which they picked up on the field. Then
originated amongst them the practice of *dismounting*
by turns when *the ground was favourable,* and thus
engaging the enemy in skirmishing order. I have
myself seen them in this way beat cavalry very
superior to them in numbers, and infantry, when
either the cavalry or the infantry attempted to
attack them singly. In such cases the infantry
soldiers opposed to them were afraid of the mounted
men, who stuck close to their dismounted comrades
with the led horses, and these dismounted men were
ready to jump into the saddle at any moment and
rush upon the enemy, if they gave way or were
driven from their cover.

'*To this manner of skirmishing I attribute the
success of the Cossacks during the campaign on the
Elbe and the Rhine, and the decided superiority
they acquired over the enemy's cavalry, in all
outpost work and detached warfare.*'

The opinions of General Stephen D. Lee on this
question of mounted rifles are so much to the point,
that they are quoted here as the views of an officer
of great experience in actual war. In his letter to
me before mentioned, he says : ' The repeating rifle
makes him a mounted rifleman, and is all-important

since the great improvements in firearms as to range and efficiency, and on foot the cavalry man is almost the equal of the infantry soldier, lacking only in metal, and under ordinary circumstances his weapon is just as effective. He does not hesitate to engage infantry as formerly.

'The equipment of the cavalry man with the recent repeating rifle, and revolvers of modern invention, in my opinion has increased his efficiency proportionally more than either the infantry or artillery arm has been by the inventions applicable to those arms. It enables the commanding general almost to detach an army-corps of infantry with the celerity of cavalry for an important blow, at a distance or even on an extended battle-field, for a critical flank. Almost in all ages the cavalry man has held himself superior to the infantry man, but when brought to the actual test before unprejudiced judges, has had in almost every instance to yield to the stolid infantry man, for whom he always had and still has a deep respect. Now he has some excuse for his proud assumption, for he is almost the equal, and the respect of the two arms of the service is mutual; the infantry not having the cavalry in contempt as formerly. A large body of cavalry as now armed is a match for almost any emergency. And it is an army in motion, and on a flank its blow is terrible,

and against communications, magazines, &c. its
damage disastrous.'

Napoleon even, the great Napoleon, has given his
testimony in favour of this description of service, and
his remarks strongly support the formation of
mounted rifles. He says: 'Cavalry of all descriptions
should be furnished with firearms, and should know
how to manœuvre on foot. Three thousand light
cavalry, or three thousand cuirassiers, should not
suffer themselves to be stopped by a thousand infantry
posted in a wood or on ground impracticable to
cavalry, and three thousand dragoons ought not to
hesitate to attack two thousand infantry should the
latter, favoured by their position, attempt to stop
them.'

˙CHAPTER III.

THE COMPARATIVE MERITS OF THE DIFFERENT ARMS.

WE will consider here the different arms which have been in use in mounted forces, and the comparative advantages and disadvantages connected with each, taking into consideration—

1. THE SWORD.
2. THE LANCE.
3. THE CARBINE.
4. THE PISTOL.

1. *The Sword.*—This arm has been from time immemorial the weapon *par excellence* of the cavalry; and although great changes have been made in the shape and dimensions of swords, nevertheless all species of cavalry have until lately invariably carried them. In the Confederate war for independence, however, large bodies of what were called cavalry, but were in reality mounted riflemen, did not carry the sabre at all.

The cavalry of the line should undoubtedly be

armed with the sabre, which should be light, very
sharp, and nearly straight. The scabbard should be
well lined with wood to preserve the edge of the
sword, and the weapon should, if possible, be one
capable of cutting down an adversary at a blow.
Captain Nolan, in his 'History and Tactics of Cavalry,'
has so thoroughly gone into this question of the
sharpness of the swords, and has proved his position
so conclusively by examples of the Sikh horsemen in
the Indian wars, that there should be no longer any
doubt on .this point, and consequently no necessity
to go over that ground again.

A serious question, however, has arisen since the
last war in America, as to whether the revolving
pistol has not taken the precedence in the *mêlée* over
the sword. I have no doubt that this idea will be
scouted by many of my brother officers in the cavalry
as absurd and contrary to the whole traditions and
genius of our service. If there is one principle which
the works on cavalry lay down more positively than
another, it is that cavalry using the sabre will always
overcome cavalry using any description of fire-arms.
This was undoubtedly correct formerly, when the old
flint-lock horse-pistol was the weapon used, an arm
comparatively speaking worthless; for the shaking
on the horse was apt to derange the powder in the
pans, or the flint might miss fire, or the fire not

reach the powder ; and even when it did go off, the chances were that the ball had shaken out, and if not, that it would not carry straight.   In those days it may easily be imagined that a body of troops depending on such arms, in preference to good swords, would certainly be defeated, and deservedly so.

But now, with revolvers the whole features of the case are changed.   These arms will carry from 200 to 300 yards, and comparatively good shooting can be made with them up to 75 or 100 yards, while in a *mêlée* they are most deadly weapons.   When considering the revolver, we will give a number of instances which occurred in the war in America, showing the value of this arm as compared with the sword.

Although so much has been written about the deadly effect of the sword in the *mêlée*, experience shows that the losses are not so heavy as would be supposed.

Colonel Harry Gilmor, a distinguished light cavalry officer, who served in the army of Virginia, has published an account of his operations, entitled ' Four Years in the Saddle.'   I shall quote many passages out of his book in the following pages, and from his writings and conversations with him, I know that he has a very high opinion of the revolver as a cavalry weapon.   In his work, p. 116, he gives an example of the difficulty of inflicting a deadly wound with a sabre. 'There was a man in command of one of the companies who waited for me till I was just upon him, when he fired but missed me. Seeing this he threw up his hands and cried "My God, Mr. Gilmor, don't kill me." "I don't know you," said I, making a cut at his head. His hat was looped up to the crown, and the double thickness of felt was all that saved his worthless life.'

Major Scott, in his 'Partisan Life with Mosby,' gives an anecdote of one of Mosby's men as follows: 'During the pursuit Bob Walker had a hand-to-hand fight with a Federal soldier, the latter using his sabre, the other clubbing his carbine. Both combatants were severely bruised and cut, but Walker, who is very strong and brave, as well as very active, succeeded in disarming and capturing his opponent.'

Colonel Heros Von Borcke, in his 'Memoirs of the Confederate War for Independence,' gives an account of a night surprise, in which two Southern cavalry regiments charged through each other in mistake. He says: 'The 1st and 3rd Virginia under this mutual delusion had charged through each other in a splendid attack, before they discovered their error, which was fortunately attended with no worse consequences than a few sabre cuts.'

Captain Nolan, p. 116, gives another example as

follows : 'In the general attack made on October 2, 1799, on the positions occupied by the enemy at Bergen and Egmont-op-Zee, the 15th Dragoons formed part of the cavalry under Colonel Lord Paget (now Marquis of Anglesey) attached to the force commanded by Sir Ralph Abercromby.

'After forcing the enemy to fall back for several miles, the cavalry advancing along the beach, as the infantry gained ground among the sand hills, the column halted in front of Egmont. The British artillery moved forward to check the fire of the enemy's guns, and two troops of the 15th Light Dragoons advanced to support the artillery. Lord Paget posted the two troops in ambush behind the sand hills, and the French general, thinking the British guns were unprotected, ordered 500 horsemen forward to capture them. The guns sent a storm of balls against the advancing cavalry. A few men and horses fell, but the remainder pressed forward and surrounded the artillery. At this moment the two troops of the 15th sallied from their concealment, and dashing among the assailants, drove them back upon their reserves, and then returned to the liberated guns.

'The opposing squadrons having rallied, and ashamed of a flight before so small a force, returned to the attack. They had arrived within forty yards of the

D

15th, when a third troop of the regiment came up, and a determined charge of all three troops drove the enemy back again with loss, the 15th pursuing above half a mile.

'The loss of the 15th was three men and four horses killed; Lieut.-Colonel James Erskine, nine men and three horses wounded.'

Here two troops dashed into 500 victorious French horsemen, and after a *mêlée* drove them off. Then the 500 French returned, and met at the charge, the English reinforced by one troop; a second fight ensues, and yet in both conflicts only *three* English are killed. This does not speak very highly for the sabre as a deadly weapon.

Nolan also mentions that at the battle of Heilsberg, June 18, 1806, a fight took place between a division of French cuirassiers and two regiments of Prussian Horse, in which it was said that a French officer came out of the fight with *fifty-two* new wounds upon him, and that a German officer, Captain Gebhart, received upwards of *twenty* wounds. Imagine a man receiving fifty-two lance and sword wounds without loss of life or limb. How many shots from a revolver would a man receive before being more seriously injured?

Compare these cases with the defeat and capture of Captain Blazer's squadron of Federal Cavalry by a

squadron of Mosby's partisan regiment under Major
Richards, in Virginia, in November 1864. The
numbers were about 100 men on each side. Major
Scott, speaking of it, says: 'A hand-to-hand combat
then ensued, in which the superiority of the revolving pistol to the rifle was soon demonstrated.
Many of Blazer's men were killed and wounded in
the first shock, and the rest of his command soon
gave way. . . . Richards lost, besides his wounded,
Hudgins, who was killed. Blazer's loss was *twenty-
four* men killed, *twelve* wounded, and sixty-two prisoners and horses.' This was in killed and wounded
thirty-six out of a hundred—more than one third,
while killed, wounded, and prisoners, comprised
virtually the whole force. The proportion of killed
to wounded is also an extraordinary proof of the
deadly effect of the revolver.

The present method of slinging the sword is too
noisy. If the rings into which the straps of the
sling buckled were solid, it would prevent the jingling of the rings, and the pliability of the strap
would be quite sufficient play for the sword. In
the Mexican War, in 1846, the Mexican cavalry
were armed with a sword carried *under* the left leg,
whereby it was prevented from dangling about, a
pistol or two, an escopet or short musket, and a
lasso, which they could throw with amazing dexterity

and effect. This could hardly have been a convenient method of carrying the sword, but it would prevent the noise which the present system entails.

Colonel Brackett, speaking of the sabre, in his 'History of the United States' Cavalry,' says: 'The sabre in Indian fighting is simply a nuisance—they jingle abominably, and are of no earthly use. If a soldier gets close enough on an Indian to use a sabre, it is about an even thing as to which goes under first.'

Hozier, in his 'Seven Weeks' War,' an account of the war in Germany in 1866, gives an instance of a party of Prussian hussars defeating a squadron of Austrian lancers at the battle of Presburg, but it must be remembered that this was on the last day of the war, and that the Austrians were much discouraged by former defeats. He says: 'While the artillery fight was going on, the dark green hussars on the right began to move quickly forward, and rushed in full career against the foremost squadron of Austrian lancers. These did not stand motionless now. Slowly at first, and then more quickly, they began to advance against the hussars ; and when the two squadrons came within a few hundred yards of each other, both urged their horses to their utmost speed, and with a mighty clatter dashed together.

'The rough embrace lasted but for a moment—then

the lancers scattered and fled, for the hussars were stronger and better mounted, and their mere weight smashed the lancers' ranks. These pursued a short distance, capturing several prisoners, but they could not follow far, for the other squadron of lancers looked threatening, and the hussars had no reserves near at hand.

In the ' History of Morgan's Cavalry' an account is given by General Duke of a charge by Morgan's men upon a Federal regiment of infantry at Shiloh in 1862. He says: ' We came close upon them before the Federals fired. They delivered one stunning volley, the blaze almost reaching our faces, and the roar rang in our ears like thunder. The next moment we rode right through them, *some of the men trying to cut them down with the sabre, and making ridiculous failures, others doing real execution with gun and pistol.*'

General Stephen D. Lee says : ' Nearly all the cavalry used by the Confederate States, and in fact by both sides, was nothing more than mounted riflemen. The sabre was done away with by the Confederate States' Cavalry pretty well, and rarely used in action by either party, and in my opinion has lost much of its merit since the revolver has been brought to such perfection. . . . The sword is a good weapon, though but little used during the recent war.

It has lost much of its effectiveness by the improved revolver, with which the cavalry man will make the dashing charge with more confidence. My experience was that the cavalry man was timid with his sabre in fighting against the revolver, and for the least excuse will drop the sabre for the revolver, and in many instances is compelled to do so in actual conflict by irregularities of ground, obstacles, &c. I don't see well how the sword can be dispensed with permanently, as some such weapon is required in case ammunition should be exhausted; but if any weapon is to be dispensed with, I should say the sabre in preference to the rifle or revolvers. These latter two, rifle and revolvers, are indispensable. In every instance under my observation, the revolver replaced the sabre with the morale, with the trooper, and against the enemy.

'Again, in the hand-to-hand conflict, which rarely occurs now (owing to the improved firearms), the momentum or pluck decides the affair before the eighteen rounds in hand are exhausted. And the momentum with good cavalry is as readily obtained with the revolver as with the sabre; my observation being that the sabre is timid against the good revolver. The revolver is the all-important weapon with the cavalry man *in motion*, and is indispensable in his equipment.'

2. *The Lance.*—This is a most efficient weapon when used by a thoroughly-trained man, but in the hands of raw levies it is perfectly worthless. In carefully-disciplined cavalry of the line, intended for charging alone, the lance has a terrible moral effect upon the enemy, and without doubt is a most deadly weapon in the shock of closing squadrons, or the shock of cavalry against squares. When the fight, however, degenerates into the *mêlée,* then the lance is awkward and cumbersome.

Montecuculi said that 'the lance was the queen of weapons for cavalry.' For cavalry proper it seems that history has shown that he was right.

Nolan is opposed to the lance. One of his arguments against it is, that the pennons attract the fire of artillery, and in single combat they betray to the adversary where the danger is, and thus enable him to avoid it. And if they sometimes frighten an adversary's horse, the animal shies, and carries his master out of reach of the point, which, if not decorated, might have run him through the body. If this is so, and the adversary's horses shy from the flags, their line would be disordered, their charge broken, and even if the lancers did not inflict serious wounds, nevertheless the main result would be beneficial. But still, if the flags are an injury, they can easily be done away with.

The Polish lancers at Albuera, getting in rear of General Stewart's division, annihilated Colborne's brigade of British infantry, and must have left a strong impression on the minds of the English soldiers of the power of the weapon. This instance is almost the only one on record where British infantry were destroyed by cavalry charging.

Colonel Ponsonby, writing of Waterloo, says : ' The lances, from their length and weight, would have struck down my sword long before I lost it, if it had not been bound to my hand.'

At the battle of Aliwal, January 28, 1846, the 16th Lancers made a brilliant charge against the Sikh infantry and artillery. Two squares were broken. The artillerymen were speared, and in the desperate hand-to-hand encounter which ensued, the lance made fearful havoc amongst the crowded foot soldiers. And this was not against indifferent infantry, for these Sikhs actually advanced on our British cavalry to attack them.

In this charge Captain Pearson of the 16th rode into the square at the head of his men, and went through it first.

In 1832–34, General Bacon's lancers did good work in the service of the Queen of Portugal. Captain Griffiths charged a squadron of the enemy in this war with only seventeen men, and routed them, killing *six* of his opponents with his own lance.

In this same war a fight took place in Torres Novas, between a regiment of the enemy's cavalry and some lancers, in which the latter, without losing a man, killed or wounded about *fifty* of their opponents.

Adjutant Dynon of the 16th Lancers has constructed a lance which appears to be the best pattern for this species of weapon.

General Halleck, in his work on ' Military Art and Science,' says that in a regular charge in line, the lance offers great advantages, hence some military writers have proposed arming the front rank with lances, and the second rank with sabres. This idea I do not coincide with. Cavalry should be drawn up and manœuvred in the rank entire, and in the *mêlée* the revolver, as before stated, is a wonderfully effective weapon. Lancers should always have swords as well as lances, as they never dismount to fight, and the swords are therefore not in the way.

It must always be remembered, however, that the lance is only of use in the hands of well-drilled men. With recruits no arm could be more ill-suited. Colonel Heros Von Borcke gives a striking example of the truth of this maxim. In speaking of a fight

which took place in June, 1862, near Richmond, he
says :

‘ One of these encounters, an affair of a few minutes,
was with a newly-organised regiment of Federal
lancers.   They stood 300 yards from us in line of
battle, and presented, with their glittering lances, from
the point of each of which fluttered a red and white
pennon, and their fresh well-fitting blue uniforms
turned up with yellow, a fine martial appearance.
One of our regiments was immediately ordered to
attack them, but before our Virginian horsemen got
within fifty yards of their line, this magnificent
regiment, which had doubtless excited the liveliest
admiration in the Northern cities on its way to the
seat of war, turned tail and fled in disorder, strewing
the whole line of their retreat with their picturesque
but inconvenient arms. . . . I do not believe
that out of the whole body of 700 men more than
twenty retained their lances.   And their sudden and
total discomfiture furnished a striking proof of the
fact that this weapon, formidable enough in the hand
of one accustomed to wield it, is a downright ab-
surdity and incumbrance to the inexperienced.’

Colonel Von Borcke is no doubt right in the con-
clusions he draws as to the value of this arm to the
inexperienced, but it seems very clear that a body of
cavalry, receiving an attack at the halt in the manner

above described, would be likely to run away under any circumstances, and without reference as to how they might be armed.

Sir Archibald Alison, in his account of the charge of Latour Maubourg's cuirassiers at Leipsic in 1813, and of their defeat by the Russian cavalry, says: 'With resistless force, Orloff Denizoff's men, all chosen cavaliers from the banks of the Don, bore down on the flank of the French cuirassiers, immediately after they had captured the guns, and when their horses were blown by previous efforts, their *long lances were more than a match for the cuirassiers' sabres.* In the twinkling of an eye the whole hostile squadrons were pierced through and routed, four-and-twenty of the guns retaken, and the French cavalry driven back with immense loss to their own lines.'

General Lloyd, who fought in the 'Seven Years' War,' and whose ideas in many instances were far in advance of his times, says: 'Cavalry arms must be a *lance* seven feet long, a sabre four feet in length, and a pair of pistols.'

Colonel Brackett, United States' cavalry, speaking of the Mexican War, says: 'The Mexican lancers were far from being a contemptible enemy, and many of them were admirable horsemen.' 'With the lance they were greatly our superiors, and used that weapon with great effect both at Buena Vista and at San Pascual.'

I shall here quote again from Hozier's 'Seven Weeks' War,' giving an account of a fight between the ninth regiment of Prussian Uhlans and a regiment of Austrian hussars, in the town of Saar, on July 10, 1866: 'In the market-place an exciting contest at once began. The celebrated cavalry of Austria were attacked by the rather-depreciated horsemen of Prussia, and the lance, "the queen of weapons," as its admirers love to term it, was being engaged in real battle with the sword. The first Prussian soldiers who rode into the town were very few in number, and they could not attack before some more came up. This delay of a few minutes gave the hussars a short time to hurry together from the other parts of the town, and by the time the Uhlans received their reinforcements, the Austrians were nearly formed. As soon as their supports came up, the lancers formed a line across the street, advanced a few yards at a walk, then trotted for a short distance, their horses' feet pattering on the stones, the men's swords jingling, their accoutrements rattling, and their lances borne upright, with the black and white flags streaming over their heads. But when near the opening into the broader street, which is called the market-place, a short sharp word of command, and quick stern note from the trumpet, the lance-points came down and were sticking out in front of the horses' shoulders, the horses broke into a steady gallop, and the lance-flags fluttered rapidly from the motion through the air, as the horsemen, with bridle hands low and bodies bent forward, lightly gripped the staves and drove the points straight to the front.

'But when the Prussians began to gallop, the Austrians were also in motion. With a loose formation and a greater speed they came on, their blue pelisses, trimmed with fur and embroidered with yellow, flowing freely from their left shoulders, leaving their sword arms disencumbered. Their heads well up, carried the single eagle's feather in every cap straight in the air. Their swords were raised bright and sharp, ready to strike, as their wiry little horses, pressed tight by the knees of the riders, came bounding along, and dashed against the Prussian ranks as if they would leap over the points of the lances. The Uhlans swayed heavily under the shock of the collision, but recovering again, pressed on, though only at a walk. In front of them were mounted men striking with their swords, parrying the lance-thrusts, but unable to reach the lancers. But the ground was also covered with men and horses struggling together to rise, loose horses were galloping away, dismounted hussars in their blue uniforms and long boots were hurrying off to try to

catch their chargers or to avoid the lance-points.
The Uhlan line appeared unbroken, but the hussars
were almost dispersed.   They had dashed up against
the firmer Prussian ranks, and they had recoiled,
shivered, scattered and broken, as a wave is broken
that dashes against a cliff.   In the few moments
that the ranks were locked together, it seems that
the horsemen were so closely jammed against each
other that lance or sword was hardly used.   The
hussars escaped the points in rushing in, but their
speed took them so close to the lancers' breasts that
they had not even room to use their swords.   Then
the Prussians, stouter and taller men, mounted on
heavier horses, mostly bred from English sires,
pressed hard on the light frames and the smaller
horses of the hussars, and by mere weight and
physical strength bore them back and forced them
from their seats to the ground, or sometimes, so rude
was the shock, sent horse and man bounding backwards, to come down with a clatter on the pave-
ment.

 'The few Austrians who remained mounted fought
for a short time to stop the Prussian advance, but
they could make no impression on the lancers.
Whenever a hussar made a dash to close, three
points bristled couched against his chest or his
horse's breast, for the Austrians were now in in-

ferior numbers in the streets to the Prussians, and the narrowness of the way would not allow them to retire for their reserves to charge. So the Prussians pressed steadily forward in an invulnerable line, and the Austrians, impotent to stop them, had to fall back before them. Before they had gone far through the town fighting this irregular combat, more Prussian cavalry came up behind the Uhlans, and the Austrians began to draw off. The lancers pushed after them, but the hussars got away, and at the end of the town the pursuit ceased. One officer and twenty-two non-commissioned officers and privates taken prisoners, with nearly forty captured horses, fell into the hands of the Uhlans as the trophies of this skirmish. Some of the prisoners were wounded, a few hussars killed, and two or three Prussians were left dead upon the ground.

'One or two of the privates taken prisoners were Germans, but by far the greater number were Hungarians, smart soldier-like looking fellows, of a wiry build. They looked the very perfection of light horsemen, but were no match in the *mêlée* for the tall strong cavalry soldiers of Prussia, who seemed with one hand to be able to wring them from their saddles and hurl them to the ground.'

I quote again from Hozier's history, with reference to the cavalry figt at Königgrätz. Speaking of the 3rd regiment of Dragoons, he says: 'Much did the officers of this regiment complain of the absence of epaulettes, which they estimated would by defending the shoulder have saved half the men they had left behind them—a complaint which was to some extent borne out by the fact that the ultimate overthrow of the cuirass regiments of Austria was due to the arrival of some of Hohenlohe's Uhlans, who took them in flank. Then, though the heavy horsemen turned upon Hohenlohe's men, their swords were shivered upon the brass plates which lay upon the shoulders of the Uhlans, for these, unlike the rank and file of the rest of the Prussian cavalry, carried epaulettes, and though the blows were aimed at the head, the smaller object was nearly always missed, and the sharp edge descended only to be dented or broken upon the protected shoulder, while the Uhlans, with their lances held short in hand, searched out, with their spear heads, unguarded portions of their antagonist's bodies, or dealing heavy blows with the butt-ends of their staves, pressed through the thick ranks of the heavy horsemen, marking their track with great heaps of dead, dying or wounded.'

3. *The Carbine.*—This weapon is certainly the proper arm for dragoons or mounted riflemen, and such improvements have been made of late years in

the manufacture and patterns of carbines, that they now compete favourably with any species of firearm in use.

The Spencer carbine is generally admitted to be the best description for general use, and the Sharp and Snider rank next in efficiency. It is said a plan has been arranged by which the load for the Spencer, seven or eight cartridges, are made into a huge cartridge, and loaded at once, taking no more time than for a single one. If this system will work well in practice it will leave little to be desired in the Spencer carbine.

The tube or magazine of the Spencer should be attached by a small chain or thong of leather to the rifle, as in action there would probably be some danger of its being lost.

These carbines are sighted for 900 yards, which is more than is necessary—400 yards or even less is quite enough. Men should be taught that they should not commence fighting until they get close to the enemy. This firing at 600 or 700 yards or upwards has a very demoralising tendency, and will make good material very bad soldiers. On this same principle cavalry of the line meant for charging should be carefully educated in the idea that the fighting does not commence until they begin to ply their swords or use their lances or revolvers, and if they work on

E

this principle, to use a Hibernicism, the fighting
will be over before it commences, for the infantry,
accustomed to keep their enemy at long distances,
by means of the arms which they confide in, will
lose heart if they find the fire has not the effect they
anticipated and hoped for.

The carbine should be carried in a long bucket
hanging behind the trooper's right thigh, and attached to the saddle. This is the plan adopted in
Her Majesty's 13th Hussars, and I suppose in the
other light cavalry regiments. There should be no
swivel on the pouch-belt, but a simple pouch carrying a good supply of ammunition; and it would be
well for each man to carry a reserve on his horse
in one of the wallets, as with the breech-loading
weapons the waste or consumption of ammunition
is frightful.

Long Enfields for mounted rifles or dragoons are
a most clumsy weapon. Colonel Gilmor in his
book says : 'Lomax had three brigades of Virginia
Cavalry, armed principally with Enfield rifles, and
these useless things for mounted men had nearly
ruined the whole command. I would rather command a regiment armed with good oaken clubs.'

The carbines should be rarely or never used by
dragoons while mounted. They are not suited or
intended for use on horseback. The men should be

dismounted to use them with effect, and if the enemy are too close to allow this course to be pursued, then the revolver is the proper arm to be employed. Major Scott, in Mosby's operations, says on one occasion: 'They fiercely assaulted the Federals with revolvers at close range, who replied with carbines; but the superiority of the revolver, as in the case with Captain Blazer, was soon evident.'

Before the time of Gustavus Adolphus, the old fashion of charging was something of this kind: 'The regiment rode up briskly till it came within pistol shot of the enemy. The first rank then discharged their pistols or carbines, and if the enemy were thrown into disorder, continued the charge; if not, the first rank wheeled round to the rear of their comrades and reloaded, while the second and other ranks in succession followed the manœuvres which the first had just executed.' Gustavus Adolphus ordered his cavalry to ride close up to the enemy's line, and discharging their firearms, draw their swords and dash in among the troops opposed to them.

Cavalry of the line should not have carbines.

General Lloyd, who wrote a history of Frederick the Great's campaigns, seems to have had such correct views, that we will make a few extracts here

from his work, which was published as far back as
1766.

'The Hussars and such troops as generally act
singly may be permitted to continue the use of
muskets, but those who are formed and ranged to
act in a mass and sword in hand ought not to carry
them, because they are expensive, troublesome, and
totally useless.   .   .   .   .   .   .

'The light cavalry and Hussars must be armed
in the usual way; because, as they are often sent a
reconnoitering, where infantry cannot follow them,
they must have muskets that they may be on equal
terms with the enemy.

'If it (the carbine) was constructed so as to be
loaded at the breech, and the centre of gravity
thrown farther back near the lock, it would not be
so top-heavy as at present, and would be much more
advantageous in action.   Marshal Saxe invented one
of this kind which he gave to his regiment of Uhlans,
but it had many inconveniences which may be easily
remedied.   This species of gun will be particularly
useful to the cavalry.'

It will astonish most people who read of the wonderful effect of the new rifle, the needle gun in the
war of 1866, to hear that the same species of firearm
had been in use over one hundred years ago.   I
have also been informed that there is now in the

Tower of London a breech-loading rifle over two hundred years old.

Before concluding this section, it will not be amiss to insert here an extract from General Duke's 'History of Morgan's Cavalry,' in which the general gives his views on the comparative merits of the different weapons; and as they are the opinions of an officer of great experience, one who had practically tested them in the hands of his own men as well as in those of the enemy, and as they are contrary to the popular ideas on the subject, they will probably be of interest to the reader.   It is as follows :—

'The weapon which was always preferred by the officers and men of the command was the rifle known as the "Medium Enfield." The short Enfield was very convenient to carry, but was deficient both in length of range and accuracy. The long Enfield, without any exception the best of all rifles, was unwieldy either to carry or to use, as sometimes became necessary on horseback. The Springfield rifle, nearly equal to the long Enfield, was liable to the same objection, although in a less degree. Now that the military world has finally decided in favour of breech-loading guns, it may seem presumptuous to condemn them; but so far as my experience goes they are decidedly inferior. When I say inferior, I mean not so much that they will not carry far nor accurately,

although a fair trial of every sort I could lay my
hands upon with the Enfield and Springfield convinced me of the superiority in these respects of the
two latter; but that for other reasons they are not so
effective as the muzzle-loading guns. Of the two
best patterns, the Sharp and the Spencer, I have
seen the Sharp do the most execution. It has been
the verdict of every officer of the Western Confederate
cavalry, with whom I have talked upon the subject,
and it certainly has been my experience, that those
Federal cavalry regiments which were armed with
breech-loading weapons did least execution. The
difference in the rapidity with which men dropped
when exposed to the fire of an infantry regiment,
and the loss from that of a cavalry regiment of equal
strength, even when the latter fought well, ought of
itself to go far to settle the question, for the Federal
infantry were all armed with muzzle-loading guns.

'A close study of the subject will convince any
man that the very fact of having to load his gun will
make a soldier comparatively cool and steady. If
he will stay to load at all, and fix his mind upon
what he is doing, he will become cool enough to take
aim; while if he has only to stick in a cartridge
and shoot, or turn a crank and pull a trigger, he will
fire fast, but he will fire wildly. I have seen some
of the steadiest soldiers I ever knew, men who were

dead shots with an Enfield, shoot as if they were aiming at the sun, with the Spencer. The Spencer rifle would doubtless be an excellent weapon for a weak line to hold works with, where all the men were accustomed to note the ground accurately and would therefore be apt to aim low, and it is desirable to pour in a rapid continuous fire to stagger an attacking line.

' It is perhaps a first-rate gun for small skirmishes on horseback, although for those our cavalry decidedly preferred the revolver. But in battle, when . lines and numbers are engaged, accurate and not rapid firing is desirable. If one-fiftieth of the shots from either side were to take effect in battle, the other would be annihilated. If rapid firing is so desirable, why do the same critics who advocate it also recommend the use of the bayonet?

' It is folly to talk to men who have seen battles about the moral effect of rapid firing, and of " bullets raining around men's heads like hailstones." That is like the straggler's excuse to General Lee that he was "stung by a bomb." Any man who has ever heard lines of battle engaged, knows that, let the men fire fast or slow, the nicest ear can detect no interval between the shots: the musketry sounds like the incessant unremitting crash of a gong; even cannonading, when one or two hundred guns are

working, sounds like the long roll of a drum, and
the hiss of bullets is perfectly ceaseless. Good troops
will fight well with almost any sort of guns; mean
troops will not win, no matter how they are armed.
If the matter were investigated, it would probably
be found that the regiments which won most dis-
tinction in the last war on this continent on both
sides, fired the fewest number of rounds.

'Nearly every man had a pistol, and some two.
Shortly afterwards, when they were captured in sufficient numbers, each man was provided with a pair.
The pistol preferred and usually worn by the men
was the army Colt furnished to the Federal cavalry
regiments. This pattern is the best and most effective of any I have ever seen.'

Hozier in his ' Seven Weeks' War,' gives an instance of the use of the breech-loading carbine by
cavalry. Speaking of a skirmish of the Prussian
advanced guard, consisting of the 2nd Regiment of
Dragoons of the Guard, with some squadrons of
Austrian Lancers in front of Tischnowitz, he says:
' But the lieutenant commanding the small Prussian
advanced guard, seeing that he was too weak to force
his way, and fearing to be surrounded and cut off,
retreated a short distance to where a slight rise in
the ground gave him a certain advantage of position,
and there drawing up his little force awaited an

attack, but with no intention of meeting it with the sword. While his men were yet retiring they were unbuckling their carbines, and before they had turned to stand, their quickly-loaded arms, constructed on the same principle as the needle gun, were ready to fire. And not too soon, for the Austrians had begun to advance quickly, and were defiling over the bridge, prepared to form line and charge, when a sudden volley from the Prussian carbines made them pull up sharp, half surprised, half frightened to find that a carbine could be of any use except to make a noise or smoke in the hands of a mounted man. But the Prussians did not wait to observe the discomfiture of their enemies; their officer only noticed that they were in too strong force to be allowed to get near his much smaller band, and again he retreated a little distance, and so quick were the dragoons with their loading that their carbines were almost ready to fire again before they turned to retire. The Austrians again formed to charge, and again before they had settled in their stride a rapid volley stopped their career. Again the Prussians retired, and again faced about ready to fire another volley. Again the Austrians came on, and again the fire of dragoons stopped them short; but this was the last time, for the whole of the first squadron of the dragoons were now up, and had

formed line beside the few who had hitherto prevented the advance of the lancers.

'Then the dragoons advanced to charge, and the
Austrians, glad to exchange the chance of close
quarters for the fire of the carbines, came forward
to meet them. Both sides advanced steadily : the
lancers with their spears in rest came on in an apparently impenetrable line, but the dragoons, with
sword points to the front and their horses well in
hand, bore steadily down upon them, in the last few
yards let their horses go, and dashed in through the
points of the lances. Their commander, Major Von
Shack, went down grievously wounded, but his men
thought of his fall only to avenge it, and rushed in
so close to the lancers that their spears were useless,
smiting them heavily with their keen bright swords.
A few moments only the *mêlée* lasted ; then the
lancers turning flew towards the town. The dragoons
pursued, but their officer kept them well in hand,
and they did not lose their order. When the street
was gained the lancers turned again, the swordsmen
thundered down upon them, and by sheer weight and
strength of blows bore them backwards along the
street. The fight was long and hard. The men, too
close together to use their weapons, grappled with
one another ; the horses, frightened and enraged,
snorted, plunged, reared, and struck out. But the

Prussians had superior weight and strength, and pressed their antagonists back along the streets to a wider space in the centre of the town, where a high image of the Madonna carved in stone looked down upon the fray.   Here an Austrian officer, hurled from his saddle by a tall Prussian dragoon, had his brains dashed out at the foot of the monument, and another Austrian bent backward over the cantle of his saddle, had his spine broken by the strength of his assailant.   The light Austrian men and horses had no chance in this close conflict, and soon they were obliged to turn, and fled down the street to where their supports were drawn up behind the town.'

4. *The Pistol.*—There is no doubt that the revolver is beyond all odds the best pistol for mounted forces of any description.   Colt's revolver is a splendid weapon, but it should be loaded with detonating cartridges so as to save the capping.   There is a modification of this pistol, which is loaded by taking the cylinder out and dropping the six cartridges from the rear into the chambers, and then the cylinder is returned to its place and fastened in.   There is then in the butt a shoulder or flange that rests against the cartridges to keep them in the cylinder.

Any arm that requires to have two parts separated while loading has not reached perfection, for mounted men particularly, for one of the detached parts may in confusion under fire be so easily lost. For this reason the tube of the Spencer carbine should be attached to the rifle, as already mentioned, with a thong or small chain; although it is not impossible to so modify the arrangement of filling the magazine as to do away with a detached tube altogether.

The revolver might be improved in the loading by having a portion of the shoulder or flange, which holds the cartridges from falling out, arranged so as to fold back on a hinge, or better still to slide back sufficiently to leave an opening over one chamber from the rear to drop in one cartridge at a time, and then by revolving the cylinder each chamber would come in turn under the opening, and be loaded with great facility. This would add very little to the complication or expense of the arm, and would make it more rapidly loading than any weapon in use. The cylinder would still be guided by the same spring which turns it with such precision now, in bringing each chamber in turn to its position as an exact prolongation of the barrel. This spring would also bring each chamber opposite the opening in the flange for loading. By this plan the cylinder could be turned with one hand and the cartridges dropped in with the other as rapidly as they could be got out of the pouch, and the slide going back with a spring

the pistol would be ready for use. This arrangement
would also provide against the detaching of the
cylinder from the pistol while loading.

A revolver on this principle has been patented and
is a very superior weapon. I have seen one, but I
do not know the name of it. The only fault with it
is the arrangement for throwing out the shell of the
exploded cartridge; this ought to be easily remedied.

The revolver is apparently the most deadly arm
that has ever yet been invented, and experience has
shown that in practice this is most certainly the case.
The sword, lance, carbine, long rifle, or cannon, do
not have the same murderous effect; the reasons for
this are numerous. In the first place, it is only used
at short range, when men are mingled together in
close fighting, and most of the shots tell. Then it is
not a weapon that is aimed by two sights requiring
care and steadiness in the adjustment. The man
merely looks at the object and pulls the trigger, and
the sympathy between the hand and eye is much
more likely to carry the ball straight, than an attempt
at mechanical and mathematical precision of aim
under fire, when men do not distress themselves with
too much accuracy in bringing the two sights and the
object into a right line. If men were taught, even
with long range rifles, to look at the objects, never
to mind the sights, but make their own allowances

for the elevation of the muzzle for the range, the
firing would be much more effective than under the
present system ; because men are taught that which,
under fire, nine out of every ten will not follow. The
best sportsmen are those who look at the objects they
fire at without sighting them at all along the barrel.
Indeed we have known of splendid shots who always
when shooting kept both eyes open, certain proof that
they used no sights.

Again, in close fighting, the revolver's bullet cannot
be warded off like a sword or lance thrust. If it
strikes, the wound is severe.   It does not require the
speed or weight of the horse to give it impetus as
does the lance, or the perfect training of the charger
which is necessary for an effective use of the sabre
when mounted. Again, it reaches farther than sword
or lance, and men armed with these weapons might
easily be shot down before having an opportunity of
getting near enough to use them.

In support of these views, I will cite some instances of the use of the revolver against all arms. I
know that most of my comrades in the cavalry force
will be opposed to these ideas, repugnant as they
are to the whole traditions of the force; in fact, I
was a warm supporter of the sabre, and used to
think that nothing could withstand it.   But the
Confederate war for independence, and the infor-

mation it has given us, has shaken my views considerably, as well as the constant and numerous conversations I have had with scores of cavalry officers, who have fought through the war, and who base their opinions upon their own observation and experience.

Colonel Gilmor, in his 'Four Years in the Saddle,' gives several striking instances of the value of the revolver. Once when being pursued by some Federal cavalry, he says: 'While they were pulling down the fence I reloaded three chambers of my revolver, and as they closed upon me, I wounded one very severely and disabled another. This they thought did not pay, so they left me to myself.'

Speaking again of a fight in a road, in column, with a body of Federal cavalry, he says: 'Both columns were at a charge, and . as we closed upon each other, I being some distance ahead of the rest, happened to kill one of the first set of fours at a second shot; when he fell their column broke.'

Again, on another occasion, he says : 'At this moment their commanding officer rode out towards me, after ordering his men to charge, but only two or three followed him. As he rode up I made a quick dash, fired and killed him almost instantly with the last load in my pistol. With drawn sabre,

I continued the charge followed by eight men, took possession of the bridge, killing one more, and drove them to the edge of the town.'

He gives another account of a charge of the 3rd Virginia cavalry, which shows how useless sabre-charging is unless the ground is thoroughly suited: ' But the gallant 3rd dashed on in splendid style, with their long bright sabres raised in *tierce point*, and with a wild ringing yell, to rouse the horses and carry dismay to the hearts of their foes. But when within 150 yards of the barricade, a deadly fire poured into their ranks, which emptied many a saddle, and threw the column into some confusion. They pushed on, however, *right up to the stone fence*, killing men behind it with the *pistol*, and tried to make a gap, but that was impossible for mounted men to do, and the poor fellows were forced to fall back out of range, and reform the regiment, now looking no larger than a good squadron.'

Again, in another skirmish, he says: ' I reserved my fire till he came within twenty paces, steadied my horse with the bit, took a long sure aim, and Somers fell dead from his horse.'

Speaking of another fight, Colonel Gilmor says : ' I saw the lieutenant run down under the river bank and several throw up their hands in token of surrender, but just as I thought all had given up, a sergeant mounted his horse and dashed at me, calling out to the men to follow him. " There are only five men," said he; " don't surrender to five men." Kemp had his revolver out, and killed the brave fellow before he came within reach of my sabre. But the rest had taken courage and began to mount and come at us, with balls whistling round our heads. *Had I drawn my pistols instead of sabre several would have fallen,* for we were at *close quarters.'*

In another place he· gives a striking example of the comparative merits of the sabre and revolver, as follows : 'We had nearly all got through a fence, when I saw Kemp engaged with a powerful fellow, who was closing in upon him with sword upraised. Kemp always carried two pistols ; in one he had but one load, that he fired upon his adversary but missed, then threw the pistol at him and struck him in the breast. The trooper closed in upon him before he could draw his second pistol, and seizing him by the hair tried to drag him off the horse, at the same time lashing him across the shoulders with his sabre. Kemp held down his head and took it all, the while trying to draw his pistol. I had cut my way to him, and had raised myself in the stirrups with uplifted sabre to cleave the fellow's skull, when Kemp discharged his pistol into his stomach and he was free.'

F

Again, he says : ' They did not move, however, until
the column had fairly struck them full in front, when
the whole battalion gave way and ran like mad—
friend and foe all mixed up together, cutting and
slashing at each other right and left. *Very few
pistols were used or our loss would have been twice
as heavy.*'

Again, speaking of a fight with the sabre with a
Federal officer, he says : ' My sabre flashed a rear
cut. He caught it on his pistol barrel. At the same
instant his horse bounded alongside. I rose up in
the stirrups to give a cut in front. In the former
stroke I was obliged to turn the sabre in tierce, and
had not time to take again the proper grip, therefore
more of the flat than of the edge struck him, breaking
the blade in the middle. The blow was a heavy one,
and would have cleft his head open to the throat had
it struck fair. As it was the concussion must have
killed him, but for the thick felt army hat. The man
rolled from his horse but was on his feet in an instant. At the same moment I saw some one lean
over on his horse and shoot him through the head.'

Captain Nolan tells of a Sikh horseman who at
the battle of Chillianwalla challenged the English to
single combat, and unhorsed three dragoons (the first,
a lancer, had the lance-pole severed and his forefinger
taken off at one blow) before he was *shot* down.

And he cites this case to show what a splendid weapon a sharp sword is. Now, how much better it would have been for the English to have sensibly shot the fellow first thing, rather than to have waited until three men had been killed or wounded. This case is certainly the strongest proof of the value of the revolver over the sword that could be produced; for here is a *splendid horseman*, a *perfect swordsman*, with a *pattern sword*, SHOT DOWN !

Some instances from Major Scott's ' Partisan Life with Mosby' will not be out of place here. In one place he says: ' Baron Massow, who was with Chapman's party, distinguished himself in the fight. Having emptied his pistol he recurred to his sword, and dashed into the midst of the flying enemy. Captain Reid, whom he passed in his rapid career, by a shot from his revolver inflicted upon him a dangerous wound, which brought him to the ground. Chapman, seeing his friend fall from his horse, spurred forward to engage the man by whom he had been shot, and when within three feet of Reid fired, killing him instantly.'

Again, in speaking of another fight between a party of Mosby's men under Major Richards, about 100 in number, and a scouting party of Federal cavalry of about the same force, in which the partisans used the pistol mainly, and where the Federals were tho-

roughly defeated, he says : ' Richards sustained no
loss in this fight, but the loss of the enemy was considerable, *twenty-six killed and wounded, fifty-four
taken prisoners*, and eighty horses.'

Major Scott gives an account of a gallant action
by a Federal lieutenant, which also proves the power
of the revolver. ' With a few men Wiltshire was
approaching through a lane which leads from Berry-
ville, the residence of Colonel Daniel Bonham, as
a Federal officer, who proved to be Lieutenant Eugene
Ferris of the 30th Massachusetts Infantry, was seen
to pass rapidly from the house to the stable, which
was situated in a corner of the yard. Wiltshire and
Gill, who were riding fifty paces in advance of their
comrades, passing through the gate which admitted
them to the yard, dashed up to the stable door in
which Ferris was standing. Without drawing his
pistol Wiltshire demanded a surrender, " Never with
life," replied Ferris, and as his adversary was attempting to disengage his pistol, he inflicted on him
a mortal wound in the neck. A little after, Gill,
who was somewhat to Wiltshire's left, fired, but
Ferris, being protected by the door-post, was not
struck, and at once fired on Gill, inflicting a disabling
wound. By this time the rest of the party had
arrived on the scene of combat, and opened a rapid
fire on the Federal officer, who disdaining to fight

under cover, stepped into the open space in front of the stable, and engaged in what appeared to be a hopeless contest. But it was hopeless only in appearance, for, begirt with pistols, he was a skilful shot, and had the additional advantage of being on foot, so that almost all his balls took effect. Soon the gallant officer was master of the field. It was death to stand before that unerring pistol. Orrick and Bartlett Bolling had both been wounded, and Orrick in addition had been thrown from his horse. Seizing Wiltshire's horse, which he found at the gate, Ferris directed his orderly—who, crouched in the stable, had taken no part in the conflict—to mount and follow him; but before taking his departure, he advanced some paces towards his adversaries, who had returned back to the lane, and fired at them two parting shots. He then sprang into his saddle, and turned his face toward his camp.'

At the battle of Leipsic, in 1631, four troops of the Imperialist cavalry charged up to the very heads of the Swedish pikes, and with their pistols picked off every ensign in Lumsden's regiment.

Colonel Von Borcke also gives an instance of the use of the pistol in pursuit. He and Captain Farley of the Confederate army were pursuing the officer commanding a Federal squadron. He thus describes

it: ' At every demand that we made for his surrender, he only spurred his horse into a more furious
gallop, occasionally turning to fire at us with his
revolver. But each moment I got nearer and nearer
to him ; the long strides of my charger at last brought
me to his side, and I was just raising myself in the
saddle to put an end to the chase with a single
stroke of my sabre, when at the crack of Farley's
pistol, the fugitive, shot through the back, tumbled
from his horse in the dust.'

Colonel Von Borcke gives another instance, of
Captain Bullock of the 5th Virginia Cavalry, who, in
attempting to rally his men, had his horse shot
under him ; ' and before he could get on his legs
again, found himself surrounded by the Yankees,
who demanded his surrender ; Bullock, however, responded with two shots of his revolver, killing two of
his adversaries,' and then made his escape by flight.

At the charge of the Light Brigade at Balaklava,
Colonel Jenyns, C. B., 13th Hussars, who was at that
time a captain in the same regiment, while making
his way back during the retreat to the English lines,
on a horse which was mortally wounded, was intercepted by three Russian cavalry, an officer and two
men. His horse was so weak from loss of blood
that he could not use his sword, so he drew his

revolver, and held the whole three at bay for some time. At length the officer made a dash in upon him with his sabre, but the colonel shot him before he came within reach of him. The other two molested him no further, and he reached the lines safely.

CHAPTER IV.

ARMS OF CAVALRY AND DRAGOONS.

I lay it down, however, as a maxim, that the cavalry should be arranged and distributed so that it may act more or less in every kind of ground.—*General Lloyd.*

HAVING in the last chapter discussed at length the comparative merits of the different arms suitable to mounted forces, we shall here proceed to consider how to distribute them among the two species of cavalry which we advocate, taking each in turn.

1. *Cavalry of the Line.*—Although it must be admitted that the great changes in the firearms of the infantry, and in the field artillery, have considerably affected the power of cavalry proper to overcome the other arms of the service, still there can be no doubt that it is carrying the principle too far to say that these improvements are to do away with cavalry proper for ever.

The opportunities in which a charge in line can be made with effect will not be so numerous or so certain as formerly; but still the occasions will arise, and chances will offer, and then the result of success will be so great as to amply compensate for the trouble and expense in preparing to profit by them. For this reason one-third, or one-fourth at the very least, of the mounted force of an army should be real cavalry, armed as such, educated as such, and taught to believe that nothing can withstand a well-executed charge, when the nature of the ground will permit it to be made with effect.

This force, which should be called the heavy cavalry, should be armed with the lance and sabre and the revolving pistol; one-half of them, or a somewhat similar proportion, being armed with sabres and revolvers alone, and the remainder with lances in addition.

This force should have no carbines. They should only be allowed to fight at close quarters; and the moral effect of this training would have a wonderful influence, not only on themselves, but also on the enemy. General Rosser's views, before quoted, are very strong on this point, and, as is stated in a former page, infantry accustomed to fight at long range will not stand a charge as well as men who have been in the habit of coming into close quarters.

The heavy cavalry man should carry his sword on the ordinary belt around the waist without a sabretache; the revolver on the right side in a holster on the sword-belt, and the pouch on a cross-belt as has been the habit hitherto. The lance also should be carried in the present method.

Although, in speaking of the comparative merits of the sabre and lance, I have not given them for *deadliness* as high a place as the revolver, still it seems for cavalry intended for charging infantry (who should be first shaken by artillery or infantry fire) that the sword has a great moral effect among retreating foot soldiers, and can be used to great advantage in pursuit, especially if the men are taught to apply the point as well as the edge. Again, if in the pursuit men are very much mixed up together, they might not be able to use the revolver with effect for fear of hitting and wounding friends as well as foes.

As the swordsman, however, has his revolver as well in his belt, he can readily revert to it if he sees that circumstances are favourable to its use, or that it is to his advantage to draw it. The lancer in the same way has both sword and revolver as a reserve.

2. *Light Dragoons or Mounted Rifles.*—The Spencer carbine should be THE weapon of this

branch of the service.   They should be trained
more particularly to its use, and taught the power
of accurate firing on foot as a means to defeat the
enemy.   The men ought also to be armed with two
revolvers to be worn around the waist.   It does not
seem absolutely necessary to carry two revolvers,
although Morgan's cavalry did, as well as most of
Gilmor's and Mosby's.   The officers of both services
should be armed with a sword, and one revolver to
be worn on the belt.

The carbine should be carried, as mentioned in
another place, in a bucket on the offside of the
saddle, and if dragoons or mounted rifles have
sabres at all, they should be attached to the saddle
and not to the man.   They might easily be hung on
the near side opposite the carbine, and slung so that
they could readily be drawn in case of need.   They
should not be so long or heavy for dragoons if hung
in this way as for the heavy cavalry, as they are
merely to be used as a reserve arm in extraordinary
circumstances, and are *not* to be looked upon as *the
weapon* of the dragoon.

It would be better for the dragoon to be without
a sabre altogether than to carry it around his waist,
because nothing can be more troublesome, noisy, or
awkward to a man skirmishing or fighting on foot,
and the occasions on which he would require it would

be rare. Even then, if it was attached to the saddle it would be just as useful, and be out of the way in mounting.

Another plan might be arranged with dragoons, by arming every fourth man with a sabre to be worn around the waist, as well as with a carbine and revolver. These should be the men who hold the horses while the others fight on foot, and in case of requiring a few swordsmen they would be ready. The only difficulty about this is, that the formation would be broken up if one-fourth were called out to use the sabre ; so perhaps the plan of carrying the sword on the saddle is the best.

The revolvers with dragoons should be carried, one on the left side on the waist-belt, the butt to the front, as on that side the right hand can draw it more readily than on the other ; the other as a reserve on the right side, the butt to the rear, to be only drawn in the case of emergency.

There should be a suspender or cross-belt over the shoulder, attached to the waist-belt, to support it, and to prevent the whole weight pressing upon a man's waist. The same plan should be adopted with cavalry proper, as the pressure on the waist is very apt to injure him seriously, when riding long distances.

General Stephen D. Lee says in the letter before

quoted from: 'The proper and best armament for the cavalry man, by which I mean all mounted men, is the light repeating rifle, and two large sized six-shooters (revolvers), and the sabre so arranged as to be left with the horse when the cavalry man is dismounted. With this equipment the cavalry man is always ready for the charge with confidence, and can always be used dismounted, either against cavalry or infantry.'

General Fitzhugh Lee, who commanded the cavalry of the army of Northern Virginia during the late war, and who gained the very highest reputation as a cavalry general, says in a letter received by me from him, that the best arms for cavalry are 'Colt's navy size revolver, Sharp's breech-loading carbine, and the French sabre.'

CHAPTER V.

THE DRESS OF CAVALRY.

Who comes in foreign trashery
Of tinkling chain and spur,
A walking haberdashery
Of feathers, lace, and fur.—*Scott.*

WITH reference to the uniforming of cavalry, there is no doubt that the most simple dress is the best. It need not, however, be rough or ill fashioned. A soldier should be comfortably and neatly dressed, and be smart in his appearance and carriage.

At times the dress of cavalry has been most absurdly foppish and dandified. The Polish hussars of the time of Charles XII. were very richly accoutred. 'They march,' says Voltaire, 'attended by several valets who lead their horses, which are adorned with bridles plaited with silver and silver nails, and sometimes made of massive silver, with large housings trailing after the Turkish manner.'

In modern times the Emperor of Austria's body-guard, from their splendid equipment and purely parade duty, have obtained the *soubriquet* of 'The Silk Hussars.' A great deal of this useless toggery is still retained in our cavalry equipments, and whatever effect it may have among the idle lovers of tinsel and pageantry it is certain that it is entirely inconsistent with practical soldiering.

Sir Charles J. Napier says: 'Our hussar's old clothes bag contains jackets, breeches of all dimensions, drawers, snuff-boxes, stockings, pink boots, yellow boots, eau de Cologne, Windsor soap, brandy, satin waistcoats, cigars, kid gloves, tooth-brushes, hair-brushes, dancing spurs, and thus a light cavalry horse carries twenty-one stone.'

Dr. Ferguson also says: 'It seems decreed that the hussar and the lancer is ever to be a popinjay. A show of foreign fooleries, so laced, and looped, and braided, that the uninitiated bystander wonders how he can either get into his uniform or come out of it.' In peaceable times there may be no objection to dressing cavalry in a gaudy uniform; it may induce recruits to enlist, and may serve to encourage a certain kind of *esprit de corps*. But when cavalry are to be used let them leave their full dress at home, let them wear nothing but their working dress, and have that as serviceable as possible.

For an undress or working dress, dragoons should
have a stable jacket made long in the waist, buttoned
up in front, with a standing collar hooked in front,
not too tight or stiff.   The jacket should be loose
and easy, especially in the sleeves and across the
chest, and it requires no ornaments for the men,
the collar and cuffs merely showing the facings.   An
edging of lace and small shoulder-knots should
distinguish the officers.   A light bar of tempered
steel or light chain shoulder-strap on the shoulder
would add little to the weight, and would be
specially useful to the heavy cavalry as a protection against sword-cuts.

The overalls should be ordinary trousers, with the
stripe on the outside seam, and should be worn with
strong jack-boots, reaching to the knees.   Nolan
recommends a bar of steel down the outside of the
boot; we do not see any necessity for this either
for cavalry of the line or light dragoons.   The ordinary jack-boots are beyond all doubt the best for
mounted men.   They are a great protection against
the crushing in the ranks, and would also protect
the man's leg from bruises and contusions in many
circumstances.

These boots would keep the men's feet dry when
dismounted, and would also save the overalls, which
are constantly getting torn.   The lower parts es-

pecially soon get rotten from the mud and dirt
which is constantly splashed on them in service.
The straps also, when short boots are used, are an
incumbrance to the men when mounting, or when
acting on foot.

Again, cavalry or dragoons on service are continually getting their legs, from the knees downwards, muddied and wet, and when the men have
to bivouac at night, and to sleep with their clothes
on, they suffer much if the trousers are damp
and cold, hanging about their ankles and feet. If
jack boots are worn, however, they can be pulled
off when the men lay down to sleep, and the trousers
will be dry and comfortable underneath.

The Governor-General's body-guard, Upper Canada,
were dressed in this manner during the Fenian
raid on Fort Erie in 1866, and both myself and
the officers and men all experienced the benefit of
these boots, sleeping as we had to, night after night,
in our uniforms.

Nolan suggests that cavalry should wear gauntlets,
with a steel guard on the outside of the left one as
high as the elbow, to protect the bridle arm. With
heavy cavalry this would be an improvement.

The jacket, if made rather long, is a better dress
for service than the tunic. Soldiers should have no
loose clothes or flaps about them, the dress should

G

fit closely without being at all tight.   Men on service
often get wet through ; if they move about and exercise themselves till they get dry, and they dry all
over equally, there will not be much harm done.
But if men wear tunics, all the water in the upper
part will drip to the skirt, and, it not being affected
by the heat of the body, will remain cold and wet
around the man's hips long after the rest of his clothes
are dry.

As for the head-dress, it should be light and not
too tall ; a forage cap, such as the English cavalry
wear, is a good covering, and presents a soldierly
appearance.   It is cool, easy, light, and is not in the
way in going through rough ground, or in using the
sabre.

Heavy cavalry might wear a light helmet strengthened with wires or steel spring bars, but made as
light as possible.   There is no necessity to have them
so heavy as they are made now.

There is nothing more useless than a tall heavy
shako or busby.   The weight of them with the plume
acts with greater effect on the dragoon than it would
on a dismounted soldier, for the shaking and plung-
ing of the horse, as well as the resistance of the air
when moving fast, renders the wearing of them
excessively painful.   I have worn both styles of head-

dress, and can speak from experience as to the sensation of torture endured in wearing them.*

Dr. Ferguson, Inspector-General of Military Hospitals, in his 'Notes and Recollections of a Professional Life,' says: 'A heavy headpiece is everywhere a disqualification and a hindrance to the wearer, for to heat and cumber the brain, which, being the source of all our powers and faculties, ought ever to be freest, can never be justified.'

There is a hat worn by the United States cavalry, as well as by the Confederate cavalry, which is a very serviceable head-dress. It is a felt 'wide-awake,' or 'rowdy,' made of rather soft felt, with a rim or flap about 3½ or 4 inches wide: a hat familiar to theatre goers as that worn by 'Fra Diavolo.' It is a most comfortable and useful headpiece, and has a great

---

* Colonel Jenyns, 13th Hussars, while reading the manuscript, made the following memorandum, which I insert in full, as the opinion of an officer of far greater experience than myself. I have never been able to become accustomed to the weight on my head, and whenever possible, have shirked wearing the shako or busby. There is no doubt, however, that a busby would be a protection to the head, which a forage cap would not :—

'I have worn, during twenty-three years' service at home and in the field on active service in all climates, shako very *light* and no plume ; ditto very heavy with a plume two feet high, cloth helmet like a hunting cap, forage cap, cocked hat, and busby ; and for service would far prefer a tolerable-sized *busby without plume,* with a plume for parade. A busby properly made keeps off more sun than any other head-dress, is as warm as a fur cap in winter, and resists a sword cut even more than a helmet.   S. G. J., Col.'

many advantages. It is light, soft, and easy to the head, it is a protection against the sun, it sheds the rain, it is not tall, can be worn anywhere, through woods even, men can sleep in it, and with the rim looped up with a feather, it presents a very picturesque appearance. It is not a soldierly-looking covering, but gives men rather a guerilla or banditti-like appearance; this is the only fault about it; in every other respect it is the best head-dress worn in any country. The plain felt hat is worn universally in the Southern States, and is a decided improvement on the ' stovepipe ' silk hat so fashionable now.

Besides the articles before mentioned, dragoons should be provided with two flannel shirts and two pairs of socks, they do not require anything more, any other stores of clothing should be kept with the army baggage. One shirt on the man's back, and one pair of socks on his feet, and a shirt and a pair of socks and a tooth brush in his wallet on the saddle, and a man has all he wants on active campaigning. When a lull comes and men are stationary or in garrison, then let them have more. When on service, the men's hair should be cut very short, and they need carry merely a comb, but no brushes, except for their horses—and even for these, the brush alone should be sufficient.

If the men had a pair of light short boots or shoes

to wear about their quarters or in camp, it would be a great comfort to them, and the weight and space taken up would not be of much importance.

On the occasion before referred to, I ordered my men to be provided as I have here stated, and we found it quite sufficient. I ordered the busbys and tunics to be left at home. We took no valises, but we carried all we required in the two wallets in front of the saddle. I took no more with me than the men, except some paper, a map of the country, a 'manual of outpost duties,' pencil, and a pair of field glasses, all of which I carried in one of the wallets. We used to get one shirt and a pair of socks washed while we were wearing the other, and by working it that way alternately, we managed very well.

By this plan a great saving is effected in the weight. Men should never be allowed to have their valises while campaigning, for they will be sure to fill them as full as they can hold, and the horses suffer. If they must have valises near, they should be carried in waggons in rear of the army, but there is no necessity for them.

As an example of the accumulation of baggage that will take place if not rigorously prevented, and of the annoyance and incumbrance it is to an army, I quote with permission from General Early's manuscript notes of his personal recollections of the war.

Describing the evacuation of Manassas in 1862, he says :—

'About two weeks before the evacuation took place, division commanders were confidentially informed of the probability of that event, and ordered to prepare their commands for it in a quiet way. Up to that time there had been no apparent preparation for such a movement, but an immense amount of stores of all kinds and private baggage of officers and men had been permitted to accumulate. Preparations, however, were commenced at once for sending the stores and baggage to the rear. Owing to the fact that our army had remained stationary so long, and the inexperience in campaigning of our troops, there had been a vast accumulation of private baggage by both officers and men, and when it became necessary to change a camp, it was the work of two or three days. I had endeavoured to inculcate proper ideas on this subject into the minds of the officers of my own immediate command, but with very indifferent success, and it was very provoking to see with what tenacity young lieutenants held on to baggage enough to answer all their purposes at a fashionable watering place in time of peace. After the confidential instructions for the evacuation were given, I tried to persuade my officers to send all their baggage not capable of being easily transported and for which they did not have immediate necessary use, over the railroad to some place in the rear out of all danger, but the most that I could accomplish was to get them to send it to Manassas Junction. This was generally the case with the whole army, and the consequence was that a vast amount of trunks and other private baggage was accumulated at the Junction at the last moment, for which it was impossible to find any transportation. This evil, however, was finally and completely remedied by the burning which took place when the Junction itself was evacuated, and we had never any great reason subsequently to complain of a plethoric condition of the baggage.'

A few men in every troop should carry small axes or hatchets in leather cases, attached in some way to the saddle. These are of the greatest use for many purposes; for breaking down fences, making breast-works, cutting wood for fires, making huts and shelters, cutting down telegraph poles, and in many other instances. It is absolutely necessary that cavalry should always have a number along with them, and for this reason some of the men should carry them, rather than have them conveyed in waggons. In a wooded country like Canada or the United States, they are more required even than in Europe.

In winter the men should have flannel drawers,

warm woollen socks, an extra flannel shirt, and a thick pelisse or overcoat, warmly lined, to reach down as far as the top of the jack boots.

The dragoons or cavalry should also have a long coat with sleeves, and split up a little behind to spread on the horse, and made so that the belts might be worn over it in case of need, as well as under it. The cloak without sleeves is very awkward and clumsy.

A large blanket is necessary also to sleep with, and in case it might be required for protection against rain, a hole could be made in the centre, and then in case of necessity the dragoon could wear it with his head through the hole, the blanket falling around him from his shoulders, in the manner adopted by the trappers and hunters on the western prairies.

An officer of cavalry, and especially of light dragoons, should carry with him always a watch, pen, ink and paper, a good pair of field glasses, a map of the seat of operations, a small pair of compasses or dividers, and a pocket compass.

We will conclude this chapter with the remarks of Hozier on the dress of the Prussian troops, as they bear upon the point, and support to a certain extent the views here expressed. He says : 'The Prussian foot soldier marched under almost every disadvantage which dress could inflict. His helmet was horrible both as to comfort and appearance, his clothes were uncomfortable, the trousers, without gaiters, hung clammily against the calf on a rainy day, or collected inside them a layer of mud, which rubbed uneasily against the ankle. The inconvenience of the dress was shown whenever a battalion started to march; the first thing the soldier did was to divest himself of his helmet and sling it from his waist-belt, where it dangled uncomfortably against his legs, he unbuttoned his coat, and after a few days' experience scarcely ever omitted to stuff the lower parts of his trousers into his boots, which thus afforded a gaiter, with the advantage of requiring neither buttons nor straps, as do those in most armies. Prussian officers themselves acknowledged that the dress of the army could not be compared to that of the Austrians, either for efficiency or appearance. It only shows what splendid stuff they are made of, when they performed such prodigies of marching as marked their victorious course under these disadvantages, and also weighed down by their heavy knapsacks, which, although of a better construction than those of most armies, *were hardly required, and though present, were seldom looked into* in the actual campaign. Railways and improved roads have made great alterations in the necessities of a warrior, both by shortening the duration of campaigns and facilitating transport. Europe will never again see any decently organised army waiting many weeks for the arrival of a siege-train for the carriage of which all available transport is required, so that from want of means of sending stores forward, the troops in the front are shivering in tattered clothes and suffering painfully from unbooted feet. Soldiers need no longer be weighed down by heavy loads upon their backs, held back from their real use, marching and fighting, to be converted into beasts of burden. A spare shirt, a change of shoes, and a pot of grease, is about all that a foot soldier need carry with him besides his arms, ammunition, and some food.'

Again, describing the entry of the Prussian army into Berlin after the war, he says: 'A gap of some hundred yards separated the Jägers from the 2nd Brigade, first in which came the 2nd Regiment, men and officers marching in forage caps. There was not a helmet to be seen in their ranks, for on going into action at Trautenau this regiment to a man *threw away their heavy helmets,* and thus rid themselves for the campaign of a cumbrous head-dress in a manner which did not draw forth such un-qualified approval from the military authorities, as did their conduct on the line of march or under fire.'

CHAPTER VI.

THE HORSE AND HIS EQUIPMENT.

Ἐὰν οὖν, ἔφη ὁ Σωκράτης, παρέχωνταί σοι τοὺς ἵππους οἱ μὲν οὕτως κακόποδας ἢ κακοσκελεῖς ἢ ἀσθενεῖς, οἱ δὲ οὕτως ἀτρόφους ὥστε μὴ δύνασθαι ἀκολουθεῖν, οἱ δὲ οὕτως ἀναγώγους ὥστε μὴ μένειν ὅπου ἂν σὺ τάξῃς, οἱ δὲ οὕτως λακτιστὰς ὥστε μηδὲ τάξαι δυνατὸν εἶναι, τί σοι τοῦ ἱππικοῦ ὄφελος ἔσται; ἢ πῶς δυνήσῃ τοιούτων ἡγούμενος ἀγαθόν τι ποιῆσαι τὴν πόλιν;—Καὶ ὅς· Ἀλλὰ καλῶς τε λέγεις, ἔφη, καὶ πειράσομαι τῶν ἵππων εἰς τὸ δυνατὸν ἐπιμελεῖσθαι.—XEN. Memor. iii. 3.

As before stated, the value of cavalry or dragoons depends upon the quality and condition of their horses. If these are bad and out of condition, the cavalry will be correspondingly depreciated in value. In fact, the horses are far more likely to be laid up, to be destroyed, to fall off in strength than the men, but if they can only be kept ready for work, the men will not be wanting.

As it is the strength and lasting qualities of the horse which make the mounted man formidable, the animal should not be made to carry any unnecessary weight, which must always detract from those qualities in a greater or less degree.

But in reducing the weight, the strength or power of the man should not be diminished; the dead weight, which cavalry carries now a days, is what kills the horses. Fancy horses carrying nineteen and twenty stone—266 lbs. and 280 lbs.—when the men can be tall enough and strong enough at ten or twelve stone, and the trappings can easily be brought under four or five stone more. No horse should carry over seventeen stone, all told. As before remarked, no valises should be taken on active service on the horse. And the personal baggage of the men ought to be reduced to the lowest possible point.

Cavalry or dragoons equipped in the lightest manner would destroy a force in which the horses were overloaded in a very short time, by operating so as to give them a great deal of harassing marches.

The best saddle for mounted corps, as far as my limited experience goes, is the present English Hussar saddle with the numnah. Its great fault is its extremely heavy weight. The United States and Confederate cavalry used the M'Clellan saddle, copied from the Mexicans, and they have a very high opinion of it. I have ridden on one merely to try it, but in my opinion it will not compare with the Hussar saddle, either for the seat of the man, or for the convenience of carrying the kit. It is used with a blanket under it, folded to the proper shape. This is a disadvantage in saddling in a hurry, if the blanket is unfolded.

General Rosser is strongly in favour of this saddle. He says, in his letter already quoted from: 'The M'Clellan saddle is by far the best I ever saw for cavalry. It is strong, light, and *comfortable to man and horse.*' General S. D. Lee says: 'The C. S. trooper considered himself fortunate in getting a M'Clellan tree.' General Fitzhugh Lee says: 'I think there is no comparison between what is known in this country as the M'Clellan saddle and any other.'

The attention of the reader is particularly directed to the remarks of a general officer of high rank in the Confederate States of America on the question of the cavalry saddle. They were kindly written at the request of the author, and are inserted in full in the Appendix, and will well repay an attentive perusal.

During the summer of 1866, my corps formed a chain of outposts, covering a camp of observation at Thorold, from the Niagara Falls along the Niagara River to Fort Erie, and along the shore of Lake Erie as far as Point Abino, making a line of nearly forty miles. The work of constantly patrolling at night was very heavy on the men and horses, as we had not force sufficient for the duty. I had not enough of the Hussar saddles for all the men, so some twenty were obliged to use the ordinary hunting saddles. Among the horses using the Hussar saddles, there was not one sore back, but among the others, the greater number almost immediately were laid up, and I was obliged to order that, as the men took their turn for duty, they were to use the military saddles, the men lending them to those who were without them when their turn for patrolling came. This saved further trouble.

The importance of the saddle has been acknowledged by all cavalry officers. The following letter of Oliver Cromwell, quoted by Captain Nolan, may well be reproduced here.

'Wisbeach, this day, 11th Nov. 1642.

' Dear Friend,

' Let the saddler see to the horse gear. I learn from one, many are ill served. If a man has not good weapons, horse, and harness, he is as nought.

' From your friend

' OLIVER CROMWELL.

' To Auditor Squire.'

The present bridle and bit in use in our regular cavalry serves the purpose very well, and cannot well be improved upon.

The system of riding in the English cavalry is also

a very good one, in spite of all the criticisms which it received at the hands of Captain Nolan in his work, and although we cannot speak from experience or personal observation, still we have no doubt that the English cavalry are the best horsemen in the world in any army. Nolan's criticisms have given the English dragoons a bad reputation in foreign countries, but the criticisms were unfair, and carried to too great an extreme. See what Colonel Brackett, in his 'History of the United States Cavalry,' says upon this point: 'As to riders, the United States cavalry under the old system had few superiors. The English as a general thing are wretched riders, and it is no wonder that they are almost universally whipped whenever they go into battle. The "bumping" up and down on their saddles is not only excruciating to themselves, but ruinous to their unfortunate animals. Nolan, in his work on cavalry, speaks in most disparaging terms of the English cavalry, as does Lieut.-General Sir Charles James Napier : and no doubt justly so, as it is hard to imagine a more helpless body of men than they are. Poor Nolan himself lost his life while charging at Balaklava, where the English horse was entirely cut to pieces by the Russians.' It is to be wondered where this officer received his *historical* education.

We will leave it to the reader to determine in his

own mind which custom is likely to produce the best horseman :—

The custom of the English gentlemen, who amuse themselves by, and whose favourite sport is the chase, riding across country after the hounds on blood horses; whose race horses are all bred for running, and where trotting races are rarely met with ; or—

The custom of Yankee gentlemen, to drive fast trotting horses, in light easy buggies, with a rein in each hand, a cigar between the teeth, and hat cocked upon one side of their heads, from one tavern or saloon to another, stopping at intervals to take a ' smile ' or to make up a trotting race with some comrade. The richest and most prominent men among them take no pride in a saddle-horse, rarely keep one, while as high as $38,000 has been paid for a fast trotter, independent of any other qualification. Men whose only idea as to the management of a horse's mouth (or ' hands ' in sporting language), one of the most essential points in horsemanship, is to haul as hard as they can with both hands, and shout in order to increase the pace of their trotting nags.

Which custom or habit is likely to produce the best riders?

If Colonel Brackett could only see Her Majesty's 13th Hussars manœuvring over the roughest ground at a speed which would astonish the smartest cavalry they have. If he could only see them skirmishing through oak scrub, across fields, over fences, as I have, without ever seeing a man thrown, unless his horse came down with him—a very rare occurrence— I fancy his eyes would be opened, and he would go back to his comrades and tell them they had never seen any riding in their lives, and did not know what was meant by the term.

Colonel Brackett, although his knowledge of military history is sadly deficient, and his education in that particular neglected, has nevertheless seen a good deal of service in the Mexican war, as well as during the Confederate war for independence, and in his work gives a good many valuable hints as to the management of cavalry horses. He says:

'Another subject has impressed itself strongly upon my mind, which is the fact that in our regular service the horses are groomed too much. I cannot say that this applies to the volunteers. In my own experience the fault with them lies the other way. What I mean is, that in the winter time, when the weather is cold, and the horses, as is almost always the case with us, are without suitable shelter, the grooming the horse one hour at day-break, and one hour just before sunset, is absolutely hurtful. Some cavalry officers who have been taught certain rules

H

insist upon the men keeping at work steadily one
hour on each horse without any regard to time,
place, circumstances, or anything else.   Now in the
fine stables which the military of France and Great
Britain have, it may do well to keep the horses
looking sleek-coated, giving them each day gentle
exercise ; but with us, who have our poor animals
trembling the great part of the winter from sheer
cold, it is worse than nonsense to tear up their hides
each day by means of the currycomb and brush.
The pores are left open, the skin is scratched, and
the wretched animals stand crouched up all night
suffering from the effects of this well-meant but ill-
administered grooming.   The condition of our poor
horses sometimes in winter, is such as to make any
heart susceptible of pity feel the most profound
sorrow.   But this I do not find fault with in actual
campaign : both men and horses must suffer, but do
not let us cavalry people make our only friends, our
horses, suffer unnecessarily.   British and French
officers may think this singular advice, but they must
recollect that their cavalry force is small compared
with ours, and they have every convenience to make
themselves and their horses comfortable, good stables, plenty of forage, and nice roads to travel upon.

  ' In cold weather care should be taken to see

that the horses are well blanketed during the night, and if necessary, men should be detailed to keep the blankets on, as horses are apt to rub or kick them off. No man can be a good cavalry officer unless he is continually on the alert, looking out for the welfare of his horses. Cavalry soldiers generally do well enough for themselves, but cavalry horses must be looked after.

'Horses' shoes should be inspected frequently, as in spite of every care, shoes are sometimes left on too long, and sometimes they are knocked off, and the horse on a rocky road becomes lame at once. The Indians never shoe their horses ; the hoofs of their animals become as hard nearly as flint. They go over the rockiest roads with our cavalry chasing them, and as soon as the shoes of our horses are torn off by the rocks they become disabled, and the Indians laugh at our efforts to overtake them.

' The shoeing tools of the farrier should consist of a shoeing knife, a toe knife, a shoeing hammer, a clinching iron, a clinch cutter, a pair of pinchers, and a rasp. What is known as a " buttress " should never be used, nor ought a shoe to be put on while hot, any more than is sufficient to show that it is of the right shape. When starting on a march, each horse ought to have two shoes at least fitted,

so that the farrier will have nothing to do but to
nail them on, in case any are lost while travelling.
Altogether, too little attention is paid to shoeing by
cavalry officers. Whatever relates to the care and
training of his horses is a part of his profession,
and the smallest matter ought not to be neglected.'

So important is it that the horses' shoes should be
attended to, that the shoe-cases should always contain a complete set of shoes fitted to the horse, and
nails, and when one is taken out to replace a lost one,
another should be made and returned to fill up the
vacancy at once, otherwise in the vicissitudes of
actual campaigning, the supply will soon fall off,
and the command then becomes worthless. An
officer of cavalry cannot pay too much attention
to this.

Colonel MacDougall, Adjutant-General of Militia,
Canada, the author of the 'Theory of War' and
other valuable military works, has issued a set of
regulations for the use of volunteers on active
service. In reference to the infantry, he says the
officers should look carefully after the men at night
after marching, and see themselves, that the men's
feet are bathed, the inside of the heel of the sock
soaped, and the men's toe-nails cut. He says
negligent officers will ridicule this as an excuse

for their laziness and neglect, but a good officer will omit nothing that will add to the efficiency of his men. In this he takes the right view, and cavalry officers will do well to keep in mind the principle, and look carefully after their horses' feet and backs.

CHAPTER VII.

FORMATION OF CAVALRY AND ELEMENTARY DRILL.

On doit chercher sans cesse, avec un soin scrupuleux, à-simplifier les exercices de la cavalerie, que tant d'innovateurs de nos jours ont mal-à-propos compliquées. Dans ces vues, il faudra nécessairement former et faire combattre cette troupe sur un front peu étendu.

Mottin de la Baime.

THE tactics of cavalry have been continually changing, since the first period of their use to the present time. This has been caused by the changes in the arms with which they have fought, and the tactics and weapons of their opponents.

Among the Greeks the cavalry were organised in squares and lozenges, and sometimes in eight ranks in depth; there being two or three paces' interval between each man, to give them room to use their weapons. Their arms were generally the lance and the sword, with sometimes the javelin added; they also carried bucklers in many instances.

The Roman ' turmâ,' or troop, consisted of thirty-two men in four ranks, and the interval between the 'turmæ' appears to have been equal to the front. The Grecian ἴλη, or troop, consisted of sixty-four men, and the interval between them was equal to the front.

Under Henry II. of France, cavalry were formed again in oblong squares, and in ten ranks. Henry IV. fixed the depth at six ranks.

Gustavus Adolphus diminished the unwieldy size of the squadrons, and reduced the depth, first to four ranks, and then to three. Tilly drew up his cuirassiers ten, and his light cavalry six deep— Wallenstein eight and five respectively.

In France, in 1766, cavalry were formed in two ranks, which has been the universal custom for many years in all the armies of Europe.

Now, however, the opinion seems to be fast gaining ground, that the rank entire or single rank formation is decidedly the best for cavalry and dragoons. General Bacon used that formation in Portugal, in 1833–4 ; and many letters have been published from our best cavalry officers in favour of it. The Duke of Wellington was a supporter of this principle, as also was Lord Vivian and Lord William Russell.

General Rosser says: 'I much prefer the *single rank* formation to the double. It is more easily managed, and nothing like so many accidents occur.'

General Fitzhugh Lee, however, does not coincide with the others, he merely recommends that the rear rank should rein back. In his letter to me he says : ' My experience in the old United States army, as in the service of the Confederate States, is decidedly in favour of the double rank. You can never get ground sufficient to manœuvre large bodies of cavalry by the single rank system, and in charging by platoon, company, or squadron front, the advantage of the single rank can always be obtained by directing the rear rank to hold their horses back a little, until the interval is attained.'

The squadrons should be told off in divisions, troops, and by fours, in accordance with the regulations for the cavalry issued by the Horse Guards, but the system of pivot flanks should be entirely done away with. The troops should be instructed to work as well inverted as any other way, in fact there should be no such thing as inversion. Colonel Jenyns, 13th Hussars, has received permission to work his regiment on the non-pivot principle, and it answers admirably, and gives twice as much facility in manœuvring as the old system. No corps could be more pliable, more in hand, more ready in field movements than that gallant regiment, as drilled and exercised by its accomplished commander. If all the cavalry regiments are as well up in field drill, in riding, in swordsmanship, in *esprit-de-corps*, as Her Majesty's 13th Hussars, the British dragoons leave little to be desired on these points. I, who have been accustomed to the old system, have been forcibly struck with the ease and extreme rapidity with which this regiment can skirmish across country, through bush and broken ground, and rally at once on any given point.

In everything, except the pivot system in the field movements and the double rank, the instructions in the 'Regulations' are quite sufficient for the Heavy Cavalry or cavalry of the line; but, as the non-pivot drill has not yet come generally into use, I have applied to Colonel Jenyns for a copy of his system, by which he instructs his regiment. With great kindness and courtesy he has complied with my request, and I have inserted in the Appendix his reply in full, detailing his whole system. I cannot urge too strongly upon my readers the advantage of studying attentively these ideas and practical remarks of one of the most gallant and distinguished cavalry officers in the British Army.

Now with reference to dragoons.

This force must necessarily be drilled and instructed, in addition to all the movements required when mounted, to dismount rapidly, form up on foot, advance, retire, take ground right or left, form column, deploy, skirmish, remount suddenly, and act on horseback as occasion may require. By this means cavalry are brought to the highest pitch of usefulness. The rapidity of movement of the lightest of cavalry is gained, with the ability of the best infantry to skirmish or attack on foot on any description of ground. It was by the power of fighting in this way that the cavalry were able to effect such results during the Confederate war for independence. It was by this system that General John H. Morgan, at the head of less than 1,200 such horsemen in his first Kentucky raid, during twenty-four days travelled nearly 1,000 miles, captured 17 towns, destroyed all the government supplies and arms in them, dispersed about 1,500 home guards, and paroled some 1,200 regular troops, losing in killed, wounded, and missing about 90 during the whole raid.

It was by adopting this system of using cavalry that Sheridan in 1865 cut off the retreat of Lee's army, and caused its surrender at Appomatox Court House, thereby ending the war. Sir Henry Havelock, in his work on ' The Three main Military Questions of the Day,' places great stress on this instance as a strong proof of the value of cavalry dismounted in a pursuit, and to a certain extent he is right. But it must not be forgotten that the South were completely exhausted at that time, and overpowered by overwhelming numbers, and would probably, although not so quickly, have surrendered from sheer inanition. Sir Henry Havelock also rates Sheridan too high. Sheridan was as poor an officer for the popular reputation he had as ever lived, unless perhaps General Grant. Both these men were lucky enough to come into command after the strength of the South had been worn out in numerous fruitless victories over M'Clellan, M'Dowell, Pope, Burnside, Meade, Hooker, &c.

M'Clellan and Sherman were the only generals the North had, and they were very fair officers, but of course not to be compared with Lee or Stonewall Jackson. Colonel Hasbrouck Davis seems to have had more of the real cavalry spirit than any cavalry officer of the North, although I have never heard what became of him. I suppose he was not a politician, or we should have heard more of him. General Averill was also a most skilful and efficient cavalry leader, very far superior to Sheridan.

General Morgan used his force purely on the principle we advocate for dragoons, and therefore it will not be out of place to insert in full General Duke's description of Morgan's tactics, as contained in his ' History of Morgan's Cavalry.' He says : ' The ideas which the experience of the last eight months had suggested regarding the peculiar tactics best adapted to the service and the kind of fighting we had to do, were now put into practical shape. A specific drill, different in almost every respect from every other employed for cavalry, was adopted. It was based upon a drill taught in the old army, for Indian fighting, called "Maury's skirmish tactics for cavalry," I believe, but as that drill provided for the employment of but very few men, and ours had to provide for the evolutions of regiments and eventually brigades, the latter was necessarily much more comprehensive. The formation of the company, the method of counting off in sets, and of dismounting, and deploying to the front, flanks and rear for battle, were the same as in Maury's tactics, but a great many movements necessary to the change of front, as the kind of ground or other circumstances required it to be made in various ways, to the formations from column into line and from line into column, the methods of taking ground to the front or rear in establishing or changing line, the various methods of providing, as circumstances might require, for the employment of all or only part of a regiment or brigade or for the employment of supports and reserves,—all these evolutions had to be added. It would be uninteresting to all but the practical military reader, and unnecessary as well, to enter into a minute explanation of these matters.'

'If the reader will only imagine a regiment drawn up in single rank, the flank companies skirmishing, sometimes on horseback, and then thrown out as skirmishers on foot, and so deployed as to cover the whole front of the regiment, the rest of the men dismounted (one out of each set of four, and the corporals remaining to hold the horses) and deployed, as circumstances required and the command indicated, to the front of either flank, or to the rear of the line of horses, the files two yards apart, and then imagine this line moved forward at a double quick, or oftener a half run, he will have an idea of Morgan's style of fighting.

'Exactly the same evolutions were applicable for horseback or foot fighting, but the latter method was much oftener practised.   We were in fact not cavalry but mounted riflemen.   A small body of mounted men were usually kept in reserve to act on the flanks, cover a retreat, or press a victory, but otherwise our men fought very little on horseback, except on scouting expeditions.   Our men were all admirable riders, trained from childhood to manage the wildest horses with perfect ease, but the nature of the ground on which we generally fought, covered with dense woods, or crossed by high fences, and the impossibility of devoting sufficient time to the training of the horses, rendered the employment of large bodies of

mounted men to any good purpose very difficult. It
was very easy to charge down a road in column of
fours, but very hard to charge across the country in
extended line, and keep any sort of formation. Then
we never used sabres, and long guns were not exactly
the weapons for cavalry evolutions. We found the
method of fighting on foot more effective. We could
manœuvre with more certainty, and sustain less and
inflict more loss—" The long flexible line curving
forward at each extremity," as an excellent writer
described it, was very hard to break ; if forced back
at one point, a withering fire from every other would
be poured in on the assailants. It admitted too of
such facility of manœuvring, it could be thrown about
like a rope, and by simply facing to the right or left,
and double quicking in the same direction, every
man could be quickly concentrated at any point
where it was desirable to mass them.

'It must be remembered that Morgan very rarely
fought with the army ; he had to make his command
a self-sustaining one. If repulsed, he could not fall
back and reform behind the infantry. He had to
fight infantry, cavalry, artillery, take towns when
every house was a garrison, and attack fortifications
with nothing to depend on but his own immediate
command. He was obliged, therefore, to adopt a
method which enabled him to do a great deal in a

short time, and to keep his men always in hand, whether successful or repulsed. With his supports from 40 to 500 miles distant, an officer had better learn to rely on himself.

'If General Morgan had ever been enabled to develope his plan of organisation as he wished, he would have made his division of mounted riflemen a miniature army. With his regiments armed as he wished them—a battalion of two or three hundred men appropriately armed, and attached to each brigade, to be used only as cavalry, and with his battery of three-inch Parrots and train of mountain howitzers, he could have met any contingency. The ease and rapidity with which this simple drill was learned, and the expedition with which it enabled all movements to be accomplished, chiefly recommended it to Morgan. I have seen his division, when numbering over 3,000 men, and stretched out in column, put into line of battle in 30 minutes.'

CHAPTER VIII.

MORALE.

L'effet moral est pour les trois quarts dans la puissance de la Cavalerie
General De Brack.

THE first Napoleon has said that 'the moral' in war is to 'the physical' in the ratio of three to one. There can be no doubt as to the correctness of this principle—in fact, it seems as if a still higher place should be given to the former. History has shown that in all ages the *morale* of the soldiers has had a most important influence on the result of battles, even where the mere physical force has been arrayed on the opposite side.

At the present day, however, when men do not fight at close quarters, but with deadly weapons at longer distances, the physical force is rarely or ever brought into play; never, in fact, in the infantry, and only rarely in the cavalry. Now, therefore, the moral effect is what decides battles, and the art of war resolves itself simply into the art of improving the *morale* of your own men and depressing that of the enemy.

Take for example two lines of infantry marching towards each other. They will never close, and the greater physical power of one line press back the weaker force of the other; but first one will waver, then halt, and finally fall back, with a greater or less degree of order, in accordance with the courage and discipline of the troops. In the same way, cavalry charging infantry will often turn on receiving a volley in their faces. It is not the physical force of the volley which does this, because those who turn are not those who are struck, but the mere moral effect on the minds of the men produces the result.

There is, in fact, no limit to the successes which will be gained by forces with a high *morale* over extraordinary odds, where their opponents are in a demoralised condition.

The elements which contribute to the *morale* of soldiers in battle are almost innumerable, and, as I have said, every officer should pay great attention to this point. We will mention a few circumstances which have their influence upon this mysterious feeling in the men's minds.

Confidence in their commander is one of the most important points in giving a good *morale* to troops.

I

Stonewall Jackson for many reasons had so won the confidence of his men, that it was impossible to defeat them when he was in command. And for the same reason the enemy were so demoralised by his presence before them, that in some battles, fugitives flying from the front line calling out ' Jackson is coming ' have spread a panic into the reserves, without their even having been under fire. This certainly is a good example of moral power over physical.

Winning the first battle in a war is also of the greatest importance in improving the spirits of the troops, and depressing the confidence of the enemy. A victory at the commencement of a campaign has its effect through the whole period of hostilities. This was clearly shown in the Confederate war for independence. There were several theatres of operations, one in Virginia 'on to Richmond,' and the other main one in the south-west. In Virginia the first battle, that of Bull's Run, was a brilliant victory for the Southerners, and the consequence was, that in that portion of the country the *morale* of the two armies never changed, that of the South being very high, while that of the North was very low. The result was that Lee's army were never really defeated and routed, and only succumbed in the end to overwhelming numbers and want of supplies of every description. But even in the last sad days for the South, before the surrender at Appomatox Court House, the *morale* of the Southern troops was good, and the army, like a lion at bay, retired slowly, sullenly, and in order, dealing heavy blows on their pursuers when pressed too closely.

On the other theatre of operations, the taking of Fort Donelson and the retreat of Albert Sidney Johnston's army from Bowling Green gave the *morale* to the enemy, and the South never recovered from it during the whole war.

Taking the initiative has a good effect on the minds of the soldiers. In the same way, cavalry charging cavalry which awaits it at the halt will always succeed, because the *morale* must be better in the charging force. History proves this conclusively.

Napoleon says: 'The worst plan to adopt in war is . always that which is the most pusillanimous or commonly called prudent;' and that 'True wisdom consists in an energetic resolution.' This is one of the most important points in war. The more one studies military history the more he will become convinced that the first great quality of a general is a sound judgment, but that the next is an indomitable energy and an iron will; without this the best judgment in the world is worthless.

Energy, indefatigable, indomitable energy, is perfectly invaluable in a general.   Every great captain
has been distinguished for this quality.   Alexander,
Turenne, Marlborough, Napoleon, Suwarrow, Lee,
Stonewall Jackson, all possessed it in the highest
degree.

In one critical period in the army of Virginia, one
of General Jackson's staff expressed his fear that the
army would be compelled to fall back.   The General
replied sharply : ' Who said that ? No, sir, we shall not
fall back ; we shall attack them.'   And he did attack
them, and defeated them completely at Chancellorsville in a day or two afterwards.   His only order,
after getting his men into position, being his favourite
battle-cry : ' Press forward.'   This was his message to
every general, and his answer to every enquiry.
After he was mortally wounded after dark, his only
message to General Lee was that ' the enemy should
be pressed in the morning.'   It was this indomitable
will and fiery energy that improved and strengthened to such a remarkable degree the *morale* of
his men, and so demoralised his opponents.

General Breckinridge mentioned an instance to
me which occurred in his campaign in South-Western
Virginia in 1864. He was endeavouring, with a small
army, to defend the salt works against a force some
five times as large as his own.   They had attacked

him in a difficult position, and it was only by the most strenuous exertions, and the greatest courage on the part of his men, that he could hold his position till dark. The enemy were outflanking him and threatening his rear, when he thought of a bold plan to extricate his army, and inflict a blow upon his opponents. He discovered a narrow path over the mountain and quietly took his troops that way during the night, round to the rear of the enemy, whom he attacked by surprise before day. The Federals thought they were reinforcements come to Breckinridge's assistance; and becoming rapidly demoralised, retreated hurriedly in different directions, Breckinridge closely following them and taking a number of prisoners.

This was a striking example of the moral effect of a bold energetic course. Most generals would have endeavoured to effect a retreat before superior numbers, which would have soon changed the *morale* and given the benefit of it to the enemy.

Men should always be led to believe that their numbers are much larger than they are: it gives them confidence, misleads spies, and has its effect upon the enemy. Napoleon decreed levies which were never raised, and increased his returns of all kinds, so as to give his troops confidence in their numbers and equipment.

M'Clellan called his forced retreat to the James
River, in 1862, a strategic change of base.   This may
or may not have had any effect on his troops, but
one thing is certain, that at Malvern Hill, after six
days of defeat, they held their ground against heavy
attacks, encouraged by the gunboats which assisted
them.

The system of target firing and the experiments
which I have referred to in another chapter, are of
little use in actual fighting, and the deductions drawn
from them are simply silly; but as a means of improving the *morale* of the infantry soldier, by the
effect on his mind in giving him confidence in his
weapon, they may be useful, and the truth of the
deduction in that case is of no importance.   In fact
the only advantage in a breechloader, is in the confidence it gives the man, and the effect it has on
the *morale* of the enemy.   As far as regards the
practical effect in action, and the numbers killed and
wounded in proportion to the numbers engaged, there
is no doubt that more loss was occasioned by the old
rifle loaded with a patch and which used to be fired
only a few times in a whole action.

Marshal Marmont speaking of the battle of
Busaco in Portugal on September 27, 1810, where
Massena made an attempt to force the English
position, when he might have turned it, and was

repulsed with the loss of 6,000 men says: 'The result of this unfortunate combat changed the *morale* of the two armies, and diminished on our side that blind confidence so necessary to success, while it re-inspired that of the enemy. Had this event not happened, an attack upon the lines of Lisbon would probably have been attempted, and had that succeeded, the success would have terminated the war in the Peninsula.'

Kinglake, in his history of the invasion of the Crimea, treats this subject of *morale* in so graphic and interesting a manner, that we cannot forbear quoting it here before concluding this chapter. Speaking of the advance of the Highland brigade at the Battle of the Alma, he says :—

' There are things in this world which eluding the resources of the dry narrator, can still be faintly imaged by that subtle power which sometimes enables mankind to picture dim truth by fancy. According to the thought which floated in the mind of the churchman who taught to all the Russias their grand form of prayer for victory, there are " angels of light " and " angels of darkness and horror," who soar over the heads of soldiery destined to be engaged in close fight and attend them into battle.* When

* This is part of the Russian prayer for victory: 'O Lord . . . . hear us this day praying for these troops that are gathered together.

the fight grows hot the angels hover down near to earth with their bright limbs twined deep in the wreaths of smoke which divide the combatants. But it is no coarse bodily help that these angels bring. More purely spiritual than the old immortals, they strike no blow, they snatch no man's weapon, they lift away no warrior in a cloud. What the Angel of Light can bestow is valour, priceless valour, and light to lighten the path to victory, giving men grace to see the bare truth, and seeing it to have the mastery. To regiments which are to be blessed with victory the Angel of Light seems to beckon and gently draw his men forward. What the Angel of Darkness can inflict is fear, horror, despair, and it is given him also to be able to plant error and vain fancies in the minds of the doomed soldiery. By false dread he scares them. Whether he who conceived this prayer was soldier, or priest, or soldier and priest in one, it seems to me that he knew more of the true nature of the strife of good infantry than he could utter in common prose, for indeed it is no physical power which rules the conflict between two well-formed bodies of foot.

Bless and strengthen them, and give them a manly heart against their enemies. Send them an Angel of Light, and to the enemies an Angel of Darkness and Horror, to scatter them and place a stumbling-block before them, to weaken their hearts and turn their courage into flight.'

'The mere killing and wounding which occurs whilst a fight is still hanging in doubt does not so alter the relative numbers of the combatants as in that way to govern the result. The use of the slaughter which takes place at that time lies mainly in the stress which it puts upon the minds of those who themselves remaining unhurt are nevertheless disturbed by the sight of what is befalling their comrades. In that way a command of the means of inflicting death and wounds is one element of victory. But it is far from being the chief one. Nor is it by perfectness of discipline nor yet·by contempt of life that men can assure to themselves the mastery over their foes. More or less all these things are needed, but the truly governing power is that ascendancy of the stronger over the weaker heart which (because of the mystery of its origin) the churchman was willing to ascribe to angels coming down from on high.

'The turning moment of a fight is a moment of trial for the soul and not for the body, and it is therefore that such courage as men are able to gather from being gross in numbers can be easily outweighed by the warlike virtue of a few. To the stately " Black Watch " and the hot 93rd with Campbell leading them on there was vouchsafed that stronger heart for which the brave pious Muscovites had prayed. Over the souls of the men in the column there was spread first the gloom, then the swarm of vain delusions, and at last, the sheer horror which might be the work of the Angel of Darkness. The two lines marched straight on. The three columns shook. They were not yet subdued. They were stubborn, but every moment the two advancing battalions grew nearer and nearer, and although dimly masking the scant numbers of the Highlanders there was still the white curtain of smoke which always rolled on before them, yet fitfully and from moment to moment, the signs of them could be traced on the right hand and on the left in a long shadowy line, and their coming was ceaseless.

'But moreover the Highlanders being men of great stature and in strange garb, their plumes being tall, and the view of them being broken and distorted by the wreaths of smoke, and there being too an ominous silence in their ranks, there were men among the Russians who began to conceive a vague terror, the terror of things unearthly, and some they say imagined that they were charged by horsemen, strange, silent, monstrous, bestriding giant chargers.* The columns were falling into that plight, we have

---

* It was from the poor wounded prisoners that our people gathered the accounts of the impression produced upon their minds by the advance of the Highlanders.

twice before seen it this day, were falling into that
plight that its officers were moving hither and thither
with their drawn swords, were commanding, were
imploring, were threatening, nay, were even laying
hands on their soldiery and striving to hold them
fast in their places. This struggle is the last stage
but one in the agony of a body of good infantry
massed in close column.'

CHAPTER IX.

CAVALRY TACTICS.

La force de la cavalerie consistant dans la rapidité de ses mouve-ments, dans la violence de son choc et dans le bon ordre qu'elle tient dans ces manœuvres.—*Warnery.*

A GENERAL commanding an army should make use of his cavalry in accordance with the proportion it bears to the other forces, and also with reference to its quality. If he has a great preponderance of cavalry, he should then employ it freely by attacking the enemy's flanks and rear, and by charges in line when the enemy are shaken and the circumstances are favourable. Even with inferior cavalry, great results can sometimes be obtained, if they are managed properly, and brought into play at the right time.

Cavalry cannot fight in a defensive position with-out the support of infantry or mounted rifles. It is more useful in attacking positions in order to clear the way to a victory, which it will often succeed in doing if it is promptly and strongly supported by the other arms, who can secure the advantages, which cavalry can so often temporarily gain; this is especially the duty of cavalry proper. In conjunction with light dragoons, its great use is to complete a victory by carrying off prisoners and trophies, by preventing the enemy from rallying, and by pursuing the beaten troops. It is also required to cover the retreat of its own broken infantry and artillery.

Dragoons are also particularly available for rapidly succouring threatened points; even for supporting weak points of lines of battle by dismounting the men, and forming them up on foot in the front of the action. Dragoons were continually used in this way in the war in America, and to good purpose.

Grand attacks of cavalry on lines of battle must be supported by artillery and infantry, otherwise their success will not be of much use. Cavalry charging batteries will almost invariably carry them, if not defeated by the infantry or cavalry supporting the guns. And then again, infantry must be at hand to hold the cannon when carried. At Balaklava, the Light Brigade charged a battery of 30 guns in the centre of the Russian lines, carried it readily, sabred the gunners, broke through the supports, and drove the cavalry in rear of the guns back upon their infantry, and mixed up in terrible confusion a

great portion of the Russian army, between some
hills and an aqueduct over which there was but one
bridge.   Had that charge been properly supported,
the Heavy Brigade sent on in support, and the infantry pushed forward, a great portion of the Russian
army would have been captured.   As it was, the
Light Brigade were sacrificed, and the sole result
was, a magnificent but useless display of bravery
and 'dash.'

Cavalry can also be used to great advantage in
being thrown upon the flank of an enemy's line of
battle.   It can do this with greater freedom than
infantry, because its speed is such, that it need not
fear to be cut off in its retreat, in case of a repulse.
It can easily rally upon the main body if not successful, while, on the other hand, if it is victorious,
the result may be the loss of the enemy's army.
Mounted dragoons are particularly useful for this
service, for they can form lines of battle on foot
after riding up with great rapidity, and slow-marching
infantry would not be able so quickly to accommodate
its movements in order to meet them to the best
advantage.   This was often practised in the Confederate war for independence by both sides, with
good effect.

Cavalry, as well as mounted rifles, should never
attack an enemy without keeping a portion of their

force in hand as a reserve. Cavalry proper should always form up in positions where they would have their front clear, and favourable for charging, and their flanks also open, except there are woods or enclosures occupied by their own troops ; otherwise, an enemy gaining possession of the broken ground, would be able to inflict great loss upon them, without the latter being able to prevent it, or attack them.

Cavalry proper, charging, should not extend too far in length ; it is better to have a small front and more reserves. The flanks by this means are better protected, success can be turned to a greater account, and disaster to one line does not affect the whole and the reserves may be able to succour the first line, and turn defeat into victory.

Cavalry should never be distributed along the front line of battle ; it should always be posted on the flanks or in rear. It is its want of defensive power which renders it unfit to form a portion of a line. A notable instance of this occurred at the battle of Blenheim, where Marshal Tallard drew up his cavalry in the centre of his front line of battle. Marlborough instantly perceived the weakness of his adversary's dispositions, and drew up his horsemen for a decisive charge upon the French centre. The opposing horse awaited the charge at the halt, were immediately pierced through and routed, and the French, divided and surrounded, were utterly defeated, and the greater proportion captured, including the commanding general. At Ramilies, Marlborough took advantage in the same way of the same defect in his opponents' arrangements.

It is necessary to be careful in ordering a charge of cavalry to have the ground reconnoitred beforehand, or to know that there are no impassable obstacles. In the Peninsular War the 23rd Light Dragoons were almost destroyed by neglect of this precaution at the battle of Talavera. It is thus described in Beamish's ' History of the King's German Legion : '—

' To check these movements General Anson's brigade of cavalry was ordered forward and it advanced at a trot, in the same order in which it had been previously formed, the 23rd Dragoons on the right, and the 1st Hussars of the legion on the left, the whole in two lines. The leading columns of the French seeing that they were threatened by a charge of cavalry, formed three squares, behind the intervals of which their light horsemen took post, and thus they awaited the advance of the brigade. After the first order to trot no further word of command was made known to the squadron officers, but as soon as the leading squadrons of the twenty-third came within range of the French artillery, the horses crowded to the left and began to canter. The hussars were now galled by the enemy's riflemen from the mountain, and several from the serrefile ranks of the regiment were killed and wounded. Arrived under the hill the brigade was loudly cheered by General Hill's division, and the encouraging shout met with a corresponding answer from the fearless horsemen who gallantly advanced upon the bayonets, the twenty-third taking the larger square which was in front of that regiment, while the hussars moved upon the two smaller squares upon the left. But just when the pace had been increased and the charge had commenced, a hollow cleft, till now hidden by the long grass, presented itself in front of the leading squadrons.

'Too late to pull up, the foremost horsemen rode headlong at the hollow, and a frightful scene ensued. Some tumbled in and over the ravine, some scrambled through it, while others leaped boldly across the chasm and gained the other side, but great disorder was the consequence. In front of the hussars the ravine was from six to eight feet deep, and from twelve to eighteen feet in breadth, while widening in front of the twenty-third; it was there also more shallow, and the greater part of

K

that regiment were able to get across, but so dispersed, and in such confusion, that they could make
no impression upon the square, and the French
artillery sweeping their ranks and fresh troops
arriving to the already overpowering mass of the
enemy, they were obliged to give way, and leaving
nearly half their number on the field, escaped from
the unequal contest.'

Cavalry should never be drawn up in long lines
one behind the other as it is sure to lead to confusion, and the mass very soon becomes unmanage-
able. Among the cavalry of Frederick the Great
it was customary when advancing to double the
extent of the intervals between the squadrons, the
second line being only partly deployed.

At Craone in 1814, the Russian cavalry though
successful in their first charge got into such disorder
that the whole mass was drawn in confusion from
the field to save it from destruction.

The flanks of cavalry must be carefully protected,
no force is so helpless when attacked in flank, as it.
At Ocana in Spain, in 1809, the Spanish cavalry
attempted to attack the French horse under Sebastiani. Napier thus describes it : ' The Spaniards came
on at a trot, and Sebastiani directed Paris with a
regiment of light cavalry and the Polish lancers, to
turn and fall upon the right flank of the approach-

ing squadrons, which being executed with great vigour, especially by the Poles, caused considerable confusion, which the Spanish general endeavoured to remedy by closing to the assailed flank. But to effect this he formed his left centre in one vast column, whereupon Sebastiani charged headlong into the midst of it with his reserve, and the enormous mass yielding to the shock got into confusion, and finally gave way. Many were slain, several hundred wounded, and eighty troopers and above 500 horses were taken.'

Cavalry should pursue vigorously, but with caution, always keeping a portion of the force in hand. The effect of the neglect of this precaution was strongly felt in the Peninsula on one occasion in 1812. General Hill had sent General Slade with two regiments of cavalry from Llera, to protect the gathering of the harvest, General Lallemande met him with two regiments of dragoons. Slade immediately attacked the French and drove them with loss, beyond the defile of Maquilla, a distance of eight miles. The English galloped rashly in pursuit through the defile, the general riding in the foremost ranks, and the supports mingled in the tumultuous charge. But Lallemande had his reserves well in hand, and turned upon the disorderly mass of English following him, broke through them, killed or wounded forty-eight men, pursued the remainder for six miles, recovering all his own prisoners, as well as capturing two officers and over 100 men from his adversary.

Horse artillery should generally accompany cavalry, and assist it in all its attacks, by shaking the enemy with its fire, before the charge is made. It should also always be attached to dragoons or mounted rifles, for as they fight generally on foot it is absolutely necessary for them to be supported by guns. General Morgan's cavalry had their howitzers well known as the ' bull pups.' And General Stuart had his horse artillery, commanded by the ' gallant ' Pelham.

We shall now give a few examples of the use of the dragoons or mounted rifles, in the war in America, in order to show the system of tactics there adopted, and the advantage and power of a mounted force of that description, if used in accordance with the genius of the arm, and with a due regard to its armament.

Just before the battle of Chancellorsville Fitzhugh Lee's brigade, and a battery of horse artillery under Major Pelham, were at Culpepper, with pickets along the Rappahanock watching the fords, when General Averill of the Federal army advanced, and attacked the picket at Kelly's Ford, overpowered it and captured more than half of its number. He then moved on in the direction of Culpepper Court House. He soon encountered Fitz Lee coming down to meet him, a stubborn and desperate fight at once began, and it was only by extraordinary valour, and with severe loss, that Fitz Lee was able to maintain himself until the Confederate cavalry being *dismounted*, and placed in good position perpendicular to the road, enabled him effectually to check General Averill's advance. The battle raged until late in the evening. Averill then withdrew and recrossed the river, the Confederates closely pursuing him.

In General Stuart's celebrated raid around M'Clellan's army through Pennsylvania in October, 1862, the tactics of his mounted rifles proved their value. He had an encounter on his return with the enemy near Poolesville in Maryland. He thus describes it in his official report : ' I ordered the charge, which was responded to in handsome style by the advance squadron (Irving's) of Lee's brigade, which drove back the enemy's cavalry upon the column of infantry advancing to occupy the crest from which the cavalry were driven. Quick as thought Lee's sharpshooters sprang to the ground, and engaged the infantry skirmishers, held them in check till the artillery in advance came up, which under the gallant Pelham drove back the enemy's force.' In this raid General Stuart at the head of 1,800 cavalry marched from Chambersburg to Leesburg, 90 miles, with only one hour's halt in 36 hours, including a forced passage of the Potomac.   A march without a parallel in history.

On another occasion a squadron of Federal cavalry . dashed up against Pelham's guns at a gallop, and having dismounted and placed a number of men behind a stone fence, not more than two hundred yards distant, poured in such a fatal carbine fire upon the gunners and artillery horses, as to seriously endanger the battery.   Two squadrons of Southern horse endeavoured to dislodge them by a mounted charge, but could not succeed, being broken by the murderous volleys of the dismounted cavalry.   It was only by a vigorous cannonading with round shot against the stone fence, that Pelham was able to dislodge them, the solid balls scattering the fragments of stone with terrible effect among the men behind it.

At the great cavalry battle at Brandy Station, 9th June, 1863, the line of battle was nearly three miles long, and an eye-witness says, 'along the woods which border the Rappahanock, the multitudinous firing of our dismounted sharpshooters sounded like the rattle of musketry in a regular battle.'

The first battle of Hartsville between Morgan's mounted rifles, and a Federal force under General

Johnson in August 1862, gives a good illustration of
the system of tactics pursued by General Morgan in
handling his men.   General Duke thus describes it:
   ' The column had gotten some distance upon the
Scottsville pike before the command to halt and
face towards the enemy had been transmitted to its
head.   And when these companies mentioned had
been formed, there was a gap of nearly two hundred
yards opened between them and the others that
were farther to the front.   Toward this gap the
enemy immediately darted.   Believing that we were
seeking to escape upon the Scottsville road, he
had thrown the bulk of his force in that direction at any rate, and it was formed and advanced rapidly and gallantly.   Throwing down the
eastern fence of the meadow, some three hundred
poured into it, formed a long line and dashed across
it with sabres drawn towards the line of horses
which they saw in the road beyond.   Companies
B. C. E. and F. were by this time *dismounted and
had dropped on their knees behind a low fence*
by the roadside as the enemy came rushing on.
They held their fire until the enemy were within
thirty yards, when they opened.   Then was seen the
effect of a volley from that long thin line which
looked so easy to break, and yet whose fire was so
deadly.   Every man had elbow-room and took dead

aim at an individual foe, and as the blaze left the
guns two-thirds of the riders and horses seemed to go
down.   The cavalry was at once broken and recoiled.
Our men sprang over the fence and ran close up to
them, as they endeavoured to retreat rapidly through
the gaps in the fence by which they had entered, and
poured in such another volley that the route was
completed.   However, they reformed and came back,
but only to be repulsed again.'   They were then
pursued by the mounted men, who followed them for
some three miles, when Johnson rallied in a strong
position on a hill, dismounted his men and formed
them up to check the pursuit.   The pursuers followed up swiftly and seeing the disposition made by
the enemy, *rapidly formed up dismounted under
cover of a hill*, and charged and carried the position
on foot.   General Johnson, his adjutant-general
Major Winfrey, and several other officers, and some
two hundred men, were taken prisoners.   General
Duke says General Johnson 'was evidently a fine
officer, but seemed not to comprehend the " new style
of cavalry" at all.'

General Duke speaking of the second battle of
Hartsville says, ' Cluke and Chenault having formed
at a gallop immediately dismounted their men and
advanced.   The open cavalry formation enabled us
with a smaller force to cover the entire front of the

enemy opposed to us, but while exposing us to less loss, made our fire more deadly. The 104th Ohio backed about twenty steps, the men striving to reload their guns, it then broke and ran in perfect disorder.' In this fight the enemy's loss was in killed and wounded over four hundred, and two thousand and four prisoners were carried off to Murfreesboro. Colonel Morgan's force was 1250 men, the enemy's over 2500 ; a more complete victory never was gained. Colonel Morgan was made a Brigadier-General at once as a reward for it, and a congratulatory order issued by General Bragg highly complimenting the command.

At the battle of Monocacy, on July 9, 1864, the Federal army, under General Wallace, was strongly posted on the eastern bank of the Monocacy to dispute General Early's passage of the river, and to cover Washington, which Early was then threatening. On reconnoitring the position, General Early concluded, that it was too strong to attempt to force by an attack in front, and was examining the river to see whether an attack could be made by crossing below the position and turning its left flank, when General M'Causland, who before it was known that the enemy had taken this position, had been ordered to cross the Monocacy, and occupy the bridges, in the effort to do so was observed crossing the river at a ford which he had discovered. This movement of M'Causland solved the problem for General Early, and the latter at once ordered General Breckinridge to move up rapidly with Gordon's division to M'Causland's assistance. The latter as soon as he had crossed dismounted his cavalry, and forming them up, advanced rapidly, full against the enemy's left flank, which he threw into confusion, and very nearly captured a battery of artillery, but the enemy concentrated upon him, and he was gradually forced back obstinately contesting the ground. M'Causland's attack gave time to Gordon's division to cross the river, gain the heights, and form up, and moving to M'Causland's support, the whole bore down upon the enemy, who were soon completely routed with heavy loss in killed and wounded, and 700 prisoners.

I have heard the particulars of this battle from Generals Early, Breckinridge, and M'Causland, and it seems to be generally conceded, that the action of the cavalry pointed out the mode in which the position could be turned, covered the passage of the river by the infantry, and thus contributed largely to the victory which ensued.

General Sheridan in his report of the first day's battle at Five Forks, gives an account which shows the value of cavalry being able to fight on foot. He says: 'A very obstinate and handsomely-contested battle ensued, in which, with all his cavalry and two divisions of infantry, the enemy was unable to drive five brigades of our cavalry *dismounted* from the open plain, in front of Dinwiddie Court House.'

'As the enemy's two divisions of infantry advanced to the attack, our cavalry threw up some slight breast-works of rails at some points along our lines, and when the enemy attempted to force this position they were handsomely repulsed, and gave up the attempt for the possession of the court house. It was after dark when the firing ceased, and the enemy lay on their arms that night not more than one hundred yards in front of our lines.'

Referring to this fight and the action of the mounted rifles in it, Sir Henry Havelock, Bart. V.C., in his very valuable and interesting work on 'The Three Main Military Questions of the Day,' says :—

'Without one thought of disparagement to our splendid cavalry, who have no more sincere admirer than the writer, it is not too much to say, that no British cavalry that he has ever been associated with, have either the arms, training, equipment, or instruction, to have enabled them under similar circumstances to play this part of independent and unsupported self-sufficing action at a distance from the other two arms.

'There is no British cavalry officer of experience in war, that reads this, but will candidly admit, that under similar circumstances, commanding cavalry, whose carbines only carry 300, or with some rifles 600 yards, his men dressed in a manner wholly unfitting them to work on foot, braced and strapped down within an inch of their lives, encumbered with long spurs and tripped up with jingling steel scabbards, he would first have fruitlessly attempted to keep back the advancing infantry by mounted skirmishers, whose fire is about as effective as that of so many boys' pop-guns, then perhaps charged repeatedly, each time with great loss to his men, then finally, consoling himself with the axiom that " Cavalry are an offensive and not a defensive arm," he would have come to the conclusion that that was no place for his troops, opposed unsupported to all three arms, and after tremendous loss of life and horseflesh, all to no purpose, would have retired on the main body, leaving the disputed ground to the enemy, *and causing the whole three days' work by which it had been gained to be done over again at some future time.*

'In a like case the action of European cavalry which has no defensive fire would have been retrograde, slower or faster, according to the *morale* of the troops and the determination of their leader, *but certainly retrograde.* The best that they could have effected without rifle fire would have been to repeat the brilliant though bootless conduct, and to suffer the heavy loss, that marked the action of the intrepid Piedmontese cavalry, that so devotedly prevented Forey from being surprised by the Austrians, and covered the formation of his troops, as they successively came on the field at Montebello in 1859, namely, to charge headlong time after time, at the cost of more than half their number, and be driven back after all. If our splendid costly cavalry are kept up for no more effectual action, or mode of fighting less ruinously expensive of the lives of brave men and magnificent horses than *that*, the sooner that a little of the light of modern change breaks in upon the directors of their organisation, and alters their training for one more capable of producing results bearing some slight proportion to the expense of their maintenance, the better. Better both for the men and officers concerned, and for the military reputation of the nation, whose defence may any day be committed to their worthy and gallant, but at present almost helpless and unavailing keeping.

' In the instance under consideration, not only was *no ground lost,* but the defence of the cavalry dismounted, using Spencer rifles, and sheltered from fire behind rails and slight earth-banks, *with their horses kept well under more solid cover farther to the rear,* was so effectual and stubborn as to cause severe loss to the two Confederate infantry divisions who assaulted them across the open, and who, after suffering many heavy casualties, drew off at night-fall, thoroughly foiled. They themselves lost next to nothing.'

These deductions, so vigorously and clearly put, show plainly the advantage of the mounted rifle principle; and it is a matter of gratification to the writer, to be so strongly supported by the views of an officer of great experience in active service; one who has learnt in the campaigns of India the same lessons which the Civil War in America has taught, and has not hesitated to advocate them through the medium of the printer's press.

CHAPTER X.

CAVALRY AGAINST CAVALRY.

Il est nécessaire que la première ligne soit suivie d'une seconde, et s'il était possible, d'une troisième de troupes fraîches. C'est sur ces principes que sont basées les règles de la formation et de l'emploi de la cavalerie, un jour de bataille.—*Archduke Charles.*

IN the above lines the Archduke Charles lays down in a few words the great principle of the employment of cavalry against cavalry in action—a maxim that has not been confined to any age, or any description of weapon—but at all times and under all circumstances has proved its truth.

The necessity of having reserves of fresh troops in cavalry actions is, without doubt, the most important principle connected with the force, and numberless examples can be adduced to prove, not only the correctness of the rule, but also to show the absolute necessity of an adherence to its teaching.

At the battle of Würtzburg in 1796 the Archduke Charles had a good opportunity of practically testing the necessity of reserves in the cavalry fight which took place during that engagement. He thus describes it in his ' Principes de la Stratégie.' ' The Imperial Cavalry attacked the French Cuirassiers the instant they formed up. The Prince of Lichtenstein moved around Euerfeld with the light cavalry, supported by a regiment of the reserve, and directed his march between this village and the farm of Seligenstädter-Hof, against the flanks of the enemy. This manœuvre was completely successful ; the French cavalry who had *awaited the charge* without moving were overthrown, but, as generally happens, the victorious squadrons were themselves in disorder. Bonnaud charged them in turn with a part of his heavy cavalry, which came up and threw them back upon the cuirassiers who were advancing in column. Sustained by a regiment of this arm, which moved out of the line, the repulsed squadrons endeavoured to outflank the right of the French cavalry, but they fell in the line of fire of the French infantry, which occupied the little woods, and were charged by some squadrons, which, *having gained their flank* by a rapid movement, repulsed them. At this moment the French cavalry were all engaged, while the Austrians, on the other hand, had still *twelve squadrons of cuirassiers disposable*; these last advanced in close order against the enemy at the trot, broke through them, and drove them back upon their infantry. All the efforts of the general-in-chief and Bonnaud to rally them were useless.'

There is a treatise on the tactics of cavalry as opposed to cavalry contained in the account of that one action just given. Not only is the necessity of supports clearly shown, and *the fact that the victory will lean to the side which brings up the last reserves* plainly manifested, but the other two principles or maxims of cavalry actions also illustrated and proved, viz :—

2. *That cavalry which awaits the shock of opposing horsemen will always be overthrown.*

3. *That cavalry attacked in flank, while engaged in front, must give way.*

General Lloyd gives an example of the truth of the second maxim, which occurred in Frederick the Great's wars. ' Ziethen's regiment of hussars fell in with the Austrian carabineers and was repulsed, but on seeing the king's army arrive they rallied, attacked the carabineers (who imprudently *waited quietly on the spot*), broke them, drove some hundreds into a morass, where they were killed or made prisoners in sight of the Austrian van-guard, who could not relieve them, for the action lasted only a few minutes.'

It was mainly owing to the judicious use of his reserves, that Cromwell was able to overcome the

Royalist horse at the battle of Marston Moor. These fresh troops, falling upon Rupert's cavalry while engaged in the *mêlée*, completely defeated them.

At the battle of Leipsic in 1813, Murat, Latour-Maubourg, and Bourdesoult, at the head of 5,000 horse, charged the centre of the allied army, broke Prince Eugene of Wirtemberg's infantry, overthrew the light squadrons of the Russian Guard, and captured twenty-six guns; but while in the confusion caused by success, they were charged in flank by 400 fresh Cossacks of the Guard, who not only retook all the guns, but drove them back in confusion to their own lines.

Here two principles were exemplified; the last reserves, and the flank attack, deciding the result of the conflict.

Cavalry are very likely to be defeated, if surprised by the enemy before being formed up ready to meet them. It is therefore necessary to advance prepared to attack, when within reach of the enemy, and to avoid manœuvring in his immediate presence. If changes are to be made in the disposition of cavalry, a small portion of the leading troops should, if possible, be put into position quickly to charge the enemy, in order to cover the movements of the remainder, who should be formed up with the greatest rapidity. Useless words of command should be done away with, and as little repetition as possible should be required, in order to save time. It takes some seconds longer than necessary, it appears, to give the commands to a brigade of cavalry, repeated as they are by regimental squadron and troop leaders. These might be reduced somewhat, to good purpose.

In moving over broken ground towards an enemy to attack, where lines cannot well be moved in order, an advance by fours from the right of squadrons and a march in a line of columns of fours is very useful, and the line can be formed in the shortest possible time. This would be a good method of moving across a country like Canada or the United States, where the leading fours of each squadron galloping on could dismount a couple of men who would open a gap in the rail fences. If a line of skirmishers is thrown out, they should perform this duty ; this could be done in a few seconds, not even necessitating a halt of the columns. If under fire, however, the cavalry should keep in line as long as possible, in order to avoid losses, and to prevent one horse falling over another, in case of any being struck down.

Always, if possible, take the initiative with cavalry, and if the force opposed to you is so numerous as to outflank you, keep reserves in your rear to protect your flanks, while with the remainder break through the centre of the enemy's line. With your flanks guarded and reserves to support you, there should be no hesitation.

If cavalry attempts by a flank march too near to the enemy to surround or outflank him, there is a great danger of its being attacked in the flank of the column, and being defeated. As for example, the defeat of the Spanish cavalry by General Sebastiani at Ocana in 1809 as described in the last chapter.

The second or third lines of cavalry should always be in lines of small columns, in order to leave openings for the first line to retire through in case of defeat, and to enable them quickly to deploy on the heads of their respective columns. If the lines are full, the defeat of the first will carry away the other two.

After the defeat of the Russian General Sacken at Montmirail in January 1814, the Prussian General Horn was ordered with twenty-four squadrons to keep the French in check at Château-Thierry until Sacken could cross the Marne. He formed his troops in two lines of equal force, without any intervals. The French charged the first line which advanced to the attack, routed it, drove it back upon the second line, which threw it also into confusion, and the whole force was scattered in every direction.

The charge of the heavy brigade of English cavalry

through three lines of Russian horsemen in the Crimean war at Balaklava was another proof of the accuracy of this maxim.

A cavalry officer should always remember, that in a defile, in a road between high fences, or at the *débouché* of a bridge, disparity in numbers has not the same effect as in open ground, and his movements should be bolder in consequence. In covering a retreat, therefore, thirty or forty men in such situations may paralyse the action of several hundreds. On July 4, 1810, Captain Krauchenberg was falling back, with a squadron of the hussars of the King's German Legion and two guns, from Gallegos to Almeida, closely pursued by three regiments of French cavalry. On retiring over a bridge on the road, Krauchenberg took his squadron over at a gallop. Beamish thus describes what occurred : ' The enemy followed with the utmost rapidity and in column, but the Germans had the speed of the French, and Krauchenberg was enabled to draw up his squadron at the other side of the bridge before they reached it. The head of the enemy's column, however, came close after the rear skirmishers of the hussars, and the leading divisions had passed the bridge, when Krauchenberg, taking advantage of a little disorder which the hasty pursuit had caused in the enemy's ranks, suddenly charged the divisions which had passed.   Full three times the strength of the hussars were at this moment opposed to them ; but the well-timed charge succeeded, and the French were driven back in disorder.   Again they advanced, confiding in their numerical superiority, and again the Germans charged and dispersed them.   Three officers and from ten to fifteen men were cut down by the hussars, whose only loss was one horse killed and four men and two horses wounded.'   Colonel Gilmor gives an account of a fight between forty-three of his men, and a large column of the enemy on a road.   He says : ' The fight was short.   The foe was confined between two strong fences, and had they twice as many, they could show no bigger front with their 200 than we could with our forty-three.   After breaking the front their rear sections were only an encumbrance to them, and all were driven back across the hill into the town.'

Colonel Von Borcke gives an account of a cavalry fight which took place at the second great battle of Manassas, which furnishes another complete ex-emplification of the maxim that victory leans to the side which brings the last reserves into action. ' The second Virginian cavalry, under the gallant Colonel Mumford, was in the advance, and arrived at the plateau of Manassas before the two other regiments of the brigade had come up.   Here they found the Yankee horse in far superior numbers, drawn up in two magnificent lines of battle, one behind the other. Without waiting for the arrival of their comrades, the brave fellows of the 2nd, their intrepid colonel at their head, threw themselves upon the foe. They succeeded in breaking their first line by their impetuous charge, but having been thrown into some disorder by the length of the attack, the second line of the enemy, using well its opportunity, made a counter charge in splendid style, and drove them back in confused flight, shooting and sabring many of the men, the rallied Yankee regiments of the first line joining in the pursuit. At this moment we arrived with the 7th and 12th at the scene of the disaster, and, receiving our flying comrades into our ranks, we charged furiously the hostile lines, scattering them in every direction, recapturing all our men who had fallen into their hands, killing the commander of the entire force, and many other officers, among whom was the major, who had given me such a run at Verdiersville, besides killing and wounding a large number of their soldiers, and taking several hundred prisoners and horses.'

The advance in echelon is often more advantageous for cavalry than in a long line. It is difficult to advance in the latter formation without falling into confusion, or being driven back on all points at once, while in echelons of regiments or wings, you can at once take advantage of any hesitation or confusion in the enemy's ranks, without delaying to form line, when the opportunity might be lost. Again, the different parts of the echelon coming up one after the other, partake somewhat of the nature of reserves; and the enemy cannot attempt to attack the leading echelon in flank, for if he does so, he exposes his own to the next echelon coming up.

Cavalry after a successful charge should rally rapidly, while still advancing. The recall should not be sounded, for time is lost, which may easily cause the loss of the advantage already gained.

CHAPTER XI.

ARTILLERY, if unsupported by the other arms, will almost invariably succumb to an attack of cavalry. This is caused by the rapidity with which cavalry can move over the intervening space to attack batteries, and the consequent smallness of the loss which they will suffer before closing.

The history of war has abundantly proved the truth of this maxim ; in fact, it is almost universally admitted. With infantry, however, the case is very different; the time necessary for them to move under fire in order to reach a battery, is long enough to give the artillery an opportunity of destroying them before they can come to close quarters. Infantry must therefore always have artillery supports when attacking batteries. On this point Napoleon says : ' In a general system, there is no infantry, however intrepid, that can without artillery march, with impunity, ten or twelve hundred yards against sixteen well-placed pieces of cannon served by good gunners. Before it could accomplish two-thirds of the distance those men would be killed, wounded, or dispersed. We know not a single instance in which twenty pieces of cannon, judiciously placed and in battery, were ever carried by the bayonet.'

But although cavalry will always carry batteries at the charge if the ground is suitable, nevertheless it must be remembered that the success is only temporary, and that it must be supported by infantry and artillery as well as cavalry, to reap the full benefits of it.

At Balaklava, the light brigade charged and took thirty guns in position, drove their supports away, and went on beyond the battery, leaving the cannon deserted four hundred yards behind them; but no supports came up, no reserves, no assistance, and the cavalry—a few hundred only—found themselves victorious in the midst of the whole Russian army, but blown, broken, and in confusion from success; and, reduced to one-third of their original number from losses advancing under fire, they were obliged to retire, and give up all the advantages they had gained.

At the battle of Jena on October 14, 1806, Marshal Ney, by a charge of cuirassiers, captured a battery of sixteen pieces of cannon which severely galled his infantry.

At the battle of Eckmuhl the Bavarian cavalry

attached to Napoleon's army took a battery of thirty guns by a well-executed charge.

If cavalry are to attack artillery supported by cavalry or infantry, arrangements must be made to engage the supports with a portion of the force, while the remainder attack the guns.

A loose skirmishing order might sometimes be used to attack unsupported guns, because such a disposition would entail far less loss from artillery fire, than in close order and in several lines, and for a charge of this kind solidity is not required.

An extraordinary instance of cavalry attacking artillery occurred in the Peninsular War at the pass of Somosierra in 1808. The position was a very strong one, and held by the Spanish General St. Juan with 12,000 men. Sixteen pieces of artillery were planted in the pass in such a position as to sweep the whole length of the ascent, which was exceedingly steep, and very difficult to carry if obstinately defended. St. Juan had posted his men very judiciously, the infantry being entrenched in lines one above the other on both sides of the road, making the position almost impregnable. Napier describes the action in the following words: 'At day-break, three French battalions attacked St. Juan's right, three more assailed his left, and as many marched along the causeway in the centre,

supported by six guns. The French wings spreading over the mountain side, commenced a warm
skirmishing fire which was as warmly returned, while
the frowning battery at the top of the causeway was
held in readiness to crush the central column, when
it should come within range.   At that moment
Napoleon rode into the mouth of the pass, and attentively examined the scene before him : the infantry
were making no progress, and a thick fog mixed
with smoke hung upon the ascent; suddenly, as if
by inspiration, he ordered the Polish cavalry of his
guard to charge up the causeway and seize the
Spanish battery.   In an instant the foremost ranks
of the first squadron were levelled with the earth by
the fire of the great battery and the remainder were
thrown into confusion ; but General Krazinski as
suddenly rallied them, and, covered by the smoke
and the morning vapour, led them, sword in hand, up
the mountain.   As these gallant horsemen passed, the
Spanish infantry on each side fired and fled toward
the summit of the causeway, and when the Poles,
cutting down the gunners, took the battery, the whole
army was in flight, abandoning arms, ammunition,
and baggage.'

In the war in Germany in 1866, the Hanoverian
army defeated the Prussians at the battle of Langelsalza, and in this action Captain Von Einein with a

single squadron of cuirassiers, captured a Prussian battery, but Von Einein was killed in the midst of his captured cannon.

At the action of Tobitschau on July 15, 1866, the Prussian cavalry—four brigades—came upon a heavy column of Austrians, with an artillery train moving from Olmutz to Tobitschau. Colonel Bredow, who commanded the 5th Prussian cuirassiers, sought permission from General Hartman to attack the artillery train. Hozier's account is here inserted, as a good example of the use of cavalry against artillery:—

'Bredow, under cover of some undulating ground, formed his regiment in echelon of squadrons for the attack of the guns. The first squadron he kept *towards his right, to cover the flank of his attack* from any Austrian cavalry which might lie in that direction ; the second and forth squadrons he directed full against the front of the battery, *and supported the second with the third as a reserve.*

'The squadrons moved forward in perfect lines, slowly and steadily at first, seeming to glide over the field, gradually increasing their pace, regardless of the tremendous fire directed upon them, which emptied some saddles. When within a few hundred paces of the battery, they broke into a steady gallop, which increased in rapidity at every stride that

brought the horses nearer the Austrian line. All
the time of their advance the gunners poured round
after round into them, striving with desperate energy
to sweep them away before they could gain the
mouths of the cannons. Rapid flashes of flame
breaking from the mouths of the guns accompanied
the discharge of the shells, which were being blurted
forth with a nervous haste, through the thick clouds
of smoke, that hung heavily before the muzzles.
The flank squadrons trending a little away from their
comrades, made for either end of the line of guns in
expectation of finding there some supporting cavalry.
The two centre ones went, straight as an arrow,
against the guns themselves, and hurled themselves
through the intervals between them upon the
gunners. Then the firing ceased in a moment, and
the smoke began to drift slowly away, but all noise
was not hushed ; shrieks from men cut down by the
broad blades of the cuirassiers, cries for quarter, the
rapid tramp of snorting and excited horses, the rattle
of steel, shouts, cheers, and imprecations from the
excited combatants, rose up to heaven in a wild med-
ley, along with the prayers which were being offered
up by another armed host, not many miles distant
at Brünn, where, on this Sunday, the army of Prince
Frederick Charles was engaged in a solemn thanks-
giving for their hitherto victorious career. Eighteen

guns, seven waggons, and 168 horses, with 170
prisoners, fell into the hands of the Prussian force.
A noble prize to be won by a single regiment. It
lost only twelve men and eight horses, for the swell-
ing ground and rapid motion of the gliding squadrons,
baulked the aim of the gunners, who mostly pointed
their pieces too high, and sent their shells over the
heads of the charging horsemen. Of the eighteen
captured guns, seventeen were conveyed to Prosnitz.
One was too much disabled to be moved.

'While the Prussian cuirassiers were engaged in
drawing the captured guns to a safe place, a squadron of hostile cavalry deployed from Nenakowitz.
Colonel Bredow placed himself at the head of his
first squadron, and charged to cover the retreat of
his regiment's spoils. This squadron dashed with a
heavy surge upon the hostile ranks; the lighter
Austrian horsemen, borne down and scattered by
their ponderous shock, broke in wild confusion,
could not rally, and were driven far beyond Nenakowitz.'

In this fight Colonel Bredow proved himself a
dashing and efficient officer, and the above account
of it contains in fact a volume of instruction, as to
the proper method of attacking artillery. Here
Colonel Bredow protected his flanks, held a reserve
in hand, turned the flank of the guns, captured them,

and carried them off—and, by his foresight in keeping one or two squadrons in hand, was enabled to defeat an attempt of the enemy to rescue the guns. Had he thrown his whole regiment at once into the fight, the success could not have been any greater, while the chances were, that the fresh Austrian squadron, coming down upon them while disordered by success, would have defeated them.

With reference to the action of mounted rifles or dragoons against batteries, the same rules would apply as for cavalry, if the ground is suitable. But, if the guns are in a position not to be approached mounted, then the dragoons must gallop rapidly to the point nearest to the battery where they can get shelter, and then by their firearms they can soon silence the battery if they are only close enough. Through intersected ground they could also charge the batteries on foot, first getting as near as possible, mounted. Under all circumstances, the horses must always be left in a sheltered position. Dragoons should never dismount to attack a battery if they can reach it on horseback, because the swiftness of motion when exposed to heavy fire is an advantage, which will more than counterbalance all the disadvantages connected with using dragoons as cavalry. Even if dragoons have no sabres at all, or even revolvers, they should nevertheless always attack batteries at speed if the ground is at all suitable; taking care to guard their flanks, and hold reserves in hand the same as cavalry. There is nothing to prevent dragoons charging with revolvers against cannon, in fact we should prefer it and would consider it more deadly, and more likely to succeed.

But then, it must never be forgotten that any general worth the name of one, would never allow a battery to be in such a position as to be liable to be suddenly attacked by cavalry, without having some of *its own* cavalry in support. Cavalry, therefore, must be so armed and prepared as to be ready to attack cavalry the instant they have taken, or are through, a battery, or they cannot expect to hold what they have gained.

CHAPTER XII.

CAVALRY AGAINST INFANTRY.

My decided opinion is, that cavalry, if led by equally brave and resolute men, must always break infantry.—*Napoleon.*

THE physical force of cavalry against infantry is
much greater than the moral. The fire of infantry
is its only defence, but under the present system of
arming, it is a most powerful one. The bayonets and
men alone could never stop good cavalry, as has
always been shown whenever the latter have ridden
with a will and determination to succeed.

The enormous range, power, and rapidity of firing,
to which the arms of modern infantry have reached,
have reduced still further the chances of cavalry
breaking into their squares, and have rendered infinitely less numerous the favourable opportunities
in which horsemen should alone charge upon
them.

Still, however, when the ground is open and clear,

when there are no obstacles to prevent the rush of
the advancing squadrons, no shelter behind which
the infantry can protect themselves, but a fair field
between the two arms, then cavalry carefully trained,
properly armed, and with a strong *esprit-de-corps*,
riding at infantry with a will, with their minds made
up to go in, will always succeed. All they want is
'the spur and the spear and the sabre, and the
native courage of the blood horse' to depend on, and
when they fight, it should be with the rush of
the whirlwind. Their horses pushed to their utmost
speed, the men leaning forwards in their saddles,
and their eyes bent upon the enemy. The shock
should be as the crash of the thunderbolt, and although many may fall, all will not, and the survivors
will win a glorious victory, and amply avenge their
comrades.

But if the ground is unfavourable, if obstacles
prevent this system of tactics being adopted, then
the mounted riflemen come into play, and by
dismounting and advancing on foot, can fight on
equal terms with the opposing force.

Great care must be taken to teach horsemen to
believe that no infantry can stand a charge of cavalry
on an open field. If the men have not confidence,
they can never accomplish anything, and each defeat

will but serve to confirm them in the opinion that it
is impossible to be victorious.   For this reason,
cavalry should not be allowed at the commencement
of a war to charge infantry, except under the most
favourable circumstances; if they win then, it will
give them confidence, and after one or two successes,
it would be impossible for infantry to withstand
them.

Cavalry, unfortunately, if they have not confidence,
generally give way just as they have succeeded to all
intents and purposes.   They ride at a square or line,
they receive a terrible volley in their faces within
sixty or seventy yards, and instead of then rushing
on to assured victory, they instinctively recoil, rein
up their horses, and hesitate, at the very moment
when the infantry have done their worst to them,
and are, comparatively speaking, helpless.   If the,
survivors charged on under this fire steadily, in spite
of it, there never would be any difficulty about the
bayonets; the moral effect would then be decidedly
in favour of the cavalry, and the infantry would
almost invariably break before the moment of contact.   Waterloo may be quoted as an answer to this,
but it is not a fair case.   There the French cuirassiers charged down one hill, across a muddy heavy
valley, up another hill, upon an army in position in

squares *en échiquier*, with artillery playing upon them.

> And to augment the fray,
> Wheeled full against their staggering flanks,
> The English horsemen's foaming ranks
> Forced their resistless way.

No position could possibly be worse for cavalry, yet in spite of it all, Jomini claims that these brave cuirassiers broke three squares.

. In this action accounts are given of the French horsemen riding up to the squares, and cutting at the bayonets; this of itself shows that these men could not have been charging. They advanced at the trot with their horses blown. They should have been at their utmost speed on reaching the enemy, and then the physical force or momentum would have swept away men, bayonets and muskets, as if they were but broken reeds held by infants.

Adjutant Moore, of the 3rd Bombay Light Cavalry, in Persia in 1857, gave an example of the way in which a charge should be made. He let his sword hang by the sword-knot, and took the reins with both hands, and jumped his horse on to the bayonets. The horse was killed, but the square was broken and annihilated, while Moore was not even wounded.

It may also be said that horses will not face squares, and will themselves recoil from the fire. This would not be so if they were properly trained. General

Hood, Confederate States of America, says, if the reins could only be cut as cavalry go into the charge, the horses would carry their riders in every time. But the men are too apt to pull up. If the horses are well trained, this difficulty could be obviated to a great extent.

At Aliwal, Captain Pearson, 16th Lancers, jumped his horse into a square first man, and went clean through, without losing his horse or being wounded. Why could not a line of cavalry run the same chance?

Some changes, however, are required in the instruction of the heavy cavalry or cavalry of the line. At present it is often the custom at reviews to charge up to squares, receive a volley, and then go threes about or retire from the flanks. This teaches the horses that they are not required to break through, and in action they will do just as they have been taught. An example of this happened at the battle of Chillianwallah, where the 14th Light Dragoons charged to the proper distance, went 'threes about' involuntarily (the men not knowing why), and ran away, occasioning the defeat of the whole of Pope's brigade, and yet the regiment did nothing more than what the horses are often taught in reviews in the Phœnix Park.

This system should be changed. It has been suggested by Colonel M'Dougall that the cavalry should be exercised in charging dummies, and in riding over them. This would be a very good plan, especially if it could be arranged so that smoke should arise in some way from these fictitious squares to accustom the horses to it.

Another good plan is to place infantry men at intervals of about a yard, and let the horses be ridden through the intervals. At first they may be a little shy, but by treating them gently they will soon learn to walk through quietly, then trot, and then gallop. The infantry should then be directed to fire blank cartridges, the cavalry continually riding backwards and forwards, until the horses get accustomed to the firing. Then another rank of infantry can be placed behind the first, and then another, and so on until, with five or six ranks, a very heavy fire could be kept up, while the horses are taught to go through at the walk, trot, or gallop. Horses so trained would not swerve from the fire of squares in action, and in the smoke and excitement would plunge right into the infantry, if they waited long enough, which would not be likely.

There are certain circumstances which are much more favourable for a cavalry charge than others; and an officer of cavalry should always be on the look-out to take advantage of them as they arise.

When infantry is on the march and under fire, a charge can often be made with the greatest results; or when it is altering its formation, and before it is prepared to receive a charge, it will generally be overthrown by a well-timed advance of cavalry.

When infantry is engaged with infantry, a charge of cavalry will generally succeed. A good instance occurred at the battle of Mockern. It is thus described by Nolan: 'The enemy had now advanced so close that a charge of bayonets against the Prussian infantry was expected every moment. Wrapped in clouds of smoke, they came on firing, and Sohr could tell only by the whistling of the bullets that they were near enough. He passed through the line of retreating infantry, and formed, and with three cheers burst upon the advancing enemy, rode over and dispersed them, pursuing them into their own batteries. He captured six pieces of cannon at the first onset.

'The enemy's cavalry, indeed, rushed down to the rescue, but a regiment of lancers from the reserve had now joined, and they advanced together and overthrew the French, the lancers pursuing them, whilst the hussars attacked the infantry formed in squares to receive them, broke into three squares in succession, and captured nine pieces of cannon, after which they joined in the pursuit, and followed the enemy close up to Leipsic, inflicting on him a severe loss in killed, wounded, and prisoners.'

The best opportunity for cavalry to charge infantry is when they have been much shaken by artillery fire. After suffering severe losses in this way, they are more liable to be overthrown than at any other time. For this reason, horse-artillery should always accompany cavalry in the field, and these batteries, by rapidly taking a position in advance of one or both flanks, can play with effect upon the squares until the charging columns get, comparatively speaking, close to them. The fire of artillery into dense masses in that formation has a most deadly effect, and demoralises infantry very speedily.

If cavalry can succeed in gaining the rear or flank of a line of infantry unperceived, they will almost invariably destroy it. There are many instances which prove the truth of this doctrine; therefore cavalry charging and defeating a body of the enemy's horse on the flank of their army, should send a small detachment in pursuit, and immediately rally the remainder, and fall upon the flanks and rear of the infantry.

The Great Conde, at the age of twenty-one, won the battle of Rocroi by a most skilful and determined use of his cavalry. He first charged and defeated the Spanish horse on their left wing, drove them off

the field, then turned on the flank and rear of the
German and Italian infantry, and broke through
them, when, learning that his own left wing had
been defeated, he carried his victorious horsemen
along the rear of the whole of the Spanish infantry,
and fell upon the rear of the enemy's cavalry of the
other wing, who were pursuing the defeated troops.
He soon put them to rout, and returning to the field,
charged upon those regiments of Spaniards which
still sustained the fight, and at the fourth charge
succeeding in overthrowing them.   How different
was the fiery Prince Rupert's conduct when, at the
head of his Royalist cavaliers, he rode down all
before him at Marston Moor and Naseby, but allowed
his want of caution and prudence to render his impetuosity of no avail.

Having thus considered the general principles
connected with the action of cavalry against infantry,
it will not be amiss here to insert a few examples of
the operations of the two forces to illustrate the ideas
here adduced.

At the battle of Wurtzburg, in 1796, several
squares were broken by the cavalry of the army of
the Archduke Charles.

At Monterey in Spain, in March, 1809, the French
cavalry effected great results.   Napier gives the following account of the action : ' As the French ad-

vanced, the Spaniards abandoned their positions in succession, spiked the guns in the dilapidated works of Monterey, and after a slight skirmish at Verim, took the road to Puebla de Senabria; but Franceschi followed close, and overtaking two or three thousand as they were passing a rugged mountain, assailed them with a battalion of infantry, and at the same time, leading his horsemen round both flanks, headed the column, and obliged it to halt.   The Spaniards, trusting to the rough ground, drew up in one large square to receive the charge.   Franceschi had four regiments of cavalry; each regiment settled itself against a face of the square, and then the whole with loud cries bore down swiftly upon their opponents; the latter, unsteady, irresolute, dismayed, shrunk from the fierce assault, and were instantly trampled down in heaps.   Those who escaped the horses' hoofs and the edge of the sword became prisoners; but 1,200 bodies were stretched lifeless on the field of battle.'

At the battle of Salamanca, July 22, 1812, Le Marchant's heavy brigade and Anson's light cavalry of Wellington's army broke through the whole French left drawn up in several lines, captured five guns and more than 2,000 prisoners, completely destroying Thomiere's division.   It was to this magnificent charge that the Duke of Wellington was mainly indebted for his victory.

An instance of cavalry attacking infantry under favourable auspices occurred at the battle of Albuera, May 16, 1811, where Latour-Maubourg overthrew a British brigade. Napier thus describes it :

' Stewart, whose boiling courage overlaid his judgment, led up Colborne's brigade without hesitation in column of companies, and having passed the Spanish right, attempted to open out his line in succession as the battalions arrived at the summit. Being under a destructive fire the foremost troops charged, but a heavy rain prevented any object from being distinctly seen, and four regiments of hussars and lancers, which had turned the right flank in the obscurity, came galloping in upon the rear of the line at the instant of its developement, and slew or took two-thirds of the brigade. One battalion only (the 31st), being still in column, escaped the storm, and maintained its ground while the French horsemen, riding violently over everything else, penetrated to all parts, and captured six guns.'

Count de Rochefort gives an account of a charge made by a small body of Piedmontese lancers, only twenty-two in number, against an Austrian square. They broke through it, but eleven were killed and the others wounded. Colonel Morelli, commandant of the regiment of Montferrat, was one of them, and although he was wounded with a ball in the stomach, he continued to charge three times afterwards. He died on the following day. The cause of this severe loss has been the concentration of fire on a small number, making it so much more deadly. The fact of Colonel Morelli keeping up, with so severe a wound, is a striking instance of how difficult it is to give a man a blow which paralyzes him instantaneously.

At the battle of Auerstadt, a Prussian dragoon regiment charged a square of French infantry, which stood firmly to the last, and gave them a volley at fifteen paces which brought down nine officers and many men; but the Prussians were not to be stopped, they rushed in and cut them to pieces.*

At the battle of Königgrätz, 1866, a squadron of hussars attached to Fransecky's division, overthrew a whole Austrian battalion and captured its flag.

At the battle of Langelsalza, June 27, 1866, after the repulse of the Prussians in their attack on the Hanoverian army, the Duke of Cambridge's regiment of dragoons, defiling from the village of Nägelstadt, dashed forward rapidly but unsupported against the Prussians and took some prisoners; while at the same time the heavy cavalry, issuing from Merxleben, attacked two Prussian squares, broke them and captured many of them.† These Prussians were armed with the much-vaunted needle-gun, yet they

* Nolan p. 305.   † Hozier, vol. ii. p. 16,

were defeated. But it must be remembered that
the Prussian army were in full retreat, and that the
Hanoverian troops would naturally be in high spirits,
while the *morale* of their opponents would be correspondingly depressed.

The Prussian cavalry defeated the Austrian infantry at Tobitschau in 1866. Hozier says:—' As
soon as the battery had shaken the detachments of
Austrian infantry, Hartman attacked them. In vain
the Austrians attempted to form company-squares,
the horsemen were too quick for them, got among
them before their formation was complete, and made
a large number of prisoners, but however without
very severe loss to themselves.'

Before concluding this chapter, it will be well to
enter more fully into the theory of a cavalry charge
against infantry, and consider the chances and
peculiarities of the conflict.

The infantry are now armed with long-range
rifles—breech-loaders. They can commence firing
at 800 yards, and fire at the rate of five times a
minute on an average with the best breech-loaders.
Some rifles in experimenting can be fired six, seven,
and even eight times a minute, but the value of five
shots would, I imagine, be quite equal to eight shots
hurriedly, confusedly, and carelessly fired.

But at 800 yards the fire is of little or no effect.

The elevation is so great that a mistake in calculating the distance of thirty or forty yards will drop the ball in front of the line, or send it over their heads, even admitting that the aim is accurate and coolly taken.   Even as close as 400 yards, the fire is not of very great effect; and when you come within 200 yards, the old musket would hit just as hard as the present rifle and be very nearly as efficient.   There is no doubt, however, that the rapidity of fire is a great advantage to the infantry; for as firing in action is generally random shooting, the more bullets are flying about, the more chances there will be of men being hit.   But even allowing for all this, the effect of breech-loaders in action is not nearly so great as is popularly believed.

Many elaborate experiments have been made with moving targets of men, horsemen, and artillery ; and targets have been constructed representing a field-battery in position, and picked men have quietly and calmly been posted to fire at them at carefully-measured distances, over ranges well known to them, and the number of hits recorded, to show that a battery of artillery or squadron of cavalry would be annihilated in so many minutes.   These experiments are simply silly, I will not say ridiculous : and it is astonishing that sensible men will amuse themselves with such folly.   Let the squadron of cavalry or the field-battery be active opponents on an unknown range, fighting at the same time, and it would be found that many of the best shots might as well be aiming at the sun.

One constantly sees very fine ' shots' at all sorts of game, but I doubt whether a brilliant game-shot would be equally efficient if every time that he shot at a duck or a rabbit, he felt sure, if he did not kill the duck, &c., the duck would kill him.

It is astonishing what a number of shots can be fired, without any injury being done. It has been said that it takes the weight of a man in lead to kill him, that is, by infantry bullets. This is certainly the case ; and with breech-loading weapons it will take many a pound more in weight to produce the same result. It is a strange fact that the loss of life in battles has been continually diminishing in proportion to the numbers engaged, in a corresponding ratio with the improvement of projectile weapons. Statistics for two thousand years will prove this conclusively.

In the war of 1866, in Germany, the Prussians used the needle-gun. At Königgrätz the numbers engaged were—Austrians 200,000, Prussians about 260,000, of whom 60,000 never fired a shot. The casualties were some 20,000 killed and wounded on the side of the Austrians, and less than 10,000 on that of the Prussians, making a total of almost one-thirteenth of the number of men actually engaged. Hozier, speaking of this battle, says, 'Nor did the infantry fire tell except at close quarters. Whether this was due to the inferior shooting power of the needle-gun, or to the practical disadvantage of aiming under fire, seems to be uncertain.'

We here append a table, compiled from one in Hozier's book, showing the proportion of loss in some of the great battles of the last one hundred and fifty years.

Name of Battle	Year	Number Engaged	Proportion of Killed and Wounded
Hohen Friedberg . . .	1745	140,000	$\frac{1}{10}$
Prague	1757	138,000	$\frac{1}{6}$
Breslau	1757	85,000	$\frac{1}{6}$
Zornsdorf	1758	82,000	$\frac{1}{2}$ to $\frac{1}{3}$
Hoch-Kirch	1758	80,000	$\frac{1}{7}$
Marengo	1800	58,977	$\frac{1}{4}$
Austerlitz	1805	170,000	$\frac{1}{7}$
Jena	1806	200,000	$\frac{1}{6}$
Preussic Eylau . . .	1807	160,000	$\frac{1}{3}$
Friedland	1807	130,000	$\frac{1}{6}$
Talavera	1809	102,000	$\frac{1}{8}$
Borodino	1812	250,000	$\frac{1}{3}$
Magenta	1859	109,730	$\frac{1}{11}$
Solferino	1859	298,358	$\frac{1}{11}$
Königgrätz	1866	400,000	$\frac{1}{13}$

To show how few shots take effect even at short distances, I will quote one or two instances which

N

have lately occurred. At the battle of Shiloh in America, in 1862, General Morgan's cavalry charged a regiment of Federal infantry. General Duke, speaking of it, says, 'We came close upon them before they fired; they delivered one stunning volley, the blaze almost reaching our faces, and the roar rang in our ears like thunder. . . . We lost only *three men killed* and several others wounded.'

In Maryland, in 1862, two infantry companies of the Confederate army were stationed on the road leading to Hagerstown, and had hastily thrown up a small entrenchment across the road. They were charged by some squadrons of Federal cavalry. Colonel Von Borcke tells the story as follows: 'The entrenchment was concealed from view by a slight elevation of ground about forty steps in front of it, so that the Yankees came upon it quite unexpectedly. The infantry officer in command had given orders to his men to reserve their fire till the last moment, and the dense ranks of the horsemen had arrived within close range, when suddenly the volley thundered upon them, making them turn and fly precipitately. Having been myself with the infantry, I galloped forward, believing that at least half of the assailants had been brought to the ground, but found, to my surprise, that not a man or a horse had been struck down, the leaden hail having passed far above their heads. On several subsequent occasions, I had a similar experience. The haste and uncertainty of volley firing, even with the improved fire-arms now in use, made it possible in a few cases for our cavalry successfully to attack and ride down unbroken infantry.'

We will give one more instance, taken from Colonel Gilmor's book. On September 3, 1864, General Lomax, moving from Bunker's Hill towards Darkesville, in the Shenandoah Valley, came upon two regiments of dismounted men armed with Spencer rifles, seven-shooters, and holding a strong position behind a rail barricade. In front of the barricade were three long narrow fields separated by two fences. From the nature of the ground the attack could only be made from the front. Colonel Gilmor was ordered by General Lomax to charge the position, by a direct attack with the 18th Virginia cavalry. He says: 'All being ready, I ordered them forward at a regular walk, keeping them well dressed and every man well up in line. We were under fire as soon as we emerged from the wood, but I made them cross the first field at a walk. Arriving at the fence, I made them halt, throw it down, cross over, halt again, and dress up in line' before they advanced. We crossed the second field at a trot, halted, threw down the fence, crossed over, and formed the line again

before we started off. There were *not more than
five or six men shot up to that time, and probably a
dozen horses.* Everything was clear before us now,
and after the line had been dressed we moved off,
first at a walk, then a trot, then a gallop, and then I
ordered a charge.

'When we left the second fence the fire was very
severe, but the men maintained the line, and moved
forward in fine style until the order was given to
charge. Then of course there was a general dash,
and the line could not be fully preserved. The
enemy at first stood very firm, and poured into us a
destructive fire; but I have observed that it is
seldom that men stand a charge when they discover
you to be still moving on without wavering. And
so it was in this case. At first they poured in volley
after volley and cheered us as we advanced upon
them; but when we got within fifty yards of the
barricade, and still showed no sign of giving way,
they commenced breaking off for their horses, held
in a small wood to the rear. The boys seeing this
redoubled their yells, while every man strained his
horse to the utmost to prevent their escape. We
had to leap the barricade, and many of the men
were badly hurt by their horses falling on them.
The blue coats were all mounted before we crossed
the barricade, and had commenced retreating. The

18th gave a fresh yell, and chased them through and around Darkesville, capturing about forty prisoners : yet the enemy lost not a man killed, and but few were wounded.'

These instances show that *practically* the effect of the infantry fire is not very deadly over 200 yards, and that often at close range the result of the volley is not so serious as might be supposed.

We will calculate, therefore, the number of shots which a foot soldier can fire, and the comparative value of each, during the time necessary for cavalry to charge over 800 yards of clear country.

From 800 to 400 yards cavalry can advance at the trot in about one minute and a quarter. In that time some six or seven shots may be fired, but practically with little or no effect; the rapidly changing distances, the difficulty of guessing the proper elevation to strike a moving body, and the necessity of having the sights accurate, will do away with much danger from these shots.

From 400 to 100 yards—300 yards at a gallop will take about half a minute ; two shots can be fired in this time, leaving one for the last hundred yards, which can be run over in ten seconds.

Suppose now that in the last 400 yards one sixth of the men or horses are shot down—a larger proportion than is likely—the remainder are quite enough

to dash the square to atoms, if they will only then
ride on firmly. In fact, the infantry would never
stand after that if the speed was only good. The
want of effect of their weapons in which they con-
fided would demoralise them, and they would be far
more easily broken than if they had only been armed
with short range weapons, and were accustomed to
close fighting.

As already mentioned, cavalry, if defeated in attacking a square, generally give way just as they have
suffered all the loss necessary to succeed. And it is
in confusion of failure, while retreating in disorder,
that the weapons of the foot soldiers have the most
effect—their aim is generally better when firing into
a retreating mass. There is no doubt whatever, if it
could only be discovered, that it would be shown that
in all the instances where infantry have defeated
cavalry, with heavy loss, that at least three-fourths
of it has been suffered in the retreat, and that
during the advance their casualties have invariably
been trifling in comparison.

Again, admitting that a good number of men and
horses are struck within the last hundred yards (the
only time at which the loss could be heavy), even
then it is surprising how few wounds even of a
mortal nature will bring down either horse or man
at once. If the man drops, the horse will still go on

if the speed is well up; and if the latter is mortally wounded, he will rarely drop within one hundred yards. There are many instances on record of the difficulty of bringing a horse down instantaneously. A charger at full speed, struck lifeless suddenly, will still have momentum enough to carry his dead body tumbling along the ground a good many yards.

Warnery in his 'Remarques sur la Cavalerie' says, 'It is necessary for a horse to be very seriously wounded to cause him to fall on the spot. I have seen one without his rider at Strigau, who had his hind leg carried off by a cannon shot, join himself to the left of my squadron, where he ran with the others during the whole battle; although we were often dispersed, at the rally he returned always to the same place, which was without doubt that which he had in the squadron he belonged to. I have seen another horse of a cuirassier fall in the grand attack in drilling at Breslau; the soldier raised him and remounted him. At three hundred paces he fell stone dead. The late General Krockow, chief of the regiment, had the horse opened, and it was found that the sword of the cuirassier had entered his heart to the depth of a twelfth of an inch.'

Hozier gives an account of the combat of Podol in 1866, in which he says, 'And the grey horse of a Prussian field-officer, with a ball in his heart, fell

heavily against the wall, kicking amid the ranks ; but
he was soon quieted for ever.'

At Garcia Hernandez, July 23, 1812, three squadrons of the King's German Legion broke three squares
of French infantry.   The cavalry were assisted in
breaking one of the squares by the fact that a horse
in the front rank, having been mortally wounded, in
his dying agony plunged wildly forward on to the
bayonets, and dashed open a great gap in the face of
the square just at the critical moment.

We have before seen that Colonel Morelli, at
Montebello in 1859, charged three times after having
received a mortal wound of which he died the following day.

General Jacob, commanding at Bushire in Persia
in June 1857, in his recommendation of officers for
the Victoria Cross, for their conduct at the battle of
Khooshab, says : ' They were all of course in front,
and were among the first to break into the bayonets,
in effecting which Captain Wren's horse was shot
in three places, one musket-ball, fired by a man of
the kneeling ranks, entering part of the horse's neck,
and coming out of his withers, without apparently
interfering with or delaying the animal's progress in
the least.   In closing with the square, also, Captain
Moore's horse received three musket-balls.

Before concluding this chapter, we must say that

there is no doubt that cavalry in charging infantry should use the revolver in riding up. It might easily have a light leather thong attaching it to the belt, which could be used to fasten it to the person in a mounted charge, the naked sword being held between the fingers and thumb of the bridle hand.

There would be many advantages in this system—and not many disadvantages. The men could fire at about one hundred yards, and again at about fifty, and still be ready to give another at the instant before contact. We have said before, the bayonets would never be in position at the shock if the horses' speed was only good; and even if they were, the pistol would be as good as the sword, because the horseman could bring down the man in front of him with his pistol more easily than with the sabre.

This firing upon the square would have a very bad effect upon the infantry, and, from the reasons before mentioned of the revolver being fired with the sympathy between hand and eye, and not by aiming, the shots would tell more surely. The fact also of the cavalry firing downwards would be likely to prevent the balls going over the heads of the enemy.

The great difficulty would be about the placing of the officers if the men used revolvers. It would hardly be safe to let them lead, or at least so many.

The squadron leader might be in front, the other officers on the flanks, and four or five men behind the squadron leader might refrain from firing, while the converging fire of the others would be most efficient.

A few shots would be sure to tell, and a very few men dropping at the moment of contact would shake a square terribly, and the bullets whistling about their ears would render their aim less effective than if they had an opportunity of firing at the cavalry without that disturbing element affecting them.

It may be said that the fire of cavalry in this way would be of no avail while the horses are moving fast. This is hardly the case. Mounted skirmishers with carbines and at rather long ranges are, it must be admitted, a humbug; but at short ranges, and firing straight ahead, the aim would be better. Men do become splendid shots with a revolver at speed on horseback. Colonel Gilmor could gallop along a road full speed, and put a bullet into every telegraph pole he passed.

Gustavus Adolphus ordered his cavalry to ride up towards infantry, discharge their pistols, draw swords, and ride in sword in hand. If that worked well in his day, why should not the revolver work ten times better now? It will carry four times the distance, will go straighter, and six shots can be fired with the greatest rapidity. It is said that it was in the hand-to-hand fight that Gustavus Adolphus wished his cavalry to be famous; he wished them to depend mainly on the shock of the charge and the keen edge of the sabre; yet he did not disdain to get all the advantage possible from his old-fashioned horse-pistols. Why then should we be too proud to use that magnificent pistol the revolver?

The cavalry in the Confederate war for independence often charged infantry with the pistol and with great success. We quote an account from Gilmor's 'Four Years in the Saddle:' 'I ordered my men to *draw pistols and prepare to charge*. As we started out at a trot we received a wild volley without much damage, though it was of buckshot and ball. Only myself and another were struck, and not till after the battle did I discover that I had a buckshot in my leg.

'In an instant we were among them; they broke and made for a deep cut in the railroad. Had they been allowed to reach that, we should have had some trouble in getting them out: but all surrendered except a part of the colour company, and they made but a feeble stand. One of my lieutenants charged these with a few men, killing the colour-bearer with his own hand while he was in the act of tearing up his flag.'

The revolver, if attached to the belt on the right side, could be dropped on the left of the horse after firing ; and if friends and foes were too much mixed up to use the pistol, then the sword could be taken out of the bridle hand, and be instantly ready for use.

CHAPTER XIII.

OUTPOSTS AND PATROLS.

The safety of an army in an enemy's country materially depends on the manner in which the outpost duty is performed. The outposts, pickets and advanced sentries, are the watch-dogs of the army, whose peculiar business is to detect and give timely warning of the approach of an enemy, as well as every circumstance which may appear to threaten its safety. An officer in command of an outpost should invariably act as if the safety of the whole army depended on his individual vigilance, and he should impress the same feeling of responsibility on the minds of every one of his sentries.—MAC-DOUGALL's *Theory of War*.

SECTION I.—DEFINITION.

THE many essential duties of a soldier which require him to leave his ranks—the cooking of rations, the necessity of sleep, the impossibility of men working or being under arms for any lengthened period, renders it physically impossible for an army to be at all moments, both by day and night, in constant readiness to oppose the attack of a vigilant enemy.

It is therefore necessary that a portion of an army

should be always under arms, and in a position to prevent the surprise of the remainder, and so to impede the attack of an enemy as to enable preparations to be made by the whole army, to resist the assaults that might be made upon it.

This object is accomplished by detaching to the front, flanks, and in some cases to the rear, a chain of guards and posts, who continually watch the enemy's movements, secure the position from surprise, and throw every impediment in the way of a hostile attack.

These guards are called outposts, and the whole system the chain of outposts. Necessity obliges this chain of outposts in the presence of an enemy to be constantly in a state of preparation; these duties are the most fatiguing and trying that a soldier is called upon to perform, and as detachments of this kind tend to weaken the main body, the chain can never be of sufficient strength to alone answer the end required.

It is customary, therefore, to preserve a portion of the main army in camp in a stricter state of readiness than the rest, so that in case an attack is made upon the outposts they may promptly support them— these bodies are called inlying pickets.

As it would be impossible to preserve a chain of sentries or posts, so numerous as not to be liable to be forced or surprised, especially at night or in foggy weather, a system has been adopted of sending small bodies along the line from post to post, as near to the enemy as possible to supply the deficiency of sentries, and to keep alive that vigilance of the men on duty which is so essential to the security of the army.

The chain of outposts consists of main guards, outlying pickets and sentries. The main guards occupy all the principal approaches to the camp, and should be of sufficient strength to resist the first shock of an attack ; these main guards detach to their front and flanks smaller parties called pickets, who cover all the approaches to the main guards, and at the same time preserve the communication with the posts on their right and left. These pickets detach sentries or videttes in front of their position communicating with the sentries of the con- tiguous pickets on the right and left, so that the sentries form one continuous chain.

In addition to this the pickets detach small parties, which march out to the front of the sentries, and taking a circle beyond the stationary posts as near to the enemy as possible, return *by the other flank* to the picket. These parties, which are called patrols, are sent out in order to obtain the earliest information of the enemy's movements, to discover any offensive dispositions in his line, and to keep alive a vigilance and activity among the sentries, without which their services would be of no avail.

It is also the duty of these patrols and advanced posts to get the earliest intimation of any change of the advanced posts of the enemy's line, of any movements in his camp, and to send in specific reports thereof; to resist attacks upon single posts, and to oppose general attacks upon the whole line, so as to enable the main body to form itself in a position for action.

It is desirable that the chain of outposts should be at an equal distance from the line; and that if there are any points where an attack is to be apprehended, the outposts should there be proportionately strengthened.

It is necessary, sometimes, in order to have all the videttes or sentries in constant communication with the pickets from which they are detached, to send forward smaller parties under command of non-commissioned officers to positions whence they can have the whole line of videttes or sentries in sight. This is only done in covered or broken ground where the picket cannot see them. The smaller parties are called intermediate posts.

The principles which regulate the distances in the disposition of a chain of posts depends so entirely upon the nature of the ground and other circumstances, that no fixed rules can be laid down. The following general principles ought to be observed, however :—

1. That the less the distance of the chain of posts from the main body, the greater must be the preparation and vigilance of the camp.

2. That the strength of the chain must be in proportion to its distance from the main body.

3. That the strength of the posts must be in proportion to the natural or artificial capabilities of the ground for defence.

5. No post ought to consist of less than three reliefs, exclusive of patrols. Reconnoitring parties consist of three to six men. The French posts always have four reliefs.

6. Cavalry posts may be thrown much in advance of infantry, *when the country is adapted to this* arm, as their celerity prevents their being easily cut off, and they can report to the rear much quicker.

7. In covered broken ground, outposts should not be far in advance of the camp.

8. It is desirable to attach a few cavalry to the important posts for the purpose of reporting quickly to the rear.

O

9. The less formidable the outposts the greater the necessity of vigilance in the main body.

10. Above all, it is absolutely necessary that the sound of a musket-shot may be heard from post to post throughout the whole line. It is also to be considered that many pickets, though weak, give more security to the main guards than a few strong ones.

Officers and men engaged on outpost duty must always bear in mind that the whole safety of the army, the success of all the operations undertaken by it, depend to a great extent upon their vigilance and activity: they should never forget that they are placed on that duty to form an impenetrable curtain behind which the army, without fear of discovery by the enemy, may execute all its movements, whilst, on the other hand, they should endeavour to find out every movement of the enemy.

A good example of an efficient outpost system occurred in Portugal in 1808, when the number and activity of the French cavalry completely shrouded Junot's position.

In 1811, the Spaniards were surprised and defeated by Marshal Soult at the Gebora, and more than 8,000 prisoners taken, while guns, colours, muskets, ammunition, &c., all fell into the hands of the French. This was almost wholly owing to the want of proper outposts.

If the army itself is in a very strong position, easily to be defended, it is not necessary to push the advance posts to such a distance as is otherwise desirable.

Colonel Adam was surprised at the combat of Ordal, by not having his outposts properly thrown out. Napier thus refers to it: 'Every officer is responsible for the security of his troops, and the precautions prescribed by the rules of war should never be dispensed with or delayed at any outpost. Now it does not appear that Colonel Adam ever placed an infantry picket on the bridge or sent a cavalry patrol beyond it. And I have been informed by a French soldier, one of a party sent to explore the position, that they reached the crest of the heights without opposition and returned safely, whereupon Mesclop's brigade instantly crossed the bridge and attacked.'

In 1862, when Stonewall Jackson reinforced Lee before the seven days' fight before Richmond, the cavalry left in the Shenandoah Valley 'drew a *cordon* of pickets across the country just above them, so strict that the befooled enemy never knew General Jackson's whole army was not in his front, until he discovered it by M'Clellan's disasters.'

SECTION II.—FORMATION OF CHAIN OF OUTPOSTS.

On the arrival of the detachments, told off for
the formation of the chain of outposts, upon the
new ground where they are to be placed, they
push forward quickly, drive in any of the enemy's
parties, and spreading out upon the roads, place
strong detachments on every approach to the camp.
These detachments are the main guards : these, then,
immediately throw out, on their front and flanks,
smaller parties which form the pickets, or *out*-pic-
kets.   These out-pickets then place their sentries
in front and to the flanks, and at once open up
communication with the pickets on either flank.

The officers in command of pickets then send
out patrols in every direction beyond the line of
sentries, to reconnoitre the ground to see if possible the position of the enemy's post, to make sure
that the sentries are all properly placed, and that
the front is clear.   It is to be particularly observed
that until the return of these patrols, the men of
the pickets are on no account to leave the ranks
for a moment, or in the case of cavalry to dismount.   Until the advanced posts are placed, the
army should remain under arms.   As soon as this
is done, the field officer's attention should be directed

to the occupation of all points of ground capable of defence, which, at the same time, command the approaches of the position.

General Crawford on the retreat to the lines of Torres Vedras in 1810, with the light division halted at Alembuer, and the weather being stormy the men were placed under cover. The cavalry had all filed into the lines, but the general sent no patrol forward, posted no pickets, and laid himself open to a surprise; the town being very much exposed to such a disaster situated, as it is, in a deep ravine. Some officers anxiously watched the heights in front, being afraid of a sudden attack : they noticed the advanced scouts of the French cavalry; the regiments were immediately got under arms, and although retiring in confusion, did not suffer much loss, and succeeded in gaining the lines, not, however, without placing the whole army in a dangerous position for a time.

When the pickets and main guards are finally posted, the officer should then use every effort to place his posts in a state of defence, by all the natural and artificial means in his power; defensive preparations of this nature protect the pickets, impede the march of the enemy, prevent surprise, inflict greater loss on the opposing forces in their efforts to carry them, and give the main army more time to prepare.

The field officer should also see that the communication between the several pickets and main guards, and between pickets and their advances, is carefully attended to, both as regards patrolling and intermediate posts.

In order to support the main guards in case of an attack in force, it is necessary, as I have before stated, to have a certain portion of the army in camp in a state of stricter preparation than the rest, so as to be able to march at once to the support of the threatened points; these are called inlying pickets. Specific reserves are also told off and ready in addition to the inlying pickets; they move to the support of their main guards by the nearest route on the first alarm.

Officers in command of outposts should be careful in posting the main guards not to push them across bridges, causeways, or through defiles, except when the main body is in position in close proximity to the defiles, and the advanced posts are not protected by artillery.

A picket ought never to be posted within musket-shot of covered ground, as opposite to the edge of a wood, or in dells or defiles of any kind, or in a position where an enemy could have any opportunity of gaining its flank unperceived.

In the day-time, and in a clear open country,

sentries need not be placed so close together or so close to the pickets as in covered broken ground, at night, or in close foggy weather.

At night or in foggy weather it is desirable, if possible, to move the position of the pickets and sentries, to draw them in closer to the main body and closer to each other, as this is apt to baffle the enemy's observation of the position of the posts during the day.

Although this is a good general rule in some cases, it cannot be followed as in case of pickets placed in rear of bridges, or at the entrance of defiles ; but in this case, if the chain falls back these special posts should be strengthened, and intermediate posts placed to give prompt assistance in case of attack. It would be prudent at night to withdraw pickets which have been in advance of bridges during the day and let them occupy the *debouché* of the bridge or causeway, with a few sentries.

Great care should be taken in placing pickets to place them out of view of the enemy's posts, as, for instance, behind hedges, buildings, groves, eminences, &c., being careful to see that the flanks and rear are open to view. Sentries should also as much as possible be concealed from the enemy, but, at the same time, should have as clear and extended a view as can be obtained.

If pickets for the sake of concealment are placed
in ravines or hollow ground, it is necessary to select
a spot as near as possible to the post, upon which the
picket and intermediate posts can assemble upon the
first alarm, as it would be impossible to strengthen a
position in a dell or ravine so as to resist an attack.

If it is necessary for a picket to occupy a wood,
it is desirable to place the sentries just within the
outer border of the wood toward the enemy, the
picket taking up a position about 200 yards within
the wood; but in a disposition of this nature the
picket, instead of waiting for the sentries to fall
back on it, will, on the first alarm, move up at once
to the line of sentries, and make a stand on the
border of the wood, so as to prevent the enemy from
having the advantage which the picket would
possess from the covering afforded by the trees. If
the sentries can be placed with advantage beyond
the wood, then the picket should be placed just
within the outer edge.

A picket should never be placed within musket-
shot of the houses of a village, or close to hedges, or
woods, for a position of this kind would be very
difficult to hold, if the enemy were to obtain possession of such cover. In case a picket is placed
near a village it should be placed on its outskirts,
on the side towards which the enemy would advance,

making arrangements to check his advance by breast-
works, abattis, &c.   If cavalry are in the picket as
well as infantry, one arm should be placed on the
road and the other concealed on one side, according
to the nature of the ground, so that one could check
the advance while the other attacked him in flank.

If several roads unite at some distance in front of
where a picket should be placed, it will take post
at proper distance from the junction, and occupy the
point of junction with videttes and sentries.   If the
point of junction is not far from where the picket
ought to be, it should occupy the point itself, and
push out videttes or sentries on all the approaches.
If two roads running parallel towards the rear of the
picket, unite at some distance in its rear, it should
be placed equi-distant from the two flank roads, and
should post videttes on both roads, and on all the
approaches.   Circumstances of locality must, however, regulate these general principles in special
cases.

High ground is very favourable for pickets, if so
situated as to admit of defending the roads, by which
the enemy must debouch.   And when the slopes towards the enemy are clear and open, affording no
cover to a hostile advance, and when the ground to
the rear will admit of supports being brought up
readily, cavalry pickets should not be placed on

ground which is only suitable for defence, but they will be effective where the ground slopes gently towards the enemy.

If cavalry and infantry are united in the picket, the cavalry should take up position in the open fields, the infantry supporting or flanking them as they can best find cover.

In posting outposts along the bank of a river, the greatest care should be taken to watch and defend those points where the river bends towards the enemy, for it is on such points that the enemy will attempt to force a passage, the conformation of the ground often enabling them from their side of the river to open a cross fire across the tongue or projection of land which is made by the bend or curve of the river. In this case small alarm posts and double sentries should be placed on these curves, the picket a little to the rear, protected as much as possible from artillery fire, with a strong main guard in the vicinity to support the picket. Under no advantages of ground can these precautions be safely neglected.

The passage of the Duero in 1809 by the Duke of Wellington succeeded only through the most flagrant negligence in picketing and patrolling the river on the part of Marshal Soult. The French guards were few, and distant from each other, while his patrols were neither numerous nor vigilant. So negligent and so badly posted were these outposts, that Col. Waters, of Wellington's staff, aided by a barber and a priest, crossed the river in a small skiff and within half an hour brought back three barges, with which the crossing was effected ; and this within a very short distance of Soult's head-quarters and in broad daylight. The French retreated in confusion and with heavy loss.

Pickets ought not to be placed on the front of bridges and causeways of great length, unless the head of the bridge is protected by a *tête-de-pont* or some strong ground. If the fire of a main guard posted near the *debouché* of the bridge can cover the retreat of the picket, it may in some instances be pushed across; but it is better to post small alarm posts or double sentries on the other side. In cases like this, materials should be in readiness to stop up the bridge or causeway, and preparations even made for destroying bridges, though in no case, except by superior orders, should any defile be barricaded so effectually as to cause any great delay in opening up again the passage. These barricades or stoppages should be made near the position to prevent the enemy from attempting under cover of night to re-establish the passage, or even approach the barricade, without exposing himself to our fire. If over a river, the obstruction ought to be made where the water is deepest, if

the river is not of sufficient depth to prevent fording
in its whole breadth.   If planks, beams, &c., are removed they should not be thrown carelessly into the
water, as they may be required for the reconstruc-
tion of the communication.

It is dangerous to post a chain of outposts too
near the main body, for the less the distance the
greater the facility of suddenly attacking the pickets in force, driving them in, and surprising the
camp or bivouac itself before the troops can form.
The only means of avoiding this danger is by imposing a much stricter vigilance among the main
body, by which the fatigue of the soldier is considerably increased.   On the other hand, if the distance
is too great the sentries and videttes cannot fall back
with as much security upon the pickets and the
pickets upon the supports, and there is danger of
portions of the chain being lost.

In-lying pickets and reserves should be instructed
in case of alarm as to what point of the chain they
are to support, so as to move up without confusion or delay.   For this purpose they must be
made acquainted with the nearest paths or roads.
In-lying pickets are sometimes employed at night
and in foggy weather in strengthening the chain
of outposts, and supplying defects in it; whenever
they are employed in this way fresh bodies are told
off to supply their place in the camp.

In some instances when the enemy is distant two marches, and the general has great confidence in his source of information, the reserves and inlying pickets are dispensed with; the patrols, especially of cavalry, being in that case constantly in motion, and detached scouring parties being also on the alert.

In case the main body is not of sufficient strength to supply a complete chain of outposts at the regular distance, the line of main guards is left out, and the chain of pickets posted at half distance. In this case the main body is in some measure the grand guard, or reserve, and must be ready to stand to arms at a moment's notice. This is only done in cases of necessity, as when the army halts for a few hours, and is under arms during the whole time, or when the enemy is at a distance.

SECTION III.—POSTING VIDETTES AND SENTRIES, AND THEIR DUTIES.

As the principal duty of sentries and videttes is to give notice to their pickets of any threatened attack of the enemy, so that they may form to resist them, and notify the posts on either side of them, the greatest care must be taken to place them in positions which will give the widest possible scope to their observation.

Those points of ground from which a clear view to the front and flanks can best be obtained, must be carefully selected on which to post the sentries. In flat level country, where there are no eminences on which to post them, church steeples, high buildings, and trees must be used to supply the place of elevated points of ground. But in these cases it is desirable, in order to save time, to place a second sentry below, in order to signal, or carry the report of the looker-out to the picket.

At night, the sentries or videttes should generally be withdrawn from the heights and placed behind the crest, as it is impossible from the high ground to see at night what is going on in the flat or hollow, while, on the other hand, anything moving over the crest of the hill (especially in clear nights) is easily seen against the sky from below. The enemy, also, to avoid being seen, would certainly direct his movements along the lowest ground. In order to obtain the full advantage, a sentry watching a road must take care that the eye does not rest on any dark background, but upon the sky, or his observation would be of no effect.

Sentries at night should be drawn closer to each other, and to their pickets, and reinforced; for the security of the whole chain, and of each individual sentry, depends entirely upon the connection and mutual vigilance. If sentries are posted on defensible heights during the day, they should be thrown forward at night so as not to lose possession of them. At night sentries depend more upon the sense of hearing than of sight, and by placing the ear to the ground the march of troops can generally be distinguished at a much greater distance than otherwise. To give full play to the sense of hearing, sentries should not be placed, at night, near mills, rushing waters, or trees; nor should they have the collars of their cloaks or coats turned up, or the ears of their caps down.

If sentries are posted double, and any movement is perceptible in the enemy's camp, such as the moving of columns, cavalry or artillery, one man runs in while the other continues his observation. If posted singly, he makes the signal previously fixed upon to the post of communication, which passes it to the picket. Cavalry videttes signal when any party from the enemy is seen approaching, by circling their horses at a walk, trot, or gallop, according to the number of the approaching force. If it be cavalry only, both videttes circle to the right; if infantry, both to the left; if cavalry and infantry, one to the right and the other to the left. If a cavalry vidette is posted singly he circles to the right and to the left in the same manner as if there was

another with him ; and, if there is a mixed force of
the enemy approaching, he circles first to the right
and then to the left, in the shape of the figure 8.
If they require a party from the picket, they place
the helmet or chaco on the muzzle of the carbine
and raise it well above the head.

When the sentry or vidette is so posted that,
from darkness, distance, fog, or wind, his voice or
signal cannot be heard or seen by the sentry of
communication, he must wait until he is certain
that the enemy is advancing towards the position,
and then give the alarm by firing. If the matter
is not urgent he must wait the arrival of the next
patrol, and report accordingly.

The sentry of communication posted between the
advanced line and the picket, on seeing the signal,
or hearing the voice of the advanced sentry, will run
in and report the circumstance to the officer in command, who will go himself or send a non-commissioned officer to ascertain the cause of it. All sentries, videttes, and advanced parties must alarm their
pickets if, during the night, the noise of artillery or
the step of horses is heard. When sentries are double,
one man may run forward some one hundred yards,
lie down, and listen with his ear to the ground.

On the approach of the enemy, the sentry gives
the alarm by firing ; and, on their nearer approach,

it is followed by a second shot—the sentry retiring slowly towards his picket, keeping the enemy in view. On a second shot from the same sentry being heard, the alarm is repeated along the whole chain, which falls back upon its picket, preserving its extended order. If the enemy pushes forward briskly, the sentries must fire repeatedly, as a signal for the whole line to fall back on the supports, being careful, in retiring, to open in the centre and form on the flanks, so as to clear the front of the pickets.

Sentries and videttes, at night, as a security against surprise, must preserve a perfect stillness, and constant vigilance; and no conversation can, on any account, be permitted. If, in spite of all precautions, a sentry or party are surprised, it is imperatively necessary for them to alarm the line by firing; and, if a man should chance to escape, he must make his way to the nearest post, and report. If anyone approaches a sentry at night, he challenges in an under tone; and, if no answer is given, he must fire and retire forty or fifty yards, re-loading immediately. If nothing follows, he will, on the arrival of the patrol sent to discover the cause of the alarm, resume his post. If the sentries are double, one reserves his fire in support of his comrade. In which case both sentries stand fast.

P

Videttes, sentries, and small parties thrown forward over bridges which have been blown up or barricaded, must fire on an advancing enemy, and retire separately or conceal themselves. They should never take refuge in houses or barns, as the enemy is sure to seek them there, and no escape is left to them.

Sentries cannot permit anyone to pass beyond their line, even when the enemy is at a distance, or the individual has a pass. A sentry has no business to examine papers or authority to act upon them; any person endeavouring so to pass must be made a prisoner, or shot if he attempts to escape.

The same precautions must be taken in case of persons advancing to the line from without. The sentries must challenge at about 100 yards; and, if the person proves to be a deserter, he must be directed to lay down his arms and walk away from them. He must then be detained until the patrol arrives, unless the sentry can signal to the contiguous post. If several deserters approach, the greatest precaution must be observed, as this is often a mask, under which they hope to surprise the post.

It was by neglect of these precautions that the Prussian army under Frederick the Great was surprised at Hochkirch, October 16, 1758, deserters coming in such numbers as to overpower the Prussian main guards.

Videttes, and sentries, will not allow armed parties in uniform, having the appearance of allies, to pass the chain of sentries until examined by a patrol. Such parties must be kept at a distance from the post, and their presence immediately reported. When patrols and rounds come up, the ordinary precautions against surprise must not be dispensed with. If posted double one man goes forward to the halted party, and finds out if all is well, the other remains ready to fire ; if all is well the word 'pass' is given, and the patrol moves on. Flags of truce are also challenged, and halted until examined by a patrol.

Sentries should notice particularly the positions of the enemy's videttes and posts, if they are within view, the hours at which they are relieved and visited, the direction and strength of their patrols, and the hours at which they go out, and also all changes in their posts, which they must report to the officer in command of the patrols, and also of the picket.

If a sentry or vidette discovers a party of the enemy within the advanced chain he must fire immediately and repeatedly, to give the alarm : and the nearest sentries or parties, if cut off from their own pickets, must make their way to some adjacent post.

When a vidette hears anything at night that

P 2

seems suspicious, he should advance a few paces, to find out if possible what it is: if the noise continues, the vidette should fire and join his outpost; but he should take care not to fire needlessly, as any animal or the rustling of leaves may have occasioned it.

If a man deserts from the advanced post the commander should be immediately informed, and patrols detached to acquaint all the videttes and outposts of the circumstance. In this case the countersign ought to be immediately changed.

When an envoy from the enemy approaches the line of outposts, he should be accompanied by a drummer or trumpeter; if not, he should be made a prisoner, and sent on immediately to the main guard and to the head-quarters. The greatest care should always be taken by videttes and sentries, as well as by officers commanding detached parties, to prevent messengers under a flag of truce from obtaining any information, either from the men of the post, or by observation. If the army is executing a movement which should be concealed from the enemy, the envoy should be detained until it is executed.

SECTION IV.—PATROLS AND THEIR DUTIES.

Patrols are of two kinds, those which patrol to the front, and those which patrol along the chain. The object of the former is to discover the enemy, and obtain information of his movements; the duty of the latter is to watch over the vigilance of the parties composing the chain, and to keep up the communication with the contiguous posts. Patrols sent out by pickets can only consist of a very few men, and the distance over which they patrol must depend entirely upon circumstances.

If a patrol moving to the front should happen to meet a strong body of the enemy advancing upon the position, it will immediately give the alarm by firing; it will then take up a position to check their advance, or will retire, according to the nature of the ground, the strength of the opposing party, and other circumstances, sending at once a man to report the fact to the picket. If the enemy advances very slowly or takes up a defensive position, the patrol will regulate its movements accordingly, keeping him in view. If the patrol is formed of cavalry, it may detach two men to observe the enemy more closely. If the opposing column pushes forward vigorously, the patrol retires, firing continually during the retreat, being careful to fall back upon one flank of the picket, upon which it is retiring. If the patrol in its advance meets a weak patrol of the enemy, it will fire the alarm to excite the vigilance of the chain of sentries, as the presence of weak patrols generally indicates the proximity of stronger bodies. It will not be necessary to fire in case the ground is very open, and it can be seen that there are not large parties near. The patrol in this case does not retire, but, posting itself on favourable ground, observes the enemy, and awaits the arrival of the next rounds. If the patrol meets a body of the enemy's troops within the advanced chain, it opens at once a brisk fire, and acts otherwise as circumstances dictate.

All sentries incapable of duty or negligence on their posts, on the arrival of the patrols are to be immediately relieved and taken back to the picket. Important information should be at once conveyed to the picket by a man detached for that purpose: important matters are reported on the return of the patrol.

The following are the general rules for sending out patrols :—

1. The main guards patrol towards their pickets and other outposts (exclusive of grand patrols), and on their flanks towards the contiguous main guards and posts of communication from whence the patrolling is continued.

2. Pickets patrol along their chain and towards the enemy, and also to the adjoining pickets and posts of communication.

3. Patrols of communication between the several posts of the chain ordinarily go every two or three hours. Patrols from the main guards to their pickets every hour, the patrolling commencing at daylight and continued at regular intervals during the twenty-four hours.

4. The second patrols march off when it is calculated that the first have reached the farthest point of their round, and so on, so that two patrols, one in each direction, are constantly in motion. The severity of this duty may in some instances be lessened by not marching off the second patrol until the return of the first. This can only be permitted when the enemy is at a distance.

5. Extra patrols are sent out when a shot is heard in the line of videttes or from a patrolling party, or if repeated firing is heard from some of the distant posts. In this case the patrol takes the nearest road to the adjoining picket in the direction of the alarm, and as every post does this the actual cause may soon be communicated, especially when cavalry patrols are employed. Extra patrols are also sent out if any movement is signalled or deserters are coming in, or in case of any special report coming in which may require investigation or attention.

SECTION V.—DUTIES OF OFFICERS ON OUTPOST DUTY.

The command of a cordon of outposts should be entrusted to a field officer, because, from his position, he is necessarily the soul of the system of defence: all the troops connected with this duty are under his orders, all reports are made to him, and from him proceed all the orders relating to the general arrangements of the chain. The field officer's post is usually fixed in a central position among those posts which cover the most important avenues to the camp—and in rear of the line of main guards. Here he should place his main reserve. His duty requires him to go the rounds from time to time, so that every part of the line of defence may be under his supervision and may feel the influence of his presence. But whenever he quits his post on visiting rounds or inspection of a portion of the chain, he leaves behind an officer whom he deputes to take charge of his bivouac, to receive reports, and to give instructions. This substitute must be made acquainted with the points of the chain he proposes visiting, and the shortest road of communication to him. If time and distance admit, his actual position should be from time to time communicated by orderly, to the officer at the bivouac.

Each picket or post must be made acquainted

with the shortest and best roads to the bivouac of the field officer, and the reserves must have specific directions, under what circumstances, what pickets, and by which roads they are to move forward in support.

At night and towards morning, the field officer stations himself with the main guard, most likely to be attacked, and notifies his position to the whole chain of outposts, and also to the reserves. He will repair to any threatened spot in case of alarm, and make his dispositions according to the circumstances ; if the alarm appear of no importance, he will leave a mounted officer with an orderly to watch the progress of affairs, and report to him in case matters assume a serious shape.

If the alarm is heard from several points at once, he sends officers, on whose judgment he can rely, to the several points, to report on the cause of such firing, remaining himself with the grand reserves, or proceeding to the most important posts, leaving careful directions where he is to be found.

In visiting the chain of posts, the field officer carefully examines the exact position of each post, corrects any faults he may see in their disposition, and sees that every part of the chain is on the alert.

The officer in charge of a post, after first making good his post, prepares and sends off his report to the field officer, as soon as the morning patrols have returned, and the old pickets have marched off. The orderly who is sent to the rear with this report, does not return to his picket, but remains at the field officer's post as an orderly, so that a certain number of men are assembled in this way, at the officer's bivouac, who are acquainted with the nearest roads to their respective posts. A second report is sent in at noon and another in the evening. These reports state the number of detached parties, videttes, or sentries; how posted, the state of communication with contiguous posts, the orders for the patrols, any intelligence that may have been obtained, as well as any change in the disposition of his own men.

The officers in command of out pickets should place an old soldier with a young one, if posted double, taking care that no man knows beforehand the post he is to occupy.

The officer commanding the post immediately opposite to where a flag of truce arrives from the enemy's lines, proceeds to the point and having answered the signal, calls upon the flag to approach; the communication is then made, or the despatches delivered over and a receipt given. If an immediate answer be required, or if the officer demands to be conducted to head-quarters or to the field officer, the officer in command of the picket will forward a report of the circumstance and place the flag in a position where the line of posts cannot be overlooked to wait until an answer is received. If permission is granted to pass to head-quarters, the flag must be blindfolded and conducted under proper escort through the lines. If the enemy's flag approaches under escort, it must be intimated to him at once that no parley will be held until it is completely withdrawn, its presence being entirely unnecessary.

No one can communicate with the flag except the picket officer, and the greatest strictness must be enforced in this respect; he must confine himself to the object of its approach, and take no verbal communication. The flag is entirely under his charge until he is dismissed or sent to head-quarters, and all communications by staff officers should be made in his presence.

SECTION VI.—RELIEVING OUTPOSTS, ETC.

The period at which an attack is most likely to be made, if meditated, is about an hour or so before dawn. In consequence of this the reliefs generally march off so as to arrive on their several posts about that time in the morning. By this arrangement the whole strength of the chain of posts is doubled at the time when a greater accession of strength is most likely to be needed. During the time occupied in the relief, the two pickets become one under the

command of the senior officer. The relief of the
videttes, sentries, and advanced posts then takes
place. While this is going on the post is handed
over to the officer of the relief, who ascertains the
number and posts of all the videttes, &c., the number
of patrols and their routes, all the information known
of the enemy's posts, together with the fullest information as to all the roads, paths, &c., between his
post and the contiguous posts, and the station of the
field officer.

The morning grand patrols go out at the time
the relief of the posts takes place; each picket at
the same time sending out their common patrols
to front and flank. These patrols are found, in
common, to enable the new pickets to become
acquainted with the roads, &c.

As soon as the morning grand patrol returns and
reports 'all's well,' the old pickets march off,
unless the weather is foggy, when they remain until
the neighbourhood is to a certain extent open to view,
or unless some movement is reported in the enemy's
camp.

The officer of the old picket on the relief should
conduct the officer of the new picket along the chain
of sentries during the relief, pointing out to him the
enemy's posts, as well as their own contiguous posts.

SECTION VII.—DUTIES OF PICKETS.

A picket should be in a constant state of readiness, prepared to stand to arms at any moment while on duty. The arms must, therefore be kept in the most serviceable condition ; the packs of the infantry piled close to the arms, and the cavalry horses saddled.

Watering parties can only be detached at the hour when it is least probable that they will be required. Only small numbers should go at a time, and they should always go armed, and should return with the least delay possible.

If the weather is very cold the picket may be permitted to place themselves around the fires before midnight. But after midnight one-half or one-third must be under arms in the strictest sense of the word; but about two hours before daybreak the whole picket is placed under arms, and remains in strict preparation until the morning patrols have returned.

Colonel Gilmor was captured through carelessness of his pickets in February 1865. He says: ' I kept scouts and pickets out in every direction, but the night they came after me, it was so cold and snowing that my men must have been housed in some comfortable log hut in the mountains.'

In the early part of Morgan's career, when only
commanding a small force, the enemy surprised one
of his pickets in a house, and in consequence of this
want of vigilance, his whole command was scattered
and many taken prisoners.   Morgan himself narrowly
escaped.   Some defect in the picket line caused his
being surprised in his quarters, and shot in September
1864, and thus one of the greatest partisan leaders
the world ever saw was lost to his cause, through want
of care in the outpost duty.   The instances of surprise from negligence and general want of efficiency
are innumerable.

Cavalry pickets feed their horses, by divisions,
three times a day—first on the return of the
morning patrols, second at noon, and third an hour
before dark.   Water should be brought, if possible ;
if not, small parties should go to water at a time :
these parties must return instantly on hearing a
shot in the advance line of sentries.   When the
enemy is very close the post should stand to arms
on the approach of night.

The men might be allowed to sit down before
midnight with their arms in their hands, by sections
or subdivisions.   Cavalry, by turns, can dismount,
but after midnight, until break of day, the infantry
should be under arms, and the cavalry mounted.

If the enemy is at a distance the severity of this

duty may be considerably lessened, especially in the day-time, by allowing repose to the pickets by turns.

When a picket has a fire it should always be placed so as to be concealed from observation as much as possible ; the alarm post of the picket should be in rear of the fire, so as to prevent the picket from being seen when drawn up, and to expose the enemy in coming up to attack them.

CHAPTER XIV.

ADVANCED AND REAR GUARDS.

We repeat that in war it is impossible to take too many precautions to prevent surprise as well on the march as in quarters.—*Gen. Dufour.*

WE have seen in the last chapter the means adopted to prevent surprise in camp and bivouac, the system of advanced posts, by which an army is protected while resting, cooking, and sleeping. We will now consider the method by which a body of troops is protected on the march, and enabled to form up for battle before receiving the attack of the enemy.

An army marching in an enemy's country or in the neighbourhood of a hostile force, must always be preceded by an advanced guard to cover the front of the column, to prevent a sudden attack, and to preclude the chance of falling into an ambuscade. Side patrols must also be thrown out to guard against a flank attack, and a rear guard to watch and protect the rear of the column and the baggage.

Any body of troops marching in a hostile country, no matter how small in numbers, must never neglect these precautions, especially if the country is much intersected; for military history is filled with instances of disaster occasioned by the absence of these parties to clear the line of march of the columns.

The proportion of the numbers of the advanced and rear guards depends so much upon circumstances, upon the character of the country, the morale of the enemy, and the size of the main force, that no fixed rule can be laid down; except that in an advance the advanced guard must be composed of the best troops in the army, while in a retreat, especially if after a defeat, the rear guard must be so constituted.

An advanced guard should generally be at the same distance in front of the head of the column as it is to the rear of it. As for example: if the column on the march extends three miles, the advanced guard should be at least that far in front. The distance must also be regulated by the nature of the ground; it should be such as to enable the main body to form in order of battle before it can be attacked.

These bodies should be composed almost altogether of mounted rifles, with a few field-pieces, in accordance with the size of the force. There is no longer any necessity for having advanced guards composed

Q

of all three arms, because this detracts very much
from the mobility of them; and the mounted rifles,
with a few guns, combine the advantages of every
arm, without the sluggishness of movement which
characterises infantry columns.

Advanced guards so constituted need not necessarily regulate their movements by those of their
own army. The mounted rifles should push on
until they strike the enemy's rear guards or outposts, and hang on them, watching their conduct;
and spreading, swarming I should say, in small
scouting parties, on every road, they should form a
screen through which nothing could pass, nothing be
seen. By this course you not only get the earliest
notice of any change in the enemy's dispositions, and
give your army the greatest possible time to prepare
in case of an attack being made upon them, but you
also retain possession of so much more country for
drawing forage and supplies from, as well as give
your army more freedom in every way.

Mounted rifles, fresh and well-horsed, need not
be endangered by being thrown two days' march in
advance of the main army, if they are only vigilant
and ably commanded.

In large armies, however, there should always be
in addition to the mounted rifles, an advanced guard
of large force, in order to dispute the approach of an

enemy to the main body. In this case the mounted rifles form a sort of advance party for the main advanced guard.

General Lloyd advocated this doctrine, and put it in practice in the campaign of 1760. At the head of two hundred chasseurs and one hundred dragoons, he kept so near the King of Prussia's army during the whole campaign, that he never lost sight of it for an hour, though the Austrian forces and the corps he belonged to were generally two or three marches off. He was always in sight of the enemy, and scarcely a day passed without a skirmish, yet in the whole time he did not lose twenty men; showing thereby the great independence and mobility of a mounted force.

The advanced guard, in moving forwards, should have, in front of it and on its flanks, scouting parties, on all the side roads, and in the fields on each side of the roads, if the country is uneven or intersected with woods, enclosures, &c. And these parties should be required to carefully examine the ground. They need not consist of more than four or five men each, and should not be so far from each other that a constant communication cannot be kept up along the whole chain of groups; in fact, it would be better for them to be in sight of one another. If the ground is very much obstructed with trees, thickets, and such

like, the number of scouting patrols must be increased, and they must move much closer together.

These men being only required to gather information, should not use their arms unless they are likely
to be taken, or have fallen into an ambuscade.   They
should try as much as possible to keep themselves
hidden from the enemy; if they come upon a body
of their opponents they should conceal themselves
where they can watch their movements, and sending
one of their number back to inform their officer, will
remain to gather up all they can learn, keeping him
informed of it, making as little noise and being as
careful not to attract attention as possible.

Ravines, dykes, hedges, walls, and even fields of
grain should always be examined, to see if an enemy
is concealed.   Houses also should be searched, one
going in, while the others remain a little way off, to
give the alarm, if necessary.   The necessity of carefully reconnoitring was well manifested at the Battle
of Luzzara in 1702, when Prince Eugene had disposed
his whole army in the dry bed of a stream ; the bank
next the French, being higher and having a low dyke,
hid the watercourse, and the ground looked perfectly
level; but by accident a French officer placing the
outposts rode up to the dyke, and immediately discovered the whole Austrian army ready to take them
by surprise.   The Austrians immediately attacked,

but the French were still under arms, and succeeded in maintaining their ground against the troops of Prince Eugene.

Before entering a village, it should be examined carefully, and the people of the place questioned as to any parties of the enemy who may be near. In a country where the people are disposed to be friendly, a great deal of information can be obtained in this way, but even then their stories must be sifted with great caution, as their fears and local feelings will often cause them to exaggerate, and even tell what is untrue, without really meaning it. When sent on to reconnoitre with my command, on our advance on Fort Erie in 1866, at the time of the Fenian invasion, I rode with the advance files in order to question the inhabitants, and it seemed as if the fears of the people had almost deprived them of their senses, for the exaggerated rumours I heard were enough to make one's hair stand on end; so wild were they that, in almost every case, I would not believe a word I heard, and the result proved that I was right. After campaigning has been carried on for some time in a country, however, the inhabitants get quite experienced, and give the most valuable information, if disposed to be friendly. Even if hostile, a good deal can be gleaned from their demeanour and general conduct under cross-examination.

While the scouting parties are making these exa-
minations the advanced guards should halt.

In a night march, which should always be avoided
if possible, the greatest silence must be observed, and,
as in the case of outposts and videttes, the sense of
hearing must be depended on, as that of seeing
cannot be exercised.

If an enemy is very near and a battle may soon be
expected, the army should be as much concentrated
as possible ; marching in broad columns and in as
many as convenient, so long as they are close together. In this case the advanced guard should
partake more of the character of a skirmish line, with
supports and reserves spread across the whole front
of the general line of columns.

In a march of this nature, on coming to a ravine
or wood, a skirmish line should be sent through it on
foot, and mounted rifles are available for this duty.
In the same way they should advance upon villages
supposed to be occupied by the enemy.

Hozier thus describes the manner in which the
Prussian army managed this duty in 1866 in Bohemia. ' As the jägers passed the bridge they threw
out skirmishers to the right and left, who went in a
long wavy line, pushing through the standing corn.
The cavalry scouts clustered thickly on the flanks of
the skirmishers, and horsemen in more solid for-

mation followed in their rear. It was a fine sight;
the long line of rifles, extending almost across the
valley, felt carefully through the crops. The Uhlans,
with their tall lances and fantastic pennons, hovered
about the flank, and the heavy masses on the road
pushed on steadily behind the centre of the light
troops.'

With small patrols without supports near, it would
sometimes be advisable, if a village could not be
turned, to go through at a gallop, pistol in hand : the
dash would often carry them through with less loss
than creeping slowly up and rendering themselves
liable to a few steadily aimed shots. Circumstances,
however, must decide these cases.

Advanced guards should never enter defiles until
flanking parties have scoured the hills on each side,
and taken possession of all points commanding the
defile. If they find a village held by the enemy's
rear guard, they should endeavour, by turning the
position, to manœuvre them out of it by threatening
their retreat. This can often be effected without loss.

Advanced parties should never allow peasants or
country people to pass them, and go towards the
enemy ; nor should rear guards allow the inhabitants
to pass them going towards the head of the column.
Whenever it is necessary to keep a march secret,
these precautions are absolutely essential, and may

endanger the loss of a whole campaign, if not carefully attended to. Napoleon's passage of the Alps,
and Marlborough's march to the Danube, were movements that required secrecy, but not so much so as
' Stonewall ' Jackson's march from the Shenandoah
valley to join General Lee in front of Richmond in
1862. As a perfect master-piece of this kind of
duty, we shall here give an account of the manner in
which his march was conducted.

In 1862, the Federals advanced on several lines
of operation against the Confederates, who were defending Richmond. M'Clellan with the main army,
with his base at Fortress Monroe, and afterwards at
the White House, was threatening Richmond from
the east, M'Dowell at Fredericksburg was advancing
from the north, while Banks was moving up the
Shenandoah valley to unite with Fremont, who was
coming from the north-west, and both were to march
on Richmond from the direction of Staunton.
Jackson, by his brilliant operations of the spring of
1862, first defeated Banks, and drove him in confusion and utter route across the Potomac, into Maryland. Hearing that a great portion of M'Dowell's
army under Shields was marching from the east
against his line of communications, while Fremont
was threatening them from the west, he made
a series of forced marches, and threw himself be-

tween them at Port Republic on the Shenandoah river. Then, making a skilful use of the bridge over the river, he first defeated Fremont on the west, and then Shields on the east, and drove them both in a northerly direction. By these operations, Banks, Fremont, and the great bulk of M'Dowell's army, were defeated, and M'Clellan alone remained, with a powerful army threatening Richmond.

The Confederate commander-in-chief then arranged his plans for concentrating Jackson's corps with his own, and attacking M'Clellan combined. It was manifestly of the utmost importance, that in drawing Jackson's corps away from the front of the *debris* of the three armies, that it should be kept secret, in order to prevent their concentration and advance upon the communications of Richmond with the west. Jackson therefore pressed them for a short distance, and drew so strict a cordon of pickets across the valley that no one could get through; the prisoners were sent to Richmond, and met several divisions of the army of that place, marching in the direction of the valley as if to reinforce Jackson; some of these prisoners were released on parole, and immediately carried the news of what they had seen to Washington; while the divisions were at once countermarched, after having served their purpose. Jackson's corps was then moved rapidly towards Richmond. A strong rear guard prevented all straggling backward, and when they encamped, all the lateral roads were carefully guarded, and all communication with the country cut off. So well was this managed, that the United States Government was thoroughly deceived, and refused to allow M'Dowell to advance to M'Clellan's assistance, because they said it would not be necessary, as General Lee's army had been weakened to the extent of 15,000 men, sent to Jackson, and that the danger of Washington City was too much increased to allow of them to permit it with safety.

Jackson's army, by the direction of their march, fell upon M'Clellan's right flank and rear, Lee also simultaneously attacked him in front, and after seven days' fighting and pursuing, M'Clellan, utterly routed and demoralised, was driven to the shelter of his gun-boats at Harrison's landing. Lee then moved north, and attacked and defeated Pope (who had gathered the other armies together), before M'Clellan could come to his assistance. We have described these operations briefly, not only as an example of the importance and necessity of great care in the vigilance of advanced and rear guards, but also as a brilliant illustration of the finest principles of strategy.

The commander of the advanced guard ought to

have the best maps of the theatre of the operations that can be procured, and verified, as much as possible, in marching over the country and by reconnoitring. Guides must also be obtained in some way, either from the friendly inhabitants, or by force if in an enemy's country. If guides are compelled to act, they must be carefully guarded by strong escorts, to prevent treachery. If an army is operating in its own country, the officers commanding regiments of mounted rifles should have lists made out of the places where the soldiers in their corps have lived, and of the localities they are most familiar with ; and by this means reference can easily be made to these lists, and the men best fitted for guides at once known without loss of time. In an enemy's country this would be of no use. Colonel Simcoe, in the American rebellion of 1776, commanded a partizan corps called the Queen's Rangers, and he acted upon this system, and was consequently rarely in want of a guide.

When the officer commanding an advanced guard reaches the position where he is to halt, he should immediately question the chief magistrate and the post-master, &c., and gather all the information possible about the defiles, marshes, roads, bridges, fords, &c., in the neighbourhood. Napoleon, in his 'Campaign in Italy,' gives a good example of the

duties of an officer commanding the advance ; and as
cavalry officers are often placed in that position,
they will do well to consider that great captain's
remarks on this duty.   He says : ' General Steingel,
an Alsatian, was an excellent hussar officer ; he had
served under Dumouriez in the campaigns of the
north, he was adroit, intelligent, vigilant.   He united
the qualities of youth to those of advanced age ; he
was a true general of advanced posts.

' Two or three days before his death he was the
first to enter Lezegno.   The French general arrived
there some hours after, and everything he required
was ready.

' The defiles and fords had been reconnoitred,
guides had been secured ; the priest, the postmaster,
had been examined; communications had been opened
up with the inhabitants ; spies had been sent out in
many directions ; the letters in the post had been
seized, and those which could give military information translated and analysed ; and measures were
taken to form magazines of subsistence to refresh
the troops.'

General Duke, in the ' History of Morgan's Cavalry,' gives full particulars of the custom of managing their advanced guard ; and as the composition
of it was somewhat original, I give the extract in his
own words.

'Before leaving Knoxville, Colonel Morgan, appreciating the necessity of having an advanced guard which could be thoroughly relied on, and disinclined to trust to details changed every day, for that duty had organised a body of twenty-five men, selected with great care from the entire force under his command, to constitute an advanced guard for the expedition. So well did this body perform the service assigned it, that the men composing it, with some additions to make up the tale as others were taken out, were permanently detailed for that duty, and it became an honour eagerly sought, and a reward for gallantry and good conduct second only to promotion, to be enrolled in "the advance."

'This guard habitually marched at a distance of 400 yards in front of the column, three videttes were posted at intervals of 100 yards between it and the column. Their duties were to transmit information and orders between the column and the guard, and to regulate the gait of the former, so that it would not press too close on the latter, and also to prevent any straggling between the two. Six videttes were thrown out in front of the guard, four at intervals of fifty yards, and with another interval of the same distance from the fourth of these, two rode together in the extreme front. These two were consequently at a distance of 250 yards in front of the body of the guard. At first these videttes were regularly relieved, but it was afterwards judged best to keep the same men on the same duty. The advanced videttes were required to examine carefully all sides, and report to the officer of the guard the slightest indication which seemed suspicious. When they came to bye-roads or cross-roads one, or both, as the case might require, immediately galloped some two or three hundred yards down them, and remained until relieved by men sent for that purpose from the head of the column, when they returned to their post.

' As soon as they notified the officer of the guard (by calling to the videttes next behind them) that they were about to leave their posts, he took measures to supply their places. The two videttes next to them in the chain galloped to the front, the other two also moved up respectively fifty yards, and two men were sent from the guard to fill the places of the last.

' When the videttes regularly in advance returned, the original disposition was resumed. If an enemy was encountered, men were despatched from the guard to the assistance of the videttes, or the latter fell back on the guard, as circumstances dictated. If the enemy was too strong to be driven by the advance, the latter endeavoured to hold him in check

(and was reinforced if necessary) until the command
could be formed for an attack or defence.   Scouting
parties were of course thrown out on the front and
flanks as well as to the rear, but as these parties were
often miles away in search of information, a vigilant
advanced guard was always necessary.   During an
engagement the advance was generally kept mounted,
and held in reserve.'

During the campaign in Pennsylvania in 1863,
just before the battle of Gettysburg, when General
Early was marching up towards York and Carlisle,
his advanced guard were in the habit of sending small
parties down every cross-road or bye-road for half a
mile or so.   These parties remained until the whole
column had passed, and then they returned and joined
the rear.

On coming upon the enemy's outposts they should
be driven in as quickly as possible, in order to endeavour to get close enough to reconnoitre the position
of the hostile forces.   Just before a battle is expected
a general-in-chief should be well to the front, as he
may often have opportunities of taking his opponent
by surprise, and of promptly acting as occasion may
offer.   Had Massena accompanied his advanced
guard on arriving at Busaco in 1810, he would have
availed himself of a most favourable opportunity of
attacking the English.   He was ten miles in the rear,

however, and when he arrived the chance had slipped through his fingers.

When an advanced guard halts it should be in a place concealed from the enemy's observation. Sentinels or videttes should be thrown out, and one half of the command kept under arms, while the other half are taking their meal. The different parts will then change places.

Marshal Marmont, in his ' De l'Esprit des institutions militaires,' gives a good example of the danger of neglecting the precaution of advanced guards, which occurred in 1814 in France. He says : 'There is in front of the village of Vauchamps, on the side towards Paris, a position advantageous and easily defensible ; it is the slope of the plateau which borders the small valley on which Vauchamps is built ; to the right and front, a wood presents the means of taking in reverse all bodies which should advance inconsiderately without having occupied it. I caused this wood to be occupied as quietly as possible, I deployed my troops on the hill, I put my cannon in battery, and we awaited the enemy.

' The corps of Kleist, the strength of which was four times that of mine, thought it had nothing to fear, and marched with extreme confidence, the troops being in column and touching without any interval between them, and even without scouting. Finding the village unoccupied, Kleist passed through it, but assailed by a murderous fire of artillery and musketry, attacked at the same time in front and flank, thrown into confusion, he flies from the village in great disorder, and our cavalry pouncing upon him, four thousand prisoners fall into our hands. From that moment the enemy, who had no regular formation, withdrew in mass until evening.'

At Königgrätz, in 1866, Benedek lost the action through not having an advanced force of cavalry or dragoons thrown out on his right flank to watch the Crown Prince's army, which he knew was in that direction. In consequence of this neglect, the Prussians penetrated into the centre of the Austrian position, and seized Chlum, the key of it, before Benedek was able to check the movement.

In pursuing a beaten enemy the advance should consist of all arms, and should push forward with the greatest rapidity, in order to prevent them from rallying. The dragoons should be sent on to endeavour to cut off the retreat of the flying masses; if able to head them off, by dismounting in a strong position, they can so easily retard the movements of the enemy that large numbers will certainly be captured. It should always be understood that in pursuing a column, it is better, if possible, to attack its flank than directly in the rear.

R

At the defile of Calliano, in 1796, after the battle of Roveredo, Napoleon having thrown the Austrians into utter confusion and rout into the defile, detached his aide-de-camp Lamarois with fifty cavalry to dash through the retreating mass and stop the head of their column. He did so, and the result was, that, checking the head of the mass, the French were able to capture several thousand prisoners.

At Sailor's Creek, in 1865, during the pursuit of Lee's army from Richmond by the Federal forces, Sheridan came upon a strong rear guard some 8,000 in number, under command of the Confederate general Ewell. Sheridan attacked the column on its flank before it reached the stream, and sending on three divisions of his dragoons, they crossed Sailor's Creek before Ewell, formed up on the high ground on the far side of the creek, dismounted, and, with their repeating fire, held the whole of the Confederate column in check until other bodies of the Federal army coming up, Ewell was obliged to surrender his whole command, after desperate fighting in attempting to break through the lines of dismounted cavalry, who checked his march.

This is a strong example of the use of dragoons armed as before suggested, and trained to fight on foot with repeating weapons.

REAR GUARDS AND THE RETREAT.

In a retreat, the most perfect discipline must be maintained in the rear guard, which should comprise the best and freshest troops in the army.

The rear guard is arranged in a somewhat similar manner to the advanced guard, but is usually weaker, and the same precautions are not required of searching ground which has already been examined, for the rear is not very liable to an attack, except in a retreat, in which case it must be much stronger than otherwise, and much more vigilant. It forms the escort of the baggage and trains while the army is advancing. It should prevent straggling, and arrest deserters, and marauders who might follow the main body.

A rear guard should have its flankers and scouting parties, as well as rear detachments, spread out to prevent a rush in on the rear of the column without notice. These parties should frequently look back to see that they are not followed. Cavalry, or dragoons, should always be attached to the rear guard to move about rapidly, and keep up the communication with the main army.

In a retreat the rear guard becomes the most important part of an army, and the duties are the most difficult and arduous that soldiers can be called upon

to perform. The *morale* of the men is much diminished, in consequence of falling back before the
enemy, while the pursuers become all the bolder, on
account of their success. Those troops who have
suffered least, should form the rear guard after a
defeat, and they must be as little encumbered as
possible. The baggage waggons are then sent on in
front of the army, or as far forward as can be arranged, so as to relieve the roads, and render the
rear columns as available as possible for defensive
movements.

As the duty of rear guards, under these circumstances, is of a *defensive* nature, a large proportion
might consist of infantry, but a heavy force of
cavalry should also be attached, as the enemy would
certainly push all their mounted force on in the
pursuit.

The rear guard should halt in all defensible positions, and check the movements of the enemy as
much as possible. They should not generally halt
in front of a defile, but on the far side of it, taking
a position on the flanks, and at the outlet, in order
to prevent the enemy from debouching. The account of the action of Captain Krauchenberg with a
squadron of the King's German Legion on July 4,
1810, described in the ninth chapter, is a good illustration of this principle.

The cavalry, or dragoons, of a rear guard should form the rear detachment, and they should defend every bridge, defile, wood, or obstruction in order to give the remainder time to continue their retreat. Under these circumstances the value of the dragoons is clearly shown; the men by dismounting will be in a position to keep back large numbers of the enemy, if the ground is intersected and defensible.

It will be well here to give an example to illustrate the method of covering a retreat in this way :—

In 1810 after the battle of Busaco, when Wellington was retiring to the lines of Torres Vedras, the rear detachment of the rear guard was composed of the hussars of the King's German Legion ; on arriving at the Mondego Colonel Arentschild disputed the passage of that river. He sent two of his squadrons across and remained on the other side, with the two remaining squadrons to check the enemy's advance. The French drove them into the ford, but some of the Germans dismounting on the opposite bank, poured in a sharp fire upon the pursuing force and covered the passage of the rear files. The enemy dismounted some men to counterbalance this, and their fire was most deadly, but the hussars held them in check until the French infantry came up, when they retired ; the retreat of their main body through a defile which lay in the rear being secured. On

several occasions during this retreat the use of dismounted cavalry was resorted to in order to give
them a defensive power in covering bridges, fords, &c.

The retreat in the immediate presence of the
enemy should be conducted by alternate masses or
lines. If lines of dismounted dragoons they could
be retired by alternate ranks, or squadrons, taking
advantage of every cover, barricading roads, bridges,
and defiles while retiring. This especially delays the
advance of the enemy's artillery.

An instance of what can be effected by a small
rear guard skilfully managed took place in Spain
in 1812. During Sir Rowland Hill's retreat from
Madrid to Arevalo, a small rear detachment of
twenty-two men of the German hussars under Lieutenant Grahn checked the enemy's progress at the
Adaja river, near Villa Nueva. Beamish describes it
as follows :—

'This picket took up a position in the hollow of
a deep roadway or defile flanked by thickly-wooded
heights, and leading from a ford of the Adaja river.
The French, having reconnoitred the position of the
picket, formed in a dense column on the opposite
bank to the number of from twelve to fifteen squadrons. Grahn, seeing the unequal contest with which
he was threatened, directed his men to put a second
ball into their carbines, and extending his little force

in such a manner as to give it the protection of the wood, he sent a report of his situation to the brigade then at Villa Nueva, about a league distant, and firmly awaited the enemy's advance. A French squadron soon appeared in motion, and crossing the ford, pressed into the defile. The hussars now opened their carbine fire, which wounding several men and horses, caused such a panic among the assailants that nearly half of them immediately crossed the river, the rest sought out for other approaches to the position of the picket but without success, and the enemy, seeing that the Germans were neither to be forced in front or flank, quietly dismounted and did not seem disposed to renew the assault.'

CHAPTER XV.

RECONNOITRING.

La base de toute opération militaire est d'abord la connaissance du terrain sous son double aspect, défensif et offensif, puis celle de la position, de la force, et si l'on peut, de la pensée de l'ennemi.— *Général De Brack.*

RECONNOITRING is necessary to procure information of the nature of the ground in front, and on the flanks of the army, as well as to discover the position, the arrangements, and the numbers of the enemy.

If a general cannot by some means obtain information of what is passing on around him, if he is unable to learn the movements of the different parts of the opposing forces, he will not only be unable to divine the intentions of the enemy's commander, in order to take his own measures to frustrate them, but also it will be impossible for him to arrange his own plans with any degree of confidence, or with much prospect of success.

There are different methods of gathering this information, and as it will often be necessary for cavalry officers to be engaged in procuring knowledge of this kind in various ways, we will consider here the principles of reconnoitring, both by armed and secret reconnaissances, and in the next chapter discuss the other means of obtaining information under the comprehensive head of 'intelligence.'

The first thing necessary in military operations (even before the declaration of war it is required) is, a good map of the probable theatre of war. Napoleon's tent always had the best map of the seat of operations on a large table in the centre, with twenty or thirty wax candles constantly burning, and a fine compass stood in the middle of them. Caulaincourt had a portable one which he constantly kept tied to his button, across his breast, and he was often required to unfold it ten or fifteen times in the course of a forenoon.

Reconnaissances are sometimes carried out in force; this is done when it is necessary to break through the line of sentries and posts which armies always throw out around them, as a screen to prevent surprise, and conceal their movements, in order by driving them rapidly in, to get into a position where the dispositions and force of the enemy can be discovered.

An officer commanding a reconnaissance in force should be accompanied by an experienced staff officer; and a practised soldier, seeing the enemy getting under arms, and forming up to oppose their advance, will very rapidly gather all the information necessary, will count their brigades and regiments, will judge of their means of resistance, and calculate the number and value of the artillery, as well as reconnoitre the natural features of the ground, and its suitability to the different arms.

This having been done, the force should retire without compromising itself, retreating carefully and steadily back upon the main army, which should send out a force to cover the retreat, if circumstances render it necessary.

A reconnaissance in force, or one of a secret character, should be composed of dragoons, with artillery attached in the first case. In advancing, the duties of a party of this kind partake very much of the nature of those of advanced guards; the scouting parties should be thrown out to the flanks and front in the same manner, but the main body must be closer, and instead of waiting for supports on coming upon the enemy, should at once push on, vigorously driving in his videttes on the pickets, the pickets on the main guards, and all together as rapidly as possible into camp. Dragoons can do this very speedily if properly and vigorously handled, and the closer they can get to the enemy's lines, the more can they discover, and the more successful will be the reconnaissance.

These parties require guides as much as advanced guards; and the officer in command should have with him a good pair of field glasses, or a powerful telescope, as well as materials for writing and sketching. If in a foreign country the commander is not acquainted with the language spoken by the inhabitants, some officer who does understand it should accompany him, to make the necessary enquiries from the peasants, who should be examined as to the size of the villages in the neighbourhood, their names and positions, the quality of the roads, and the direction in which they lead, the principal features of the rivers and streams, as well as the size of the woods, and the position of bridges, and fords, &c.

Information such as this is invaluable in many instances. A remarkable example occurred in the Peninsular War, of the necessity of being acquainted with the fords on rivers in the seat of operations. At the passage of the Tamega at Amarante in 1809, the French, after losing 180 men, and many officers, in fruitlessly endeavouring to force a passage across the bridge, at last succeeded by blowing away a part of the obstacles, and effected their crossing. At the same time there was a practicable ford near the bridge unguarded and unknown to both parties.

Everyone who is met should be questioned in the hope of obtaining valuable information, as the people of the country are almost always able to give some hints which with the aid of the map can be easily understood. The map should be tested and verified, and any necessary corrections or additions made upon it. Matters of apparently a trivial nature often assume afterwards a most important character, and have a serious effect upon the operations of armies, consequently the minutest details of information should be collected, classified, and recorded.

In the map used by General Lee at the time of the seven days' fight before Richmond, there was an inaccuracy which had a most important influence upon the operations. It appears that there were two by-roads starting from near the same point, one of which had no name, while the other was called the Quaker Road. The surveyor who made the map, by some misunderstanding, had marked down the road which had no name as the Quaker Road. General Lee, laying down his plans by this map, ordered General Magruder with his division to march by the Quaker Road to a certain position. The latter, enquiring of his guides and the inhabitants, was conducted by the real Quaker Road, which was not the one meant by General Lee. The mistake was discovered after marching about an hour on the wrong track, and Magruder was obliged to retrace his steps. Through this mistake this whole division was rendered useless at one of the most critical junctures of that memorable succession of battles.

In advancing, an officer should examine the peculiarities and formation of the country as he passes, choosing positions on which to make a stand on his falling back, if it becomes necessary for him to do so. He should arrange his plan of forming up his command in his own mind, and this will render him more confident in his movements when obliged to retreat. He should look back and examine the country from every point of view, and by so doing would be able to test better, whether his plans for forming up would require alteration.

If a reconnaissance in force, especially of dragoons, is made to some distance from the main army, and consequently it becomes necessary for the party to halt, to rest or to take food, it should be made behind a hill, or a wood, or in some position in which the presence of the troops will not be easily perceived. Sentries or videttes being thrown out in every direction concealed as much as possible, but posted so as to see the country without being seen. Small cavalry patrols could also be sent a greater distance along the roads to give notice of the approach of an enemy. If the halt is made near a village it should

be made on the far side, so as to hold possession of
it. If necessary, the commanding officer will call
upon the inhabitants to provide food for the men,
who should take their meals by turns, part eating
while the remainder continue under arms.

An officer commanding a body of dragoons effecting
a reconnaissance in force, should husband the strength
and wind of his horses, until he first strikes the
enemy's advanced parties, and then he should drive
them in at speed ; by this means he can sometimes
almost get into the main camp at their heels, taking
them by surprise by the mere rapidity of his movements. By this course he may be able to take some
prisoners from whom a great deal of information can
often be obtained. He should be careful, however,
not to let his command get out of hand.

On November 29th, 1864, General Rosser surprised the strongly-fortified post of New Creek, by
driving the pickets and videttes in at full speed
into the camp, riding in almost with them. Although the place was fortified and well garrisoned,
he captured it, taking two regiments of cavalry
prisoners, with their arms and colours, while eight
pieces of artillery, and a very large amount of ordnance, quarter-master, and commissary stores, fell
into his hands. He effected this with the loss of
only two men.

The commander should not be tempted from the object of his mission to attack parties of the enemy whom he may hear of as being open to surprise; he should stick to his instructions. If it comes in his way, he may destroy railroads, burn supplies, spike or capture cannon, make prisoners, and defeat detachments of the enemy, but he should not allow this to prevent him doing his main duty.

General Stuart of the Confederate cavalry made a magnificent armed reconnaissance in 1862 in front of Richmond, by which he gained a great deal of information as to the position of the enemy's lines, which enabled 'Stonewall' Jackson a few days afterwards to fall upon the flank and rear of M'Clellan's army with perfect confidence and with terrible effect.

In this reconnaissance, or 'raid,' as it is commonly called, Stuart made the complete circuit around the whole of the Federal army, going round their right flank, along their rear, and returning by their left flank, having, as Colonel Von Borcke says, ' destroyed the enemy's communications, burned property to the amount of millions, captured hundreds of prisoners, horses and mules, and put the whole Federal army in fear and consternation.' This partook partly of the character of an armed, and partly of a secret, reconnaissance, as they tried to avoid fighting as much as possible, and to conceal their movements, while they were quite ready to attack whatever appeared to bar their passage.

In another 'raid' by General Stuart in the same year on Catletts Station in rear of Pope's army, 'he killed and wounded a great number of the enemy, captured 400 prisoners, among whom were several officers, and more than 500 horses; destroyed several hundred tents, large supply depôts, and long waggon trains, secured in the possession of the quarter-master of General Pope 500,000 dollars in greenbacks and 20,000 dollars in gold, and, most important of all, deprived the Federal commander of all his baggage, and private and official papers, exposing the *effective strength* of his army, the dispositions of his different *corps d'armée*, and the plans of his whole campaign.'

An armed reconnaissance, in falling back after completing its task, is much in the situation of a rear guard covering a retreat, and the same rules should regulate its movements and the same principles guide its actions.

Secret reconnaissances are for the same purpose as armed, with the difference that in one case, the object is gained by force, and in the other by secrecy and stratagem. The latter should be composed of very few men as they serve the purpose quite as well and are more easily concealed, while their march does not attract any attention. With bold daring men these secret reconnaissances are most effective.

These bodies partake somewhat of the character of scouting parties, and should act in a similar manner. They should conceal their march as much as possible among woods and ravines, and through bye-roads and paths, and should act sometimes on foot, sometimes mounted, according to circumstances.

They should march out one way and come back another, in order to avoid any arrangements that might be made to cut them off. They should be composed of men who know the country thoroughly; if not they must have good guides, as they generally march by paths not much known. One man should move cautiously in front, and if any of the enemy come in sight, the party should turn aside and conceal themselves in woods, hollows, or in some way or other.

If the enemy is approaching in a large column and near the advanced posts of the army, the officer commanding the party should attack their advance in order to give alarm to the chain of posts behind, and at the same time to check its movement. If the enemy's force is small, and he cannot escape observation, he can then fight; but he should endeavour in every instance to conceal his party, if possible.

s

If near the enemy's lines he comes upon a strong column, he should conceal, himself and count its strength as accurately as he can, and send the information back to his general. Care should be taken to send several orderlies back, in order to have the greater chance of one of them getting through.

When the reconnoitring party gets as near as possible to the position of the enemy, the officer should conceal his men in some convenient place, and proceed with the guides stealthily to some mound or point where he can get a view of the camp of the hostile forces, and keeping himself hidden, with his glass he should coolly examine their whole dispositions, numbers, and arrangements, taking notes of all that he sees, and making a rough sketch of the position. This should be done, even if the sketch is very hurriedly and poorly executed. The guide should explain to him the names of the different villages and points which he can see, and this should, all be taken down. A topographical sketch might also be made, and although not accurately verified, would be very useful to a general in giving him an idea of the locality.

Just before the battle of Cedar Creek in 1864, General Early had established a signal station on the end of Massanutten Mountain, which overlooked the whole of the enemy's position. Intending to attack the enemy by surprise, General Early sent Captain Hotchkiss, his topographical engineer, with General Gordon, one of his divisional generals, to this station to make a reconnaissance, to obtain the information necessary in order to plan the attack. Captain Hotchkiss drew a sketch of the enemy's camps and position, showing how their pickets were distributed, &c. The sketch, which proved to be correct, showed the roads in the enemy's rear, and the position for crossing the river and forming up the attacking column.

On this information General Early made his plans and ordered the movements of his columns, and succeeded the day after in surprising the enemy.

Every officer of light cavalry should be able to make a topographical reconnaissance and sketch, and should practise himself in this work; occasions are always arising in war in which the knowledge will be valuable to himself, and make him more useful to his commanding officer.

Information should not be forwarded unless exact, for false reports would have a much more prejudicial effect than complete ignorance in cases of this nature.

In 1863 a false report was forwarded by a telegraph operator, after Averill had made a raid upon the Virginia and Tennessee Railroad at Salem, and started to go back, stating that he had returned to that place by reason of high water having prevented his retreat by the route by which he had come. In consequence of this report, a cavalry force under General Fitzhugh Lee, which had been sent to intercept him on his retreat, was deflected from the point to which it had been despatched in pursuit of him on another route. This enabled General Averill to make his escape by the very route which would otherwise have been closed against him.

It requires experience and study and thought to educate a man to perform this duty of secret reconnoitring well, and also great prudence, skill, and presence of mind.

If a man knows the language of the enemy, he can often by skilful ruses get himself out of difficult situations, where without adopting that course he would be captured.

A friend of the writer, an officer in the Confederate army, during the advance of General Lee into Pennsylvania, got leave to go into the Yankee lines in Maryland, to see his mother who lived there. He went in civilian's clothes, but had not been there long, when some Union woman in the village recognising him, informed the Yankee troops. The officer commanding sent a party to arrest him; they went to the next door first, so he knew they were coming after him. He arranged his plan, and

when they knocked at the door he opened it
promptly, and asked what they wanted. He was
told that they had been sent to arrest a rebel officer
who, they had been informed, was concealed in the
house. He told them it was quite a mistake, that
they were loyal people, and requested the officer to
search the house carefully. They went over the
whole place, the Confederate assisting them, and
after convincing them there was no one concealed,
he gave them something to drink, and requesting
them not to believe any more stories reflecting on
his loyalty, he politely bowed them out, and then
immediately went to the rear of the house, mounted
a horse, and rode off about ten minutes before the
party returned to arrest him, having in the mean-
time discovered their error.

General Morgan was once bringing in some
prisoners, when he rode right into a Federal regiment, which had got between him and his command.
He was halted and questioned. He stated that he
was a Federal colonel, and that his regiment was
only a short distance off, and that the prisoners were
his own men he had arrested for straggling. His
questioners much doubted his story, and said he
wore a strange dress for a Federal colonel. He
suddenly pretended to get angry, said he would
bring up his regiment to convince them who he was,
and galloped away.

Hozier in his 'Seven Weeks' War' gives the following incident which occurred after the battle of Königgrätz. 'On the evening of the battle, an officer of the Ziethen hussars, who were forward in the pursuit, rode as far as the gates of Königgrätz, and finding there were no sentries outside, rode in; the guard immediately on seeing him in his Prussian uniform, turned out and seized him, when with a ready presence he declared he had come to demand the capitulation of the fortress. He was conducted to the commandant, and made the same demand to him, adding that the town would be bombarded, if not surrendered within an hour. The commandant, unconscious that he was not dealing with a legitimate messenger, courteously refused to capitulate; but the hussar was conducted out of the town, passed through the guard at the entrance, and got off safely without being made a prisoner.'

If the guides are not friendly, they should be kept separated to prevent combinations, and to test the accuracy of their statements by comparing them with each other. Main roads should be avoided, and great silence maintained, especially at night. In passing by hills, scouts should examine the far side of them, and in the same way should examine woods, ravines, &c., which they have occasion to pass.

They should keep away from villages, especially in going out, in order to escape observation and avoid giving alarm. If it is impossible to avoid going through a village, hints should be thrown out which would lead the inhabitants to form an incorrect idea of the destination of the party, while the principal people of the place should be carefully examined, in order to get all the information possible from them. A party of this nature intending only to be away a short time, should carry enough food to last during the expedition, in order to prevent the necessity of going to villages or houses to obtain it.

If a party of this kind should arrive close to the chain of outposts of the enemy at daybreak, they should be carefully concealed, and the men forbidden to smoke or to make any noise which might lead to their detection, for it is at this time that all the posts are doubled and on the alert, and the patrols are most active and vigilant.

If the officer can get upon any commanding point with his glass where he can secretly discover what is passing on beyond the outposts, he will often be able to obtain valuable information, for at this hour the troops are usually under arms, until the return of the morning patrols.

Secret reconnaissances can often be effected more

successfully by making a wide détour, and coming
in upon the rear, for there the outposts and sentries
are neither numerous nor vigilant, and the number of
camp followers and parties continually passing about,
renders it less easy to detect small bodies of scouts
who may be moving around.   Stuart's 'raid' on
Catlett's Station was a good illustration of a reconnaissance in the rear.

In making a reconnaissance, an Itinerary should
be made by an officer of the column, showing simply
the features of the ground, alongside the road.   The
simplest way is to have paper ruled with a line down
the centre of each sheet, and a column ruled off on
each side.   The notes should be commenced at
the bottom of the sheet and carried on to the
top; the distances are marked by the length of time
taken to traverse them at a walk: the special features of the road, and the remarkable points on
right or left, defiles, bridges, declivities, marshes,
must all be marked down, as well as the side roads
which leave the main road, where they lead to, and
the distances to the nearest villages.   All other
points of importance should be noted down carefully.   An example of an Itinerary is given on the
opposite page.

Speaking of Marshal Benedek's ignorance of the
Prussian movements, before the battle of König-

These wooded heights command the road at this point.

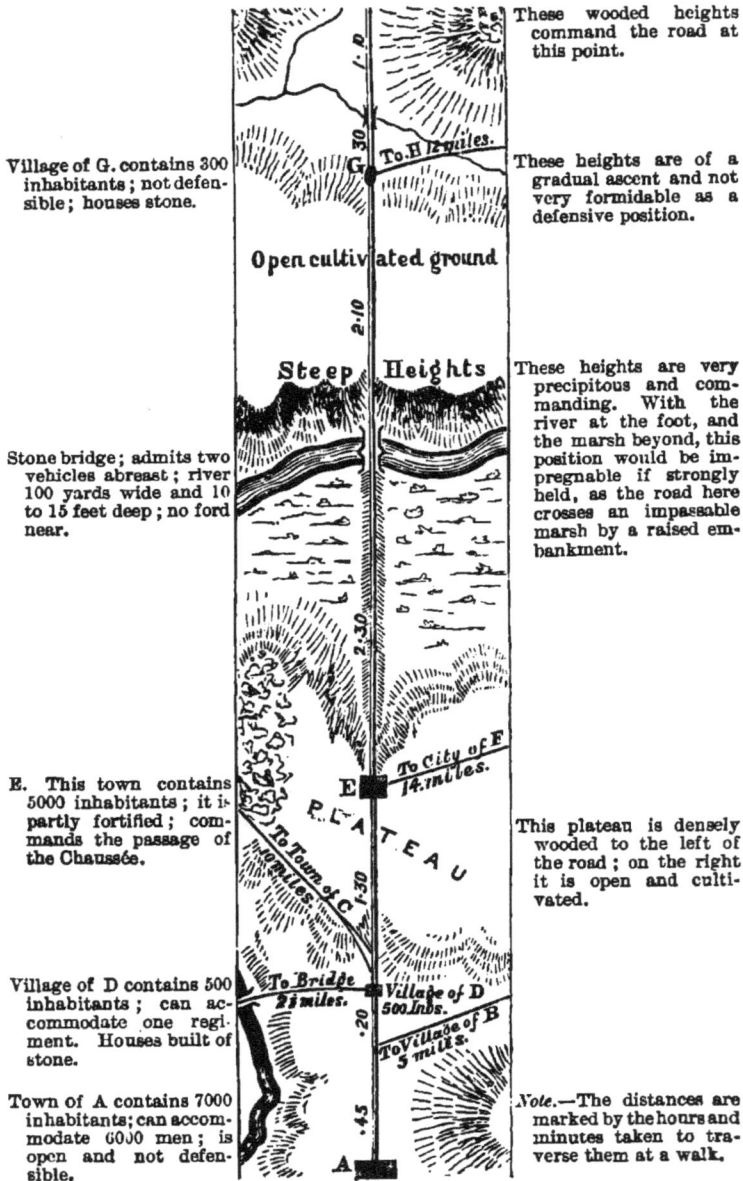

Village of G. contains 300 inhabitants; not defensible; houses stone.

To H. 12 miles.

G

These heights are of a gradual ascent and not very formidable as a defensive position.

Open cultivated ground

Steep Heights

These heights are very precipitous and commanding. With the river at the foot, and the marsh beyond, this position would be impregnable if strongly held, as the road here crosses an impassable marsh by a raised embankment.

Stone bridge; admits two vehicles abreast; river 100 yards wide and 10 to 15 feet deep; no ford near.

E. This town contains 5000 inhabitants; it is partly fortified; commands the passage of the Chaussée.

To City of F 14 miles.

E

PLATEAU

To Town of C

This plateau is densely wooded to the left of the road; on the right it is open and cultivated.

Village of D contains 500 inhabitants; can accommodate one regiment. Houses built of stone.

To Bridge 2½ miles.

Village of D 500 Inhs.

To Village of B 5 miles.

Town of A contains 7000 inhabitants; can accommodate 6000 men; is open and not defensible.

A

Note.—The distances are marked by the hours and minutes taken to traverse them at a walk.

grätz, and of the unexpected march of the Crown
Prince's army upon his right flank, Hozier in his
history says :—

' From the high bank above Königinhof, a staff
officer lying hidden in the fir wood could almost
with the naked eye have counted every Prussian
gun, every Prussian soldier that the Crown Prince
moved towards Miletin. The eyes of the Austrian
army on more than one occasion during the campaign failed. Their patrol system was very much
inferior to that of the Prussians. Its inferiority
seems to have been due to the want of military
education among the officers to whom patrols were
entrusted. In the Prussian army special officers of
high intelligence were always chosen to reconnoitre.
Properly so, for the task is not an easy one. An
eye unskilled, or a mind untutored, can see little,
where a tried observer detects important movements.
A line of country, or a few led horses, will tell the
officer who is accustomed to such duty, more than
heavy columns or trains of artillery will disclose to
the unthinking novice. The Prussian system never
failed, never allowed a surprise. The Austrians were
repeatedly surprised and taken unprepared.'

CHAPTER XVI.

INTELLIGENCE.

It is a fact, that when we are not in a desert but in a peopled country, if the general is not well instructed, it is because he is ignorant of his trade.—*Napoleon.*

THE different methods of gaining intelligence and the various ways in which information can be gleaned from the most trivial circumstances, are almost innumerable, and it will depend on the ability and skill of the general and his chief intelligence officer, whether the information obtained, with reference to the enemy's movements is complete and accurate or not.

In the last chapter we have discussed one of the most important means by which knowledge is obtained of what is passing beyond the enemy's lines, but there are, in addition to reconnoitring, many other resources open, by which to attain the same end, and we will here allude to a few of them.

A cavalry officer is so often placed in such a position as to be obliged to exert himself to obtain intel-

ligence, that he should instruct himself in the duty ;
for there is no man, however qualified he may be by
nature for a particular service, who will not be bene-
fited by devoting a little study and thought to the
subject, before he is called upon to act in earnest.

The principal means of gaining information concerning the enemy, are by the employment of secret
spies, who are sent into his camps, by intercepted
letters and orders, by deserters, by examining prisoners, and by sending staff officers to watch the enemy
from within their own lines.   Many a little incident
also connected with other circumstances will throw
light on a difficult problem.

A chief intelligence officer requires a keen knowledge of human nature, and must be an accurate
judge of character.   Such an one, cross-questioning
a deserter or prisoner, will instinctively know what
portion of his remarks to believe, and what not,
whether the man is honestly answering him, or attempting to deceive him, and will often gain an
insight into the truth, from the very attempts made
to mislead him.

Intercepted orders are above all odds the most
valuable and most complete means of obtaining information.   The knowledge gained from them is
always more certain, more full, more accurate, than
by any other means.   Intercepted letters referring to

the military movements perhaps rank next; for this reason, light cavalry should be continually hovering about the enemy, in the hope of picking up information, as well as capturing couriers, orderlies, &c., who often carry despatches containing news of value to an enemy.

In the Peninsular war, Wellington had a tremendous advantage over the French in the shape of better intelligence of their movements. The partidas, or guerilla bands, continually swarming about, frequently captured despatches, letters, &c., which not only gave Wellington a complete insight into his enemy's views, but at the same time interrupted seriously the communications between the different sections of the French army, which hampered their movements, and seriously embarrassed all their operations. After the battle of Talavera, Wellington heard of Soult threatening his communications, and the numbers of his army, by intercepted letters which the Spanish guerillas had captured.

In the Crimean war, one of the great drawbacks to the commanders of the allied army was their necessary want of intelligence, both armies being in reality besieged and stationary. Except by spies, at all times a doubtful source to be depended on, the first intelligence gained with respect to Russian reinforcements, was, generally speaking, obtained by reported telegrams, &c., from Vienna, published to the whole world.

General Lee was much embarrassed in 1862, through the accidental loss, by a general of division, of a very important order detailing the orders of march for the whole army. Lee's army was unavoidably scattered, in consequence of the necessity of capturing Harper's Ferry, where there were 12,000 men and immense stores. M'Clellan, with an army depressed by many defeats, was slowly and cautiously feeling his way, utterly ignorant of General Lee's plans, or even the whereabouts of his army. When this order was obtained, it gave him every information he required. He exclaimed on reading it,' Well, if I don't destroy Lee this time you may call me what you like!' and with confidence pressed on as fast as possible, struck a portion of the Confederates before the remainder had come up, and a desperate battle took place at Sharpsburg or Antietam Creek: It was a drawn fight, but Lee was foiled and obliged to recross the Potomac without accomplishing all that he had desired by his campaign. Had not this order been lost, the chances are that his army would have been ready, and if the Federals had been defeated, peace might have resulted in favour of the South.

An Austrian field post was captured in 1866 on

the retreat to Olmutz, which contained private letters giving information as to the demoralised condition of the army, as well as a copy of Marshal Benedek's orders for the marches of the corps, and the movements of his administrative services. A few days later the Austrian cavalry obtained much valuable information by a despatch of the Crown Prince, which they seized in a Prussian field post. In the last chapter mention is made of General Stuart capturing General Pope's official and private papers at Catletts Station. Information obtained of this sort, if real, is more valuable than any other can possibly be. Napoleon would not write general orders, but gave separate instructions to each of his subordinate officers; so if one copy was captured or lost, it would not give so much information to the enemy as by the other plan. He very rarely deviated from this rule.

The celebrated Stonewall Jackson was never known to communicate his plan in written orders, and very rarely verbally, leaving even his general officers ignorant of the point of attack. The consequence of which was, that his movements never were known to the enemy until they felt his blows.

Napoleon gave the following advice to his brother Joseph in Spain on this subject: 'We have no accounts of what the enemy is about; it is said no

news can be obtained; as if this case was extraordinary in an army, as if spies were common. They
must do in Spain as they do in other places. Send
parties out. Let them carry off the alcade, the chief
of a convent, the master of the post or his deputy,
and, above all, the letters. Put these persons under
arrest until they speak, question them twice each day,
or keep them as hostages, charge them to send foot
messengers, and to get news. When we know how
to take measures of vigour and force, it is easy to
get intelligence. All the posts, all the letters must
be intercepted; the single motive of procuring intelligence will be sufficient to authorise a detachment of
4,000 or 5,000 men, who will go into a great town,
will take the letters from the post, will seize the
richest citizens, their letters, papers, gazettes, &c.
It is beyond doubt that, even in the French lines, the
inhabitants are all informed of what passes, of course
out of that line they know more, what then should
prevent you seizing the principal men? Let them
be sent back again without being ill-treated. It is a
fact, that when we are not in a desert but in a peopled country, if the general is not well instructed, it
is because he is ignorant of his trade. The services
which the inhabitants render to an enemy's general
are never given from affection, nor even to get
money; the truest method to obtain them is by safe-

guards and protections to preserve their lives, their goods, their towns, or their monasteries.'

Another method of obtaining intelligence is by the employment of spies. Great skill is required in the management of this part of the intelligence department, emissaries of this nature being generally of a very unreliable character, and it being very difficult to test and verify their faithfulness.

A system of espionage to be successful must be extensive, because the chances of the spies learning news will be greater, while by comparing the different reports, a more accurate idea may be formed of the enemy's movements, than can be gleaned from the report of one or even two, who can only in large armies observe but a portion of the hostile forces, at a time. If a number are sent out also, and they have no communication with each other; they check each other; and by comparing their stories, it can be discovered if any and which are deceiving you.

In fighting in your own country, the inhabitants who are friendly will give a great deal of information from motives of loyalty, and their accounts can generally be depended on. Women have often given information in this way, which has been of the utmost importance. Mrs. Secord of Chippawa, Niagara Falls, in the war of 1812, walked through the woods twenty miles to warn a British force of a

T

movement by the enemy to surprise and capture it. Thanks to this information, Captain Fitzgibbon, who commanded the English, made his arrangements for their reception with such skill as to succeed in capturing the whole party. This occurred at Beaver Dams, near Thorold, in Canada West, in June 1813.

In December 1863, notice was given of General Averill's raid, mentioned in the last chapter, by a young lady who had been at New Creek, on the Baltimore and Ohio railroad, and ascertained that the horses of the cavalry were all being *re-shod*, indicating a movement of some sort. After her return home, she rode sixty miles to give information of the fact to the Confederate commander in the Shenandoah valley. This intelligence gave time for preparations to be made to receive Averill, and his force would have been captured, except for the false information received, as stated in the previous chapter.

For spies in an enemy's country, it is necessary to have money, to pay them well; for the risk is great, and the punishment in case of detection severe and prompt. If it is possible to bribe an officer of the enemy's army, as can sometimes be done, most valuable information can often be obtained. In 1809, in Spain, Marshal Victor must have had some correspondence with some officer on the Spanish staff; for Napier relates that secret discussions which took

place between Wellington and Cuesta, at which only
one staff officer on each side was present, became
known to the enemy shortly after.

In 1810, in Portugal, Massena organised a communication with Lisbon through General Pamplona.
Agents pretending to be selling sugar to the inhabitants passed out of the lines and took him the news
of what was going on inside the lines of Torres
Vedras. At the same time the Duke of Wellington
succeeded in bribing a French officer of rank, and
both generals were in possession continually of excellent information of their opponent's movements.

As an illustration of the different ways of obtaining and employing spies, I cannot do better than
here insert Napier's account of Wellington's arrangements for obtaining intelligence in this way in 1811.
He says :

' Lord Wellington had also established good chan-
nels of information. He had a number of spies
amongst the Spaniards who were living within the
French lines. A British officer in disguise constantly
visited the French armies in the field. A Spanish
state counsellor living at the head-quarters of the
first corps gave intelligence from that side, and a gui-
tar player of celebrity, named Fuentes, repeatedly
making his way to Madrid, brought advice from
thence. Mr. Stuart, under cover of vessels licensed to

fetch corn from France, kept *chasse marées* constantly plying along the Biscay coast, by which he not only acquired direct information, but facilitated the transmission of intelligence from the land spies, amongst whom the most remarkable was a cobbler, living in a little hut at the end of the bridge of Irun. This man, while plying his trade, continued for years, without being suspected, to count every French soldier that passed in or out of Spain by that passage, and transmitted their numbers by the *chasse marées* to Lisbon.'

' With the exception of the state spy at Victor's head-quarters,—who being a double traitor was infamous,—all the persons thus employed were very meritorious. The greater number, and the cleverest also, were Spanish gentlemen, alcades, or poor men, who, disdaining rewards and disregarding danger, acted from a pure spirit of patriotism, and are to be lauded alike for their boldness, their talent, and their virtue.'

Many instances occurred in the late war of the Southern people giving information of the utmost importance to their armies ; and detached parties of Union men in the same way assisted the Federal troops. It was through news carried by a Union woman that the Federals were enabled to surprise and kill General Morgan at Greenville in 1864, she having ridden some sixteen miles at night to carry the information.

A very good plan, if you can only be sure of your man and *positive* as to his fidelity, is to get him to become employed as a spy on the other side; this will enable him to get a pass to go through the enemy's lines, and give him perfect security as to his movements about their camp. In this case he should be allowed to take correct intelligence of unimportant matters every little while, in order to give the enemy better confidence in him; and by regulating yourself what information he is to convey to the opposing general, no harm can be done by telling him the truth, and if you wished sometimes to deceive, it might be more easily managed. This is a game, however, that must be skilfully played, and with great caution.

There is another method in use in the British army, by which a single officer is sent out alone, in his uniform, to watch the enemy's movements. In the Peninsular war there were several officers employed by Wellington who were of the greatest service to him: they would penetrate into the cantonments of the enemy, hover on the skirts of his columns for days, just out of musket range, and count their numbers and note the direction of their march. Col. Waters, of Wellington's staff, was distinguished

for his efficiency in this service, but Captain Colquhoun
Grant was the most celebrated of all. Napier says
of him, that he was 'a gentleman in whom the
utmost daring was so mixed with subtlety of genius,
and both so tempered by discretion, that it is hard to
say which quality predominated.'

It is also necessary to prevent the enemy from
obtaining intelligence, and for this purpose all
scouting parties, reconnaissances, secret or in force,
all officers detached for any purpose, or spies, who
can get an opportunity of destroying telegraph lines
in use by the enemy, should do so. Hozier in his
second volume, page 176, gives an account of a
Count Hasler, a Prussian staff officer, who with two
cuirassiers rode beyond the outposts to destroy a telegraph line. My Canadian readers will hardly believe
it, but the historian describes the several attempts
made, and the great difficulties they encountered,
in effecting this end, although they had a hatchet.
After trying to climb up the pole for some time, they
at last succeeded, by one standing as a prop, while
the other, starting from his shoulder, was able to
climb up and cut the wires with the hatchet. A
Canadian would have slashed down two or three poles
in as many minutes, and have cut the wires then
with the greatest ease, without requiring any prop,

and without thinking twice; for Hozier says the poles were of dry polished wood.

Circumstances apparently of a trivial nature often give much information. Clouds of dust will give indication of the march of columns, and the size of them, to a practised eye. Stuart on one occasion, wishing to lead the enemy to believe that reinforcements were coming up to the assistance of General Longstreet, sent a number of troopers, who rode along the road in long lines, dragging bundles of brush through the dust. He succeeded by this means in completely deceiving the enemy.

Stratagem may sometimes be resorted to in order to gain intelligence. At the retreat of the English army from Burgos in 1812, the rear guard destroyed the bridge over the Carion by a mine just as a French cavalry column came up. Napier describes what followed. ' The play of the mine, which was effectual, checked the advance of the French for an instant, but suddenly a horseman rode down under a flight of bullets to the bridge, calling out that he was a deserter; he reached the edge of the chasm made by the explosion, and then violently checking his foaming horse, held up his hands, exclaiming that he was a lost man, and with hurried accents asked if there was no ford near. The good-natured soldiers pointed to one a little way off, and the gallant fellow

having looked earnestly for a few moments, as if to
fix the exact point, wheeled his horse round, kissed
his hand in derision, and bending over his saddle-bow,
dashed back to his own comrades, amidst showers of
shot and shouts of laughter from both sides.   The
next moment Maucune's column, covered by a concentrated fire of guns, passed the river at the ford thus
discovered.'

At night the position and numbers of the enemy
may be roughly estimated by the camp fires, or the
glimmer in the horizon over them.   If the camp-
fires are so that they are in sight, and it is seen that
in the middle of the night they are replenished
uniformly, the conclusion may be drawn that the
enemy intend retreating, and the fires are made up
to prevent its being discovered.

Some armies use a system of signals from elevated
positions.   If the alphabet can only be discovered, a
signal officer getting in sight of a post will read with
ease the orders which are passing.   Before Chancellorsville in 1863, General Lee was informed of all the
orders which Burnside issued to his different corps by
this means.

This system of signal stations seems to be a very
good plan for conveying intelligence and orders
rapidly, subject of course to the drawback just mentioned.   General Early gives me a very favourable

account of the working of his signal corps in the Shenandoah valley in 1864 and 1865. In his memoir he says that when he was at Staunton, and Sheridan around Winchester, in the winter of 1864–65, ' Cavalry pickets were left in front of New Market, and telegraphic communications kept up with that place, from which there was a communication with the lower valley by means of signal stations, on the northern end of Massanutten Mountain and at Ashby's Gap in the Blue Ridge which overlooked the enemy's camps and the surrounding country.' Again, later in the winter, he says, ' The telegraph to New Market and the signal stations, from there to the lower valley, were kept up, and a few scouts sent to the rear of the enemy, and in this way my front was principally picketed, and I kept advised of the enemy's movements. Henceforth my efficient and energetic signal officer, Captain Wilburn, was the commander of my advanced picket line.' By this means General Early was informed for some days of Sheridan's preparations for a movement of some kind ; and as soon as Sheridan started, he was informed of it immediately, although ninety miles distant. No system of intelligence could be much better in its practical operation.

General Early also tells me he has no faith in spies as a means of obtaining information, his experience being that paid spies are worthless and unreliable.

Field telegraphs are useful for conveying orders rapidly. The Prussians used them with good effect in the last war. Napoleon III. also used them, it is said, in Italy in 1859. The difficulty about them is that a skilful operator can tap them and read every word. Stuart and Morgan both had telegraph operators on their staffs for this purpose on raids, and they were of great value to both in gathering information. Ellsworth, Morgan's operator, a Canadian, was an exceedingly expert hand, and played the most extraordinary tricks on the Federals by the manner in which he made use of the wires.

Troops of cavalry should never be told off to do duty as orderlies or couriers, to carry despatches and orders. This is a most important duty, and the best plan is to organise a corps with higher pay and a higher standing, picked men from the cavalry, good riders, intelligent, brave, and resolute, and detailed permanently for that duty. The men get more accustomed to it by practice, and the experience fits them more to be useful. This was the practice in the C. S. army. A colonel of a cavalry regiment, if left to himself to send some men for orderly duty in war, will not send away the best men from the ranks, and the consequence will be a failure in the courier service.

The value of good maps in giving information to a general has been referred to before, and there is no need to reiterate the necessity of the best maps being procured.

The presence of the Old Guard in front of Blucher in 1815, in the Waterloo campaign, informed him that the Emperor was present, and therefore probably that the French army was concentrated.

The sound of cannon gives information of a battle going on, and the direction in which it is taking place, and an officer in command of a detachment will generally be right in marching ' *au canon.*'

The stories of men on sentry must sometimes be taken with great caution, especially if the men seem much excited. General Duke gives an instance of a vidette on a bridge who was alarmed by two men in a buggy, who drove rapidly on to the bridge without heeding his challenge. He fired both barrels of his gun at them, and galloped full speed into his picket, and alarmed them so by his account of the immense number and headlong advance of the enemy, that they also came in at the gallop. The whole command got under arms, and General Duke questioned the vidette. ' He stated that the enemy's cavalry came on, at the charge in column of fours, that they paid no attention to his challenge, and that when he fired they dashed at him, making the air

ring with their yells and curses. He said that the
road seemed perfectly blue for more than half a mile,
so great was their number.'

I have been permitted by General Early to make
the following extract from some manuscript notes
of his personal recollections of the war in the Confederate States. In speaking of a false alarm under
which a rapid movement of his brigade was begun,
to meet a reported flank movement of the enemy the
day before the battle of Manassas, and then suspended
on a discovery of the falsehood of the report, he says:

' As this false alarm was rather singular in its
nature, but of such a character that any general
might have been deceived by it, I will state how it ·
occurred. A captain of General Ewell's brigade who
had been posted with his company on picket at Yates
Ford, not far below Union Mills, retired from his
post and reported in the most positive manner that
the enemy had appeared in heavy force on the
opposite bank of Bull's Run, and commenced build-
ing two bridges. He further stated that he had seen
General M'Dowell on a white horse, superintending
the construction of the bridge. As there was no
reason to doubt his veracity or courage, General
Ewell of course sent at once the information to
General Beauregard, and thence the order for my
movement. After the message was despatched, some-

thing suggested a doubt as to the correctness of the report, and the officer making it was sent in charge of another to ascertain the facts. On arriving in sight of the ford he pointed triumphantly to the opposite bank, and exclaimed, " There they are; don't you see the two bridges ? don't you see M'Dowell on his white horse ? " when the fact was, that there was nothing visible but the ford, and the unoccupied banks of the stream, which were so obstructed as to render a crossing impracticable until the obstructions were removed. It was then apparent that it was a clear case of hallucination, produced by a derangement of the nervous system consequent on a loss of sleep, and great anxiety of mind resulting from the nature of the duties in which he had been engaged. Neither his sincerity or his courage was questioned; and this affair shows how the most careful commander may be misled when he has to rely on information furnished by others.'

' It requires very great experience and a very discriminating judgment to enable a commanding general to sift the truth out of the great mass of exaggerated reports made to him, and then he has often to rely on his own personal inspection.

' I have known important movements to be suspended on the battle-field, on account of reports from very gallant officers that the enemy was on

one flank or the other in heavy force, when a calm
inspection proved the reported bodies of the enemy
to be nothing more than stone or rail fences. Some
officers, while exposing their lives with great daring,
sometimes fail to preserve that clearness of judgment
and calmness of the nerves which is so necessary to
enable one to see things as they really are during an
engagement. And hence it is that there are so
many conflicting reports of the same matters. The
capacity of preserving one's presence of mind in
action is among the highest attributes of an efficient
commander or subordinate officer; and it must be
confessed that the excitement of battle, especially
when the shells are bursting and the bullets are
whistling thick around, is wonderfully trying to the
nerves of the bravest.'

CHAPTER XVII.

MARCHES—CAMPS—SUPPLIES.

The business of an army is to march and to fight. By rapid and wisely directed marches a skilful general prepares the way for a successful campaign, reaps the fruits of victory, or escapes from pursuing and superior forces.—*General Dufour.*

Encampments of the same army should always be formed so as to protect each other.—*Napoleon.*

IF the marches of cavalry are not judiciously arranged, and the distances carefully regulated, especially in the opening of a campaign, great injury will be done to the force; the horses will soon be rendered unfit for service, and then the men will not be of much use.

Horses must be trained to long marches gradually, and when they are accustomed to it, and have been brought into a hard-working condition by practice, then they will effect forced marches without any difficulty to themselves, and without deteriorating in any degree from the effective value of the corps.

If it is necessary to march any given distance, and they are not required to keep pace with a column of infantry, the cavalry should push on at a moderate trot, say six miles an hour or perhaps a little more, the men being allowed to rise in their stirrups, as it eases the horse and man considerably ; walking the column, however, up and down hill. And if the road is perfectly level, then it would be better to walk one mile out of every three, in order by changing the pace to relieve both horses and men.

Frequent halts should be made, and the men allowed to dismount for a few minutes. This is of advantage on long marches. On one occasion, when I was making a march of some forty miles, and with horses not very fresh, at intervals I ordered the men to dismount and, leading the horses, march a couple of miles or so on foot. This was a great assistance to the horses, and did not fatigue the men, who, carrying no knapsacks or muskets, could march with ease. Forced marches could be best made in this way. I mean forced marches as regards distance, not speed.

In all cases, the precaution of an advanced and rear guard, as described in a former chapter, must be attended to with a greater or less degree of vigilance, in accordance with circumstances.

If the force of cavalry is very large, the march should be made by different detachments with intervals between to prevent crowding and confusion ;

and if there are several parallel roads leading in the same direction, the different parts of the corps can be distributed on the different roads, if the communication between them is free and open, and if they are not too distant from each other. If close to the enemy, these points must be more carefully looked to, and the point of concentration must be in possession of your own troops. The great desideratum in moving over an enemy's country is, if possible, to advance in parallel columns at such a distance that, by deploying, the intervening spaces can at once be covered in line.

Columns should never cross each other, because delay and annoyance are sure to be caused to one or other of them, and disputes may easily arise unless care has been taken to lay down accurately the manner in which the columns are to pass. No column should allow another to pass it without a special order to that effect.

Troops in summer time should always start as early as possible, the men being first allowed to breakfast. This should always be carefully attended to: men cannot work or perform any duty in a famished condition, nor horses undergo fatigue if not carefully fed. Officers should bear this in mind, keep their men and horses well fed and cared for, and they will have more influence over their men,

U

will get more work out of them, and will have more
confidence in them, than by any other course they
can take.

Stonewall Jackson, one of the grandest and finest
soldiers that ever lived, and at the same time one of
the best men that the world has seen, was excessively
careful of the comfort of his men. He had a standing
order that on the line of march, if a halt took place,
if only for five minutes to fix a plank on a bridge or
for any purpose, the troops should be ordered to
pile arms as they stood, and be allowed to lay down
in their ranks. General Early told me that on one
occasion, where a halt occurred for a few minutes,
General Jackson, who was riding by, noticed that the
officer (one of Early's brigadiers) had neglected to
cause the men to pile arms, the delay being a very
short one. The General was so much annoyed that
he immediately ordered the officer under arrest, and
it was with some little difficulty that General Early
was able to get him reinstated in his command.

Night marches are not good, for many reasons:
they are not good for the health of the men, there is
much more straggling, and they are also more liable
to surprise. If, however, the country is clear of the
enemy, and it is in midsummer, forced marches can
be better made at night ; for it is cooler, and the men
can lay by during the hot part of the day and rest.

Halts should always be made, except in extraordinary circumstances, in the middle of the day, to give the men sufficient time to rest, to cook, and to feed both themselves and their horses.

Colonel Brackett, in his ' History of the United States Cavalry,' which has been quoted from in a former chapter, makes the following remarks on marches: ' About marching too, a few lines may not be amiss. In starting out after feeding, let the horses walk about one hour, when a halt of fifteen minutes ought to be sounded. Let the men close up and then dismount. This eases the horse, gives him a chance to breathe a short time, and makes him feel better. When ready to start, tighten up the girths, which will be found to have slackened, one or two holes. Do not let the saddle be loose on the back— it should sit snug; but at the same time caution all soldiers not to draw too tightly, as I have seen some dreadful sores made on horses' sides by the ring and strap which is used on the M'Clellan saddle, and which is borrowed from the Mexicans.' * * * *

' The horses should be watered once or twice on the march, if it is convenient, and should be allowed to drink as much water as they want, provided they are moved on after drinking; but on no account should they, after marching some distance, be allowed to drink and cool. If this is permitted, in nine cases

out of ten the animals will be foundered. Officers
should be continually on their guard, watching recruits in this respect, as by its neglect many a fine
animal has been ruined.'

If a march is very close to the evening, and the
force is large, the columns should have as broad a
front as the road will allow, in order to have the
force as much concentrated as possible. If the army
is large and the ground is suitable, the cavalry will
sometimes march in heavy columns in the fields.
Infantry sometimes do the same thing, leaving the
roads clear for the artillery and trains.

Forced marches are a very great strain on cavalry
and infantry, and have a more prejudicial effect with
the former than with the latter arm. Officers of
cavalry should consequently endeavour to rest their
horses and recruit them after a forced march, in
order to keep them always in condition. If they once
fall off seriously, they can rarely be recruited again
on service. Infantry should also be kept in condition.
Crawford's brigade, which at the time of the battle of
Talavera marched sixty-two miles in twenty-six hours,
three weeks afterwards were only able, with the
greatest difficulty and after frequent halts, to reach
the summit of Mirabete, a distance of only four miles
from where they started. This was caused by previous sufferings and deprivations during the intermediate period.

Men should always carry some provisions with them in their havresacks, and some oats in their nose-bags for the horses, and waggons should accompany the troops with provisions. General Dufour says that Marshal Davoust in the Russian campaign had arranged the knapsacks of the men so that they could carry in them four biscuits of a pound weight, and under each a little bag of flour weighing ten pounds, besides two loaves of three pounds' weight each in a havresack. This, it seems, would load the men down terribly, but they would be well fed, and so many waggons would not be required. And perhaps well-fed men in good condition would march better under sixty pounds' weight than a starving man with no load to bear him down.

Cavalry on the march should never break ranks to bivouac or camp, until all the ground in the neighbourhood is examined and the outposts formed, videttes posted, and patrols sent out. These precautions should also be taken on halts on the march.

Hozier describes the manner in which the Prussian army marched in pursuit of the Austrians after the battle of Königgrätz, in the following words: ' But where the army marched all was bustle and noise, the infantry tramped monotonously along the roads, while the cavalry spread in bending lines through the fields, and behind the combatants toiled long trains of waggons which carried the stores of this large army. Along every road and every lane foot soldiers marched, and cavalry occupied the intervals between the heads of the columns, all pointing southward towards the Elbe.   For miles on either side could be seen the clouds of dust raised by the marching troops: in some places it rose from trees and woods, in others from among houses, or from the hard straight roads leading through the wide corn land, where the hot July sun poured its rays straight down upon the soldiers' heads, and made them suffer much from heat and thirst.'

Cavalry for one day or two will march tremendous distances, but they must have time to recruit afterwards: the horses will not pick up strength again nearly as quickly as the men.   Wellington once, in India in 1803, marched his cavalry sixty miles in thirty-two hours.   Lord Lake, before the battle of Furruckabad, marched, it is said, seventy miles in twenty-four hours.   In the raid around M'Clellan's army through Chambersburgh in 1862, as before stated, General Stuart's cavalry marched ninety miles in thirty-six hours, including a forced passage of the Potomac.   While General Duke mentions an instance in Kentucky where General Burbridge, in June 1864, marched nearly ninety miles in thirty hours, and surprised General Morgan's command in camp.

Care should be taken on the line of march to prevent men drinking. Some will say it is necessary to give men spirits, to keep them up. I do not see any necessity for it. I have always noticed that the men who do not drink at all stand work the best and will hold out the longest. The only case in which spirits should be allowed might be in long sieges, in trenches where the men cannot get exercised and require some artificial means of keeping up the heat of the body.

Railways are not of much use for moving cavalry. They could only be carried in small numbers, and cavalry can march so rapidly that they do not require to be moved by trains. Railways also cannot be used in an advance into an enemy's country. In June 1866, when the Fenian invasion took place on the Niagara frontier, I was sent over with some forty men of my command hurriedly to form a scouting force for the column under Colonel Peacocke. We went by steamer to Port Dalhousie from Toronto, some thirty-six miles, in about three hours. In forty-five minutes more we were in Port Robinson, a distance of some fifteen miles farther ; having unloaded the men from the vessel on to the cars of Welland Railway, and unloaded from the cars at the village. At Port Robinson, the men were fed by requisition telegraphed ahead, and in forty minutes from our arrival the men and horses were fed, the horses watered, the men fallen in, and the column on the move. We marched some nine miles in about fifty-five minutes, and reached Chippawa, sixty miles from Toronto, in less than five hours and a half, including a halt for feeding,—more than ten miles an hour, including stoppages. It must be considered, however, that we were hurried on by rumours of fighting ahead. I mention this as an instance of the rapidity that can be attained by the use of steam by land and on water in moving small bodies of troops.

Stonewall Jackson, when his army were marching along a line of railway, was accustomed to order the trains to pick up as many as possible from the rear of the column and carry them on to the front of the line of march, and place them down some distance ahead, and then go back and bring on another load. By this means the respective positions of the men in the column changed, the same men not being compelled to drag along in the rear all the time.

CAMPS.

In the Confederate war for independence the strict rules which guide the laying out of camps in European armies were not regarded or followed out. Circumstances generally dictated the position as well as the arrangement of the camps of the different corps and divisions. Tents were very rarely used when really campaigning, except for the staff officers. The men of course, of the different regiments and companies, camped close together, but the formation of the ground had its influence upon them. Captain Ross, in his 'Cities and Camps of the Confederate States,' says, 'They are much more pleasant and comfortable than if rules were strictly adhered to.' Colonel Heros Von Borcke says of General Fitzhugh Lee's bivouac: 'The camp was a novelty to me in the art of castrametation. The horses were not picketed in regular lines as in European armies, but were scattered about anywhere in the neighbouring wood, some tethered to swinging limbs, some tied to small trees, others again left to browse at will upon the undergrowth.'

This system would answer very well in America and Canada, where wood is so plentiful, and forests are scattered about everywhere; but in Europe, where often there would be a difficulty in finding places to picket horses to, the lines and picket pegs must be carried along in waggons, as well as cooking utensils and other articles that a regiment requires. In this case the camp must be laid out regularly, and according to fixed rules.

Tents should not be used in time of war; the

extra waggons they require, and the incumbrance they are on the roads, cause them to retard the army very much in its movements. Napoleon said that tents killed more men than the enemy's artillery, and held that bivouacs were much more healthy. Camps should, if possible, be situated near water, or otherwise a great inconvenience is entailed on the men in obtaining it. The men should hut themselves if the army is to halt for any time; the huts require no transportation, and are far more healthy for the troops.

In a cavalry bivouac the arms are stacked in rear of each row of horses with the saddle and bridle, unless very near an enemy, when the saddles should be left on all night with the girths slackened. The men should also always be allowed fires, except in extraordinary cases. They are a great comfort to the men, and by drying the ground around them make it better to sleep on. If possible, shelters should be constructed open towards the fires and the line of horses. Officers should bivouac with their troops; if they sleep in houses, the men do not bear up so cheerfully as if they see their officers sharing their hardships.

If not too near an enemy, the troops can be billeted in the houses and villages. The Prussian army acted on this principle to a great extent in

Bohemia and Moravia in 1866. Hozier says on one occasion : 'The towns of Przelautch and Pardubitz were entirely filled with Prussian soldiers. On every door was written in chalk the name of the regiment and company to which the house was allotted, and the number of men which it was to accommodate. The numbers appeared enormous, for the size of the houses : fifty or sixty men were sometimes billeted in a small house with four rooms, but the soldiers managed well enough so long as they could get straw to lie upon ; but here there was a great scarcity of that, and the men had to sleep as they could, on the floor or in the gardens.' Speaking of another town where the troops were billeted, Hozier says : ' Thus the town, before so noisy, grew perfectly still, and no sound was heard, except the monotonous step of a sentry, or the uneasy neigh of some restless horse ; but the arms piled with the bayonets fixed, beside each house, with the knapsacks laid close to the butts, packed and ready to be instantly taken up, told that the soldiers were ready, and that the least alarm would fill the streets with armed men ready to march.'

Napoleon's views are worth inserting here as the highest authority that can be given on anything relating to war or the management of armies. 'Tents,' says he, 'are not wholesome. It is better for

the soldier to bivouac, because he can sleep with his
feet towards the fire, he may shelter himself from
the wind with a few boards or a little straw. The
ground upon which he lies will be rapidly dried in
the vicinity of the fire. Tents are necessary for the
superior officers, who have occasion to read and con-
sult maps, and who ought to be ordered never to
sleep in a house, a fatal abuse which has given rise
to so many disasters. All the European nations
have so far followed the example of the French as
to discard their tents; and if they be still used in
camps of mere parade, it is because they are econo-
mical, sparing woods, thatched roofs, and villages.
The shade of a tree against the heat of the sun, and
any sorry shelter whatever against the rain, are
preferable to tents. The carriage of the tents for
each battalion would load five horses, who would be
much better employed in carrying provisions. Tents
are a subject of observation for the enemy's spies
and officers of the staff, they give them an insight
into your numbers and the position that you occupy,
and thus inconvenience occurs every day and every
instant in the day. An army ranged in two or three
lines of bivouac is only to be perceived at a distance
by the smoke, which the enemy may mistake for the
vapour of the atmosphere. It is impossible to count
the number of fires; it is easy, however, to count

the number of tents, and to trace out the position that they occupy.'

Camps should be on high ground, and, if possible, where wood and water can be conveniently obtained; the flanks should be protected, if possible, and cavalry with the main army should encamp, if convenient, in rear of infantry, as the latter can be got under arms quicker, and cover the forming up of the cavalry.

The outposts should always be thrown far enough forward to cover the camp and give the troops ample time to form up in order to receive an enemy. The approaches to the camp should be barricaded so as to delay an enemy advancing, and enable the main guards and inlying pickets to hold them in check with greater effect.

SUPPLIES.

The art of subsisting troops of all arms is one of the most difficult matters that a general has to attend to, especially in time of war, and in a hostile country. If the army is advancing, it becomes more difficult, because every march takes it farther from its base, and consequently from its magazines.

Troops are supplied by magazines, by purchase from the country in which the army is operating, and by forced requisitions. A system arranged by

which the first and second plans are both used
seems to combine the most advantages—the magazines forming the reserves, and the daily wants
supplied as much as possible by purchases from the
inhabitants. Provisions, even in an enemy's country,
should always be paid for promptly; it is the cheap-
est, best, and safest plan, in the long run. By this
course the people will bring their provisions into
camp with confidence, they will exert themselves to
raise crops as much as they can, and the country
will not be devastated.

Where forced requisitions are resorted to, and the
food not paid for, a different effect, and a disastrous
one, will be the result. The inhabitants will conceal
their stores so that they will only occasionally be
discovered, they will abandon their homes, there will
be nothing to induce them to sow seed again; and,
in the second year, if the war lasts so long, the
country becomes a desert, a barren wilderness.

With reference to cavalry, with which we have
more particularly to deal, the question of subsistence
is of a rather difficult character. The immense
bulk and weight of forage for a large body of cavalry
renders it almost impossible to carry the food any
distance; and horses eat so much in weight, that
waggons that could carry supplies for 1000 men
could only provide food enough for about 100
horses.

Cavalry must therefore be supplied from the immediate neighbourhood of the army; but there is this advantage, that no cooking or preparation is required for the horses, and that even when regular distribution of forage fails for a time, the horses can often pick up something to eat by pasturing in the fields around their camps.

The proper place for cavalry, however, is on the front of the army, as well as to its flanks and rear. From their mobility they can be spread over a great extent of country, and without danger of being cut off. They should therefore be thrown out in different directions, and scattered during any lull in the active operations. By this means the main army is better guarded from surprise; and the horses, from not being gathered in large numbers, are far more healthy, are much more easily fed, and, on an alarm or on the approach of active fighting, they can rapidly be concentrated on the main army, fresh and in good condition for work.

There should always be magazines of forage, especially of oats, or grain of some kind, with the main army pretty well up to the front, so that when the cavalry are concentrated for action the distribution of forage may be regular. Cavalry should have their nose-bags in good order, and endeavour always to keep a feed on hand. The men, also, should never be started on a march, or commence any operation, without having some food in their havresacks. I am much opposed to the horse being loaded down more than can be helped, but it is absolutely necessary for the comfort of the men that they should have one day's rations on hand always, so that, no matter what turns up, they have some sort of a reserve to fall back upon for a time.

As cavalry are generally scattered on the outskirts of an army, and the men are therefore generally more easily fed by requisition, they should not carry much food with them ; but with infantry it is different. Providing them with food is a difficult matter, and the waggon trains under any circumstances are enormous, so that a great gain is effected by causing the men to carry a certain amount of provisions with them. The Roman soldier carried usually fifteen days' provisions with him : active hurried operations of a campaign are often completed in that time.

Foraging should not be resorted to if it is possible for the commissariat department to obtain sufficient supplies without taking that course. There are many reasons for this. It has a demoralising tendency with the men, it has an injurious effect upon their discipline, it is annoying and troublesome to the inhabitants, and excesses are very apt to be committed. If it does become necessary, however, the steadiest troops must be employed, and any misconduct on their part promptly and severely punished.

Foraging parties should never be sent out unless the country has been well reconnoitred, and they should be strongly guarded and supported, to prevent surprise, and ensure the safe bringing in of the supplies. If the troops commit any excesses and plunder from the inhabitants, the cases should be investigated closely, the amount of loss assessed, and paid at once to the sufferers, the amount being deducted from the pay and allowances of the corps by which the offence has been committed. A few examples made in this way will have a most beneficial effect on the troops, and will quiet the fears and ill-feelings of the inhabitants.

An officer of cavalry who is often on detached duty on the outskirts of an army in an enemy's country, should always remember that nothing adds more to the credit of his corps, and his nation, than a kind and courteous bearing towards the inhabitants. No sour looks or impertinent remarks should ever cause soldiers to lose their self-command. By a dignified and imperturbable bearing, and a uniform respect to the feelings of the inhabitants, as well as to their rights of private property, they will rapidly gain friends among the people ; a circumstance which cannot fail in being productive of the most beneficial results to the whole army.

CHAPTER XVIII.

PASSAGE OF DEFILES AND RIVERS.

The passing of rivers is justly considered as one of the most difficult and dangerous operations of war.—*General Lloyd.*

THE system of passing defiles by cavalry or dragoons, was formerly very different from the plan which should be adopted now. When cavalry have long-range fire-arms, and are organised and equipped to fight dismounted, they can carry the defiles in accordance with the rules laid down for infantry, if, from the nature of the ground, the latter force would be the most suitable to attempt it.

Formerly, if the infantry had not come up, a cavalry force coming to a defile, had to adopt a very different line of action. Nolan lays down the rules which mounted men should follow in such a case; he says, 'Always pass a defile quickly.' 'Occupy half the road only, and make the men keep the near side of it, to prevent the troops getting jammed up when attacked, and to keep that side clear on which a cavalry soldier makes use of his sword (the right).'

'Before entering a defile, reconnoitre it. Wooded places and defiles of no great length are reconnoitred by making a man of the advanced guard gallop through, followed at some distance by a single horseman. If there is no direct impediment, the advanced guard then gallop through, and keep the outlet until the main body has passed out.'

'When a cavalry detachment without infantry has no choice, but is obliged to pass a defile known to be in the possession of the enemy, their best chance is to attempt it at night and at a gallop. If a barricade has been raised, the advanced party give notice, and a few dismounted men endeavour to remove it. If the obstruction is of such a nature as to be impassable on horseback and impossible to remove, the party *will have to turn back.*'

'When acting with infantry, these reconnoitre the defile, for it would be dangerous for the cavalry to find an enemy's infantry posted there on their flanks and *out of reach of their swords.*'

What arguments these few sentences of Nolan, the champion of the Sword, contain in favour of the mounted rifles! Fancy the loss sustained by a party of swordsmen galloping into a defile barricaded, and fired upon from each flank, obliged to withdraw. In almost every instance where it would be better to gallop through, it could be done as well by mounted rifles as by cavalry proper, and if the dragoons used their revolvers, a great deal better, while in case of need the men could dismount and clear the flanks of the defile by skirmishers on foot.

The flanks of a defile, the heights on either side of it, should always be reconnoitred and held by dismounted men before the head of the column enters it—and the whole column should not be committed until the outlet has been secured. Baggage waggons should never be allowed to enter until the *debouché* is in the hands of the advance force. A portion of the artillery should precede the column, in order that its fire may not be masked, but that it may open at once on the enemy if they come in range.

If the enemy show a disposition to defend obstinately the passage of a defile, every effort should be made to turn it, in order to threaten their retreat. This will often cause them to abandon their defence, and retire, leaving the defile open to the main army.

These turning movements should always be attempted by dragoons, with some guns attached, for they are not liable to be cut off, if detached to any distance from the army.

In covering a retreat through a defile, dismount a

number of men, and line the heights with sharpshooters, and at the same time overturn some waggons in the defile, or raise barricades in some way,
defending them also with dismounted men, placing
a gun in position, if circumstances are favourable.

If driven from this position, the force should be
drawn up in rear of the defile in such a manner
that they can charge simultaneously on the front
and flank of the head of the column, as it *debouchés*,
so as to prevent its having an opportunity to deploy.

Sometimes it is necessary to retreat through a
defile—always a most difficult operation. A portion
of the cavalry must show front to the rear, and cover
the passage of the remainder, who should, on passing,
line the heights with sharpshooters, who can cover
the retreat of the rear party, when they are obliged
to retire.

Nolan quotes from the life of General Sohr, an
instance of a retreat through a defile, which we will
reproduce here as an illustration of the manner in
which that officer preserved steadiness and discipline
in his squadron.

' To check the pursuit of the enemy, a strong rear
guard was pushed forward at 3 o'clock A. M., from
Weissenberg to Wurschen. The enemy was brought
to a stand by the sudden opening of our artillery,
and more than an hour elapsed before he received

sufficient reinforcements to resume the offensive, and drive in our rear guard.'—

'At the pass of Rothkretcham, to the eastward of Weissenberg, is an arm of the Lobaur stream, the passage of which was hotly contested. Sohr's squadron was formed in the plain in front of the defile, and the enemy's troops of all arms were seen pressing forward on the neighbouring heights to the north and westward. When our rear guard had effected its retreat through the defile, Sohr thought it high time to do the same, and gave the word, " Divisions," " right about wheel—march ! " '

'The enemy was near at hand, and the division wheeled about hurriedly, and almost before the command was given '—

'The experienced leader, who had an eye to the future behaviour of his squadron, immediately fronted the divisions again, and, placing himself at their head, said : " I'll have you all cut down by the enemy rather than see you work unsteadily." '

'He faced the foe ; not a sound was heard in the squadron : the enemy pressed on : and their artillery opened with round shot on the defile in his rear, cutting up the ground on both sides of the devoted band. The sudden fronting and bold attitude of Sohr's squadron fortunately led the enemy to suppose that supports were at hand, and they ordered a flank movement to turn his position. His situation became more critical every moment he remained, for the enemy's cavalry were now coming up. Still not a movement was perceptible in the squadron, till, turning his horse towards them, he gave the word in his peculiarly measured way—

' " ' Divisions ' . . . ' right about wheel ' . . ' Walk ' . . . ' March ' . . ' Threes right ; ' and in a voice of thunder, he added, ' At speed '— ' March ' ' Ride as hard as you can.' " The defile was passed almost together with the enemy. Never again did his squadron hurry. In the hour of danger the hussars looked with confidence to their leader, and " were in hand." '

PASSAGE OF RIVERS.

Bridges and fords are a species of defile, shorter, generally, than defiles proper, but more difficult to force if ably defended. On the advanced guard reaching a bridge, where the enemy is not visible, the ground on the opposite side should be carefully reconnoitred before the main body of the advance crosses over. This can be done by a few horsemen, who can gallop across, and then, spreading in every direction up and down the banks, can discover whether any hostile force is concealed.

If no force is discovered, then the different parties

composing the advance guard, cross over as quickly as possible, the same formation of flankers, &c. being resumed immediately on reaching the far side.

It is very difficult to force the passage of a bridge, if it is a long one, and the opposite bank is the highest, and the enemy have a large force of artillery posted. In this case artillery are required to concentrate such a fire upon the defenders on the other side, as to drive them away from the bridge, in order to give an opportunity for the troops to rush across. In many instances, a body of cavalry in the advance have seized a passage of a river, by charging boldly across a bridge, at a gallop, and driving away the defenders.

Mounted rifles should be dismounted in endeavouring to force the passage of a bridge, and placed along the banks, taking advantage of every cover in order to pour a rapid and sustained fire on the enemy on the opposite side. In many cases, in following up a retreating foe, they will be quite able to effect a crossing, without waiting for the main force to come up, by making a judicious use of their twofold power, of fire and speed ; as a portion mounted might often dash across the bridge at the gallop, under cover of the fire of their dismounted comrades.

The different plans for effecting a passage of a river, where there are no bridges or fords, are almost innumerable. Cavalry officers, however, should remember that where the footing is good on both banks, cavalry can always, if necessary, swim across. We have already seen that Wartensleben, in 1796, swam the Main at the head of twenty-four squadrons. This plan should only be adopted in case of emergency.

The most common kind of bridges which are used in armies, are pontoon bridges, and for narrow rivers they serve a very good purpose. Colonel Simcoe, in the American Revolution of 1776, had the bodies of his waggons so constructed, that they could be used as pontoons as well as boats, and could hold six men each. This, it seems, would be a good plan, and save a regular pontoon train to a certain extent. In Canada, or the United States, large rafts could be rapidly made, and, by crossing a cable, they could be drawn backwards and forwards, and a large number of men crossed at each trip.

At Alcantara, in 1812, Colonel Sturgeon invented a plan for repairing the bridge at that place, without the enemy being aware of his preparations. He secretly prepared a net-work of strong ropes, in such a way that it might be carried in parts. It was transported to Alcantara in seventeen carriages, cables were stretched across the chasm from beams fixed up on each side, and the net-work was drawn over, and a bridge constructed on it, which took over the heaviest guns in safety.

Stonewall Jackson constructed a bridge over the ford of the South River just before the battle of Port Republic, with waggons placed in the stream, without their bodies, the axles forming beams to support the flooring, which was constructed of loose boards from a neighbouring saw mill. There was some carelessness in the construction of it, so that the men could only cross in single file, which caused the supports to come into action very slowly, and occasioned thereby much loss.

Colonel Simcoe gives an account of the passage of the Rivanna River, in June 1781, as follows:

' The water was fenced, as it were, with spars and canoes, so as to make a lane, and the horses swam over between them; the infantry passed on the float, which held with ease one hundred and thirty men, and had been made in four hours.'

Col. Von Borcke gives the particulars of the passage of the Chickahominy River in June 1862, during General Stuart's celebrated raid around M'Clellan's army. He says:

' Two regiments and the two pieces of horse artillery were ordered, in case of an attack, to cover our

retreat; whilst all the other available men were dismounted, some of them being employed to build
bridges, the others to swim the river with the
horses.'

'A bridge for foot passengers was hastily constructed across the stream, which was about ninety
feet in breadth, and the saddles, &c., were carried
over it.

'All the swimmers took the unsaddled horses
through the river, some riding them, others swimming by their side, with one hand holding the mane,
and the other directing the horse.

'After about four hours' work a second bridge was
completed for the artillery, and more than half the
horses had reached the other side of the river.'

In the last war in Germany, the Prussians, ex-
pecting that the bridge over Riese would be destroyed,
had before the declaration of war secretly measured
it, and had caused a complete new bridge to be made
ready to put up at once.

CHAPTER XIX.

SURPRISES AND AMBUSCADES.

En effet, pour surprendre l'ennemi, il faut bien connaitre ses forces et ses dispositions. Pour s'embusquer, il faut non-seulement bien choisir le lieu convenable, mais s'y rendre sans être aperçu sans donner le moindre soupçon de sa marche.—*General De Brack.*

THE benefit of surprising the enemy is very great, in consequence of the demoralisation that always results from it. A well-planned and vigorously-executed surprise rarely fails in succeeding, if the surprise is complete, and the enemy has not the necessary time to make his arrangements to meet the attack.

A surprise can rarely or never take place, if the outpost duty is properly performed, if the officers and men on whom it devolves are vigilant and intelligent, and if the light cavalry patrols are numerous and watchful. An ambuscade is still less likely to succeed, if the duty of the advance guards and flankers is effectually executed.

If, however, your spies and scouts bring information showing that the advanced guards of the enemy are not properly organised, or that he is marching without the usual precautions, these arrangements should be made to ambuscade him, and if it can be done, the ground being favourable, the success will certainly be great. In the same way, if the outposts of the enemy are careless and negligently posted, then a surprise might be attempted by the cavalry and dragoons, as these troops can move so much more rapidly than the other arms, and would give so much less time for the enemy to prepare.

In moving to surprise an enemy, or to take up a position for an ambuscade, the march should generally be made in the night, when the movements of the force cannot be perceived. Great care must be taken to make as little noise as possible. Horses which neigh or cough should not be taken, and hard roads, where the horses' hoofs would make a great clatter, should be avoided, and the scabbards should be bound around with something to prevent them jingling.

In these night marches with a view to a surprise, great care must be taken if several columns are employed, that they do not fall in with and attack each other in the night. This has often occurred. Once, in the Peninsular War, a partizan leader with some fifty men got between two French columns in the night, and by firing upon both columns caused them to commence fighting each other. He thereupon immediately slipped off with his command, and left the enemy, butchering each other till morning. In Wallachia, in 1853, two Russian columns attempting a surprise, fell in with one another, and fought for some time, suffering very severe loss.

Rainy or foggy weather will sometimes cover a surprise, if properly taken advantage of. It is better to attack after the patrols and scouts, sent out by the enemy's outposts, have returned in the morning, following them back to camp at a distance, and allowing them to reach the posts, and give in their reports of all being quiet. The troops are usually under arms while the patrols are out, and on their return, finding nothing threatening, will allow themselves some rest. If cavalry can dash in then, they will be very likely to surprise them, while taking breakfast or watering or cleaning their horses.

The surprise of Rocquencourt, in 1815, was one of the most successful and well-planned operations of the sort of which we have record ; it partaking somewhat of the character of a surprise, somewhat of that of an ambuscade.

General Early surprised Sheridan's army at the battle of Cedar Creek on October 19, 1864, and his arrangements for the operation, as detailed in his 'Memoir,' are worth reproducing here. He says:

' Rosser was ordered to move before day, in time to
attack at five o'clock next morning; and to endeavour
to surprise the enemy's cavalry in camp, Kershaw
and Wharton were ordered to move at one o'clock in
the morning towards Strasbourg, under my personal
superintendence, and the artillery was ordered to
concentrate where the Pike passed through the lines
at Fishers Hill, and at the hour appointed for the
attack to move at a gallop to Hupps Hill; the
movement of the artillery being thus delayed for fear
of attracting the attention of the enemy by the
rumbling of the wheels over the macadamized road.
Swords and canteens were directed to be left in camp,
so as to make as little noise as possible. The division commanders were particularly admonished as to
the necessity for promptness and energy in all their
movements. And they were instructed to press the
enemy with vigour, after he was encountered, and to
allow him no time to form, but to continue the
pursuit until his forces should be completely routed.'

Ambuscades can only succeed when the enemy is
very negligent in his marches. If he takes the usual
precautions of advanced and rear guards and flankers,
with scouting parties as well to the front, it will be
impossible to ambuscade him.

In taking up a position to ambuscade an enemy,
scouting parties should surround it to prevent the

column being themselves ambuscaded, and also to arrest and detain any persons who might take the enemy notice of what was going on.

Ambuscades are usually concealed in woods, in hollows, or behind hills. Hedges also sometimes conceal a party, as well as villages, houses, &c. Fields of grain or tall grass can sometimes be used to conceal troops, and should always be searched by the flankers and scouting parties.

Circumstances, however, decide all points on service, and strict rules cannot be laid down to guide an officer in the field. A soldier of an inventive, quick genius, will see opportunities, and take advantage of them, when another in happy ignorance will never know that any chances were even open to him.

Infantry are more available for ambuscades than cavalry; they can operate on broken covered ground, where cavalry cannot reach. Mounted rifles, however, are useful for this service, by dismounting the men near and concealing the horses.

Cavalry must ambuscade farther from the road on which the enemy is marching, than infantry; they can cross over the intervening space quicker, and the noise which a body of horses will make will not be heard. The ambush ought not to be too near the road, for fear the flankers should discover them.

A body of troops in ambush should not light fires,

and the greatest silence should be preserved. The men should keep the positions in which they are placed, without moving, as that might betray their presence to the enemy.

The signal for attack should be given by the commander, and the men should carefully refrain from firing, even if discovered, until the preconcerted signal is given, otherwise the best-laid plans might miscarry.

If cavalry are attacked they should be sent by a circuitous route, to endeavour, if possible, to cut off the retreat of the enemy.

If an army is victorious, it should always pursue the enemy with vigour, but with caution, for they may easily be drawn into an ambuscade and lose the whole fruits of the success. At Marengo, that result occurred, but not by design, Kellerman's dragoons being virtually in ambush behind some vineyards.

CHAPTER XX

CONVOYS.

Le commandant de l'escorte d'un convoi doit ne jamais perdre de vue que le but de sa mission n'est autre que d'amener à bon port le convoi qui a été confié à sa garde.—Général de Brack.

AT the present day, when all civilised countries are traversed with railways running in every direction, an army operating in any of the countries of Europe, excepting perhaps Russia and Turkey, would be able to find lines of railways, with ample equipments of rolling stock, so situated, as to serve as a line of communication, and as a means of conveying to an army advancing all the supplies which it requires.

Formerly this service was performed by long tedious convoys of waggons, escorted by strong detachments of troops of all arms, but especially cavalry. These convoys wended their sluggish course by slow, tiresome marches, dependent to a great extent upon the roads and the condition of them, dependent also on the weather, which, if wet and unfavourable, would cause great delays in the arrival of the stores so essential to the comfort of an army.

This old-fashioned method had also the disadvantage of requiring immense numbers of waggons and horses, and men to attend them. These men and horses had to be fed. Forage had to be carried for them; this required more waggons, and the effective strength of an army was hardly more than the numbers employed in administering to its wants.

Now one train, with a locomotive and twelve cars worked by six or eight men, will convey 200 miles in twelve hours supplies, ammunition, &c., which under the old method would have taken some seventy or eighty waggons, as many men, 150 horses, and an escort about ten days, if the roads were in good order, and the weather favourable.

Still, even at the present time, convoys are required for shorter distances, from the nearest point on the railways to the army; and these will sometimes require to be escorted; so a cavalry officer should know somewhat of the duty, in order to be in a position to perform it, if called upon to do so.

The escort of convoys is a very difficult and delicate task if before an enterprising enemy, and requires the greatest skill and presence of mind on the part of the commander, as well as courage and steadiness on the part of the men.

Convoys should always march on the road or roads the most removed from the enemy and the least liable to an inroad from his cavalry, and they should always be escorted. A notable instance of the truth of this principle was shown at Tobitschau in 1866, where Marshal Benedek sent a train of artillery from Olmutz to Tobitschau by the road near the enemy, while the main column marched by that from Olmutz to Prerau. The artillery moved with little or no escort, and, as might be expected, were intercepted near Nenakowitz by the Prussian cavalry, and Colonel Bredow with his single regiment of cuirassiers captured eighteen guns and all their waggons, &c. The particulars of this affair are described in Chapter X. in a former part of this work.

Escorts for convoys should be composed partly of infantry and partly of dragoons. The infantry should march with the convoy; the cavalry, spreading out over the whole country, should give warning of an approaching attack, in order to enable dispositions to be made for its reception. The dragoons in that case concentrating to fight also in defence of it.

A body of pioneers should march at the head of a convoy, with a few waggons holding tools, materials, &c., in order to repair the bridges and roads where they may require it. A third of the escort might also march near the head of the column, about as much more in the rear, with the remainder in the middle.

If the road is of a sufficient width the convoy should move in double columns, as this plan shortens its length by half, and makes it so much more easily defended.

The same rules as to the halting for a few minutes at intervals, and halting to feed in the middle of the day, and most other rules which are laid down for marches generally, apply equally well to the management of convoys.

In parking convoys protected situations should be found, when possible, and the waggons containing the most valuable loads, such as documents, despatches, money, &c. should be placed in the centre of the park, with the others closed up around them. The horses should be kept inside the waggons, each team with its own waggon. The troops must take the same precautions as to outposts, videttes, &c., as are laid down in the chapter on that subject.

It is also necessary to number the waggons, in order that each driver may know his position more readily, and that questions of precedence may not arise among them. This will prevent a great deal of confusion which might otherwise occur.

A list should be carefully prepared containing a

memorandum of the contents of each waggon, its number, and the name of the driver. This is a very important measure and also tends to prevent confusion and embarrassment.

A convoy should never enter a defile without feeling confident that the outlet is secured, and the flanks not occupied by the enemy. A friend of the writer, with a small party of some twenty-five cavalry, in the war in America, once waited for a convoy in a defile where there was a road branching off from the main road about the middle of the defile. He hid his men near the junction, allowed the advanced party and many of the waggons to pass, then sending some men to overturn three or four waggons beyond the cross-roads to prevent the advance party from coming back, he then turned some twenty waggons down the track which branched off, then overturned two or three other waggons and barricaded the defile behind him, and carried off his spoils in safety—covering the retreat with a portion of his men.

Mounted rifles are more suited for this service than cavalry proper, as they are better able to fight on all kinds of ground; and it would be more than probable that a convoy, if attacked at all, would be most likely to receive the attack while moving through a defile, or in broken ground.

The numbers and composition of the escort must depend, however, to a certain extent, upon the nature of the country, the feelings of the inhabitants, the distance from the army, and the chances of attack. The ground to be passed over by the convoy should, if possible, be first carefully reconnoitred, and the march commenced, only on receipt of the most satisfactory reports as to the safety of the route.

The head of the convoy should be moved with great regularity, and at an even pace, in order to avoid confusion in the column; and if the train is very long, it would be better to divide it, leaving intervals in order to prevent the swaying and fluctuations which will always arise in a very long column; and drivers should not be allowed to halt, to water their horses, or for any purpose whatever, without permission, as it might delay all the others. Of course, in powder trains no smoking can be allowed. The waggons should not be too heavily loaded, and if one happens to break down, its load should rapidly be distributed among the others. An officer commanding an escort of a convoy, on hearing from his scouts that the enemy is approaching, should form up his command in the best disposition to meet the attack, keeping the enemy as far removed from the waggons as possible. These latter should move on as fast as they can, while the escort fight to cover their march. The escort, in case of success, should not pursue too far, as the retreat might be a *ruse* to draw them away from their charge, and their duty is to secure that before everything.

CHAPTER XXI.

FLAGS OF TRUCE.

Un parlementaire a presque toujours une double mission, dont la partie cachée est bien plus importante que la portion ostensible.— *Général de Brack.*

THE officer chosen to bear a flag of truce into the enemy's lines, should be a man of great intelligence and quickness, in order that he may gather as much information as possible from the conversation of the parties with whom he is thrown in contact, as well as from all the circumstances which occur around him while engaged on the mission.

It is desirable that he should be well appointed as to horse, arms, uniform, &c., as he will be scanned with great interest by the enemy, and a good moral effect is produced by his appearance and equipment, if of a character to produce a favourable impression. The credit of the army also demands attention to this point.

A trumpeter should accompany a flag of truce, and should be directed to sound constantly, while approaching the enemy's videttes; one of the party also carrying the white flag conspicuously displayed as they advance. The officer, as well as the others with him, ought at the same time to endeavour to see all they can of the enemy's lines, before being blindfolded, as is the usual custom. Even when blindfolded, an officer may pick up a good deal of information, by hearing what is passing on about him as he is conducted along.

In the same way the enemy will endeavour, by apparently careless questioning, to obtain information. An officer should consequently be on his guard, and so frame his replies, as, with an appearance of candour, to prevent his questioners from learning anything, but rather to mislead them, if possible.

The trumpeter will also be questioned, and should therefore be an intelligent man, and ought to be carefully warned of the importance of using great caution, in replying to any of the enquiries that may be made of him, and of being prudent in his own casual conversations. In 1809, in Portugal, Franceschi expected an attack on account of the imprudent conversation of an English officer, the bearer of a flag of truce. This had some effect in preventing Sir Arthur Wellesley from surprising him and capturing his force.

An officer of outposts will observe great caution in

allowing flags of truce to approach his lines, and will move out and meet them, making the bearers leave their escorts in a position where they cannot overlook the dispositions of his command. The bearer of a flag of truce must be halted and detained until permission be obtained to conduct him to the commanding general, or until instructions are received as to what course is to be pursued. If he is to be conveyed to the general, he should be blindfolded, unless for some good reasons it is deemed advisable not to do so.

A flag of truce should not be received unless it purports to come from the opposing general. Subordinate officers have no right to send them, and if it is attempted they should be sent back. It should never be forgotten that flags are often sent out for very different purposes from the nominal reasons, and if this is seen they should not be received.

In order to illustrate the foregoing principles the full particulars of a flag of truce, sent by orders of General Lee to General M'Clellan in 1862, near Shepherdstown, Virginia, will be inserted here, quoted from Colonel Von Borcke's ' Memoir of the Confederate War for Independence,' he having been the officer carrying the flag.

' The following day there came some important

documents and letters from General R. E. Lee, to
be transmitted to General M'Clellan, and I had the
honour to be selected by our Commander-in-chief
as the bearer of them into the Federal lines.   To
make a favourable impression upon " our friends the
enemy," I fitted myself out as handsomely as the
very seedy condition of my wardrobe would allow,
and as all my own horses were more or less broken
down, I borrowed a high-stepping, fine-limbed,
chestnut from one of my comrades of the staff for
the occasion.   General Stuart took advantage of the
opportunity to send, under my charge, a batch of
prisoners for exchange, and entrusting me with some
private messages to M'Clellan bade me proceed as
far as possible into the enemy's lines and employ all
my diplomacy to attain a large insight into his
position, to as great an extent at least as was con-
sistent with the proprieties of my mission.   About
ten o'clock in the morning, my 50 or 60 Yankee
prisoners were turned over to me by Colonel W. H.
F. Lee at his camp, and at noon I reached the
Potomac near Shepherdstown escorted by a cavalcade
of our officers, who were interested in accompanying
me, as far as the river, with my flag of truce.   This
imposing ensign consisted of a white pocket-handker-
chief on a long pole, and was borne most loftily by
one of our couriers, a handsome martial-looking

fellow, who crossed the river with it, and soon brought
me the permission to come to the opposite shore.

'On the Maryland shore I was received by a
major who was in command of the outposts at this
part of the Federal lines, who handed me his proper
written acknowledgment for the prisoners, and said
that, as for the papers and documents, I might
deliver them to him, and he would forward them at
once.   This, of course, I politely declined, giving him
to understand that despatches of such importance I
could only deliver to General M'Clellan, or should
this be impossible, to some other general of his army ;
and adding, that as I supposed General Pleasanton
to be supreme in command of this portion of the
lines, I should be glad to be conducted to him.   The
major here betrayed some embarrassment, and spoke
of impossibilities, &c., but at last concluded to send
off a mounted officer for further instructions.

'Meanwhile all the Yankee soldiers who were not
on duty came running towards me, impelled by
curiosity to see the "great big rebel officer," in such
numbers, that the major was compelled to establish
a cordon of sentries around me, to keep them at a
respectful distance.   The only camp-stool that could
be produced having been politely offered me for a
seat, I soon found myself engaged in a lively and
pleasant conversation with a group of Federal officers.

' At length, after a weary time of waiting, came the answer to the major's message that I might proceed, and a good-looking young cavalry officer was reported to me, as guide and protector. Eager to anticipate a disagreeable and awkward formality, I now asked to be blindfolded, but this was politely waived. Starting from the ford, I took a tall and singularly-shaped pine tree, which reared itself far above the tops of its neighbours, as a landmark, and with this constantly in sight, it was not difficult for me to discover that I was purposely carried about in a circle, up hill and down dale, through dense woods, and vast encampments of troops.

' My companion proved to be a very pleasant young gentleman, and inexperienced officer, who voluntarily gave me much information that he should have kept to himself, during a ride of eight miles, which brought us to somebody's head-quarters. Here I saw at a glance a considerable display of the pomp and circumstance of war. What a contrast it presented to the head-quarters of our general officers, especially to the simple encampment of our great commander-in-chief, who, with his staff and escorts, occupied only a few small tents, scarcely to be distinguished from the tent of a lieutenant. Here, a little town of canvas surrounded the magnificent marquee of the general, from which floated the stars and stripes in a reckless extravagance of bunting; numerous sentries were pacing their beats : mounted officers, resplendent with bullion, galloped to and fro; and two regiments of Zouaves in their gaudy uniforms were drawn up for parade.

'I had already found out that this was General Fitzjohn Porter's head-quarters, and it was evident enough that some very great personage was expected there. Adjoining the general's marquee there had been erected a beautiful pavilion, under which was stretched out a long table, laden with luxuries of every description, bottles of champagne in silver ice-coolers, a profusion of delicious fruit, and immense bouquets of flowers. A balloon (we have mentioned before that this means of observation was much in use with the Federal army) was rising every few minutes to the height of several hundred feet, the car secured by ropes, filled with officers, who with all kinds of glasses, were looking out narrowly in the direction of Harper's Ferry. I was not mistaken in my conjectures. As I afterwards learned, no less a dignitary than President Lincoln was momentarily looked for. Escorted by General M'Clellan the President had already inspected a great portion of the Federal army of the Potomac, and as this was to be kept a secret my visit was necessarily to be a short one.

'During the time my young companion was announcing my presence to General Porter, I directed my eye towards the river, and there stood my pine-tree, not more than three miles distant, in a straight line, plainly in view.

'From General Porter's tent I could now hear the sound of voices in excited conversation; indeed I caught several very angry expressions before my guide returned, with a flushed face, in which one could read plainly the reprimand that had been given him, and desired me to enter.

'After a brief interchange of salutations, ensued the following colloquy:—

'*Federal General:* "You will allow me to express my regret that you have been brought here, and to say that a grave fault has been committed in your coming."

'*Confederate Major:* "General, I have been long enough a soldier to know, that a grave mistake *has* been committed, but I also know that the fault is not on *my* side."

'*Fed. Gen.:* "You are right. I ask your pardon. But why did you enquire for General Pleasanton, and what in the world induced you to suppose that he was in command here? I do not myself know where General Pleasanton is. At this moment he may be on your side of the Potomac."

z

'*Confed. Major:* "Where General Pleasanton is to-day, I am certainly not able to tell; but as I had the pleasure of seeing him with my own eyes, last night, returning with considerable haste to *this* side of the river, I had the right to suppose that he was here."

'*Fed. Gen.:* (laughing) "I can have no objection to your conjecture. When do you think to join General Stuart again?"

'*Confed. Major:* "Should I ride all night, I may hope to reach him some time tomorrow morning. (I was dancing at half-past ten o'clock that same night at "The Bower")'

'*Fed. Gen.:* (again laughing) "You seem to enjoy riding at night."

'*Confed. Major:* "Very much·at this delightful season of the year."

'The General now very courteously offered me some refreshments, which I declined, saving and excepting a single glass of brandy-and-water. I then delivered my despatches, pocketed my receipt for them, and took leave of a man whom I could not help admiring for his amenity of manners and high soldierly bearing.

'We had the same long round-about ride on our return, and it was late in the evening when we arrived on the bank of the Potomac, through whose waters I was conducted half way by my friendly foe, who, as we shook hands at parting, regretted that we were enemies to each other, and said that he hoped we should meet again, "when this cruel war was over," under happier circumstances. I thanked him for his kindly feeling, and begged him to take a lesson from me as a farewell offering. Showing him my pine-tree on the Maryland shore which had served me as a landmark, I said to him: "My young friend, General Fitzjohn Porter's head-quarters, in a straight line, are not three miles from that tree. He is in command of your right wing, to deceive me you have conducted me all round the country, but I have always known where I was, and I have passed three divisions of your army. Moreover, an important personage is every moment expected at General Porter's tent, and this personage is no other than President Lincoln." My courteous adversary laughed heartily at this and said: " Well, I did not believe that in any other nation of the world there was a man who *could fool a Yankee.* You have shown me the contrary, and I accept the lesson." We then shook hands for the last time, and returned to our respective lines.'

.

ᴜ

APPENDICES.

——◆◦◆——

APPENDIX A.

COLONEL JENYNS' NON-PIVOT DRILL.

HAVING applied to Colonel Jenyns, C.B., 13th Hussars, for the details of the system of drill in use in his regiment, he has kindly complied with my request, and his reply is inserted as follows :—

SYSTEM OF 'NON-PIVOT' DRILL AS ADAPTED TO THE PRESENT ENGLISH CAVALRY DRILL BOOK.

The drill laid down in the present 'Cavalry Regulations' is not altered in any respect as to the formation or 'telling off' of a Regiment, Squadron, Troop, or Division, with these exceptions :—

1. Troop leaders ride opposite the centre of their troop on *all* occasions.

2. Squadron markers (if any, and I consider them useless) and squadron serrefiles ride in rear of their leading troops when in column, thus leaving both flanks clear.

3. The dressing is to that flank on which the squadron leaders are posted, and they always follow the commanding

officer's movements in this respect, viz. if the regiment is
advancing in column of troops, and the commanding officer
shifts from the right to the left flank.   The squadron leaders
do the same, merely giving the caution (in a well-drilled
regiment unnecessary), 'eyes left' or 'eyes right.'

Trumpet Sounds.

The only alteration necessary is the addition of one 'G,'
or two 'Gs,' before the 'wheel into line;' one 'G' meaning
'right,' and two 'Gs' 'left wheel into line.'

Advantages of the Non-Pivot System.

The great advantages of the 'non-pivot' system are
these :—

A regiment advancing or retiring in column of troops or
squadrons can at once wheel into line to either flank.

All inverted manœuvres are totally unnecessary.

All reverse flank formations are also useless.

A regiment in column of squadrons at quarter-distance
can reverse its front by simply wheeling the troops right or
left about.   A regiment in line, in order to face to its rear,
need not countermarch on its centre, but simply wheel by
troops right or left about, as this movement in retiring is
almost as quick as 'fours about.'   Officers are enabled
always to be in *front*, whether advancing or retiring, and
it is well known that many accidents have occurred in
action, owing to the simple word of command (on the pivot
system perhaps necessary), 'threes' or 'fours about,' when
the men have perhaps only one or two officers, or non-
commissioned officers as serrefiles to lead them.

In column, a regiment can form line to its front or rear,
on the *right* or *left* of its leading or rear troop.

In quarter-distance or close column it is never necessary to advance to the front from the rear squadron in order to be left or right in front; the command is simply, 'advance in column of troops' from the 'right' or 'left' of the leading squadron (the same thing).

A detached squadron sent out to reconnoitre or skirmish can rally (when recalled) at *once*, either on the right or left of a regiment in line, or in rear of a column irrespective of the former position it held in line or column.

In fact a regiment can never be 'clubbed' as it is termed, and a commanding officer is enabled *at once* to form one or two lines to his front, rear, right, or left, whether the regiment is in line, quarter-distance, or open column.

The simple rules to remember are these :—

When in *line* the right squadron is the 'first,' the next the 'second,' and so on.

When in column the *leading* squadron is 'first,' the next the 'second,' and so on.

So that at any moment if a squadron is named 'first,' 'second,' 'third,' or 'fourth' (as squadrons never retain their same position in line), a squadron leader has merely to think where he stands at the moment, either from the right in line, or the front in column.

In forming close or quarter-distance column of squadrons, the squadrons on the left in line form in rear, and those on the right in front of the same squadron (unless otherwise ordered).

In deployments, the squadrons in rear of the named squadron form on the left, and those in front on the right of that squadron. The same rule applies to troops in open column formations.

In fact in column a regiment is always *supposed* to be right in front (according to the pivot drill system).

The present Field Movements according to the Non-pivot System.

Showing that all can be performed in the same way if necessary, but that very many, and those the most complicated, are totally useless.

The movements are laid down according to the order observed in the present ' Cavalry Regulations,' dated January 1, 1865.

Parade Movements, as at present laid down in the ' Cavalry Regulations.'

Remarks.

If, however, as is often the case, the ground is limited, after marching past by squadrons, instead of each squadron wheeling at D marker, the word may be given ' *Troops* left wheel,' and the head of the column wheeling again immediately, the regiment can pass close to the rear of the band, however strong it is.

Also after ranking past by ' fours ' or ' files,' and a close column has been formed, the word may be given, ' Take ground to the left in column of troops,' each squadron wheeling by troops to the left in succession from the first squadron.

Movements from Line.

No. 1. As at present, p. 162.

No. 2. As at present, or 'advance in column of troops from the right,' and ' right wheel into line.'

No. 3. As at present.

No. 4. As at present, or ' retire in column of troops from the left,' and ' left wheel into line.'

No. 5. As at present.

No. 6.   Ditto.

No. 7.   Ditto.

No. 8.   Ditto.

No. 9.   Ditto.

No. 10.   Ditto.

No. 11.   Ditto.

No. 12.   Ditto.

No. 13.   Ditto.

No. 14.   Ditto.

No. 15.   Ditto.

Here the caution ' right in front' is unnecessary.

No. 16. Useless and complicated. ' Troops right or left about wheel.'

No. 17. Useless and complicated. ' Troops right or left about wheel.'

No. 18. As at present: a line can however be formed to the right or left at once, by wheeling the squadrons, or to the rear on any squadron by ' troops right ' or ' left about wheel.'

No. 19. As at present.

No. 20.   Ditto.

No. 21.   Ditto.

A regiment, however, if retiring by fours from the right or left, can front form line to its original rear (if such a thing should ever be necessary) equally as well as it could form line to its front when advancing.

Movements from Quarter-distance Column.

No. 1. As at present. If necessary 'deploy on the *right* of the leading squadron.'

No. 2. As at present. If necessary, 'deploy on the *left* of the third squadron.'

No. 3. As at present. But if necessary, a line in the same manner can be formed 'to the *right* on the third squadron,' or 'advance in column of troops from the left,' and 'left wheel into line.'

No. 4. As at present.

No. 5. Useless and complicated. If a close column, 'squadrons will countermarch,' if a quarter-distance column, 'troops right or left about wheel.'

No. 6. As at present. If in quarter-distance column, 'troops right or left about wheel' is simpler.

The Open Column.

No. 1. As at present, or '*right* wheel into line.'

No. 2. As at present, or 'line to the front,' 'to the *right* of the leading troop.'

No. 3. As at present, or 'line to the front on the *left* of the rear troop.'

No. 4. As at present.

No. 5. As at present, or 'line to the rear on the *right* of the leading troop,' or wheel the head of the column to the right, and when in column 'right wheel into line.'

No. 6. As at present, or 'line to the rear on the *left* of the rear troop'—or, 'troops right (or left about wheel' and 'line to the front on the right (or left) of leading troop.'

No. 7. As at present.

No. 8.   Ditto.

No. 9. As at present.

No. 10. Unnecessary. 'Advance,' and 'right wheel into line.'

No. 11. Unnecessary. 'Advance,' and 'right wheel into line.'

No. 12. As at present, ' line to the front on the right of the leading troop,' or ' wheel the head of the column to the right,' and ' left wheel into line.'

No. 13. Unnecessary. 'Advance,' and ' left wheel into line.'

No. 14. Unnecessary. It does not signify which troop or squadron leads.

No. 15. As at present, or ' to the right of the leading troop.'

From Double Column.

No. 16. As at present, or, in a regiment of four squadrons ' two lines to the front,' two lines to the right or left (by each wing wheeling into line, *a most effective movement*), or troops ' right about wheel,' and one or two lines to the original rear.

No. 17. As at present, or if four squadrons, the left column passes on, and ' right wheel into line.'

Skirmishing.

The non-pivot system obviously gives great pliability in skirmishing. A flank or central squadron can be sent out, and if driven in, it can rally anywhere in the line without creating confusion.

Conclusion.

There are, as any Commanding officer drilling his regiment on the non-pivot system will find, very many useful formations from line and column, which can be immediately made, as circumstances require ; both in the advance and retreat. A left *wing* of a regiment can support and pass through the right wing and immediately form one line to the left, or a supporting wing can form up either on the right or left of its leading wing.

In retiring from both flanks by column of troops after attacking, to allow guns to fire, or a supporting regiment to attack in succession (in a regiment of four squadrons), in order to reform the head of each wing merely wheels inwards, and the whole are wheeled into line by the commanding officer. Distances are thus ensured.

The great advantage is that it is almost impossible for a regiment drilling on the ' non-pivot ' system to be taken on the flank, as it can *always* wheel and *act* to either flank *without confusion*, which is always the case if a regiment on the pivot system finds itself ' inverted.' What regiment was ever known in action in the moment previous to attack to attempt an inverted or reverse flank formation? or any of the complicated manœuvres in the drill book which by the ' non-pivot ' system are rendered obsolete?

The antagonists of the ' non-pivot ' system urge an objection that in some formations when troops are wheeled about (instead of, for instance, a line countermarching on its centre), the line will not *exactly* occupy the same ground. Of course it will not by the breadth of a troop.

But as all drill is only an instruction for the moment of action in the field; which, in the above instance, would any cavalry officer prefer, when he finds it necessary to retire in line *under fire*? going 'threes about' or fours about'—a movement that has caused more disaster than any other?

Wheeling the troops about, thus retiring in line, officers leading?

Or, in order to preserve this exact mathematical distance, countermarching on the centre, which until the movement is completed, renders a regiment helpless, and *then* retiring with no way of fronting again to attack, perhaps an advancing enemy, without going through the same complicated operation?

Oh! say some, I would then at once wheel about and attack. Then, *why* not make it the usual drill?

What can be the use of movements (in these days of breechloading firearms with immense range) that take some minutes to execute, and when done leave you inverted, or, to those not drilled on the 'non-pivot' system, as good as 'clubbed'?

In these days, pace, quickness in formations, and pliability must be obtained in order to render cavalry efficient. Let the exactness required as to distances, &c., in order to instruct officers and men for parade movements, be enforced to the *greatest degree*, as without it men will never ride or drill decently; but it should not be carried too far in fighting manœuvres, it should never interfere with the far more requisite instruction of riding, quickness, and pliability in the field.

I know from experience that a regiment can march past and rank past as correctly and as exactly on the non-pivot as on the pivot system. In fact it can do every movement laid down in the Cavalry Regulations, exactly as specified if necessary. But the 'non-pivot' system gives immense additional powers, and it only teaches officers and men to do what they must under some circumstances do in actual combat.

I have said to officers who adhere to the old system, Suppose you were, when in column, attacked or suddenly threatened on your reverse flank, what would you do?

'*Then*, of course, I should at once wheel into line to that hand.'

Then I say why not teach your men always to do so if necessary? Would it add to the men's confidence at the moment of attack to find themselves suddenly ' clubbed,' as they have always been taught to consider it? A contingency they have always been warned carefully to avoid.

Everyone that has been engaged in actual operations in the field when cavalry meet cavalry, knows that the instant opposing bodies *meet*, formations are at once destroyed, officers and men are personally engaged; the successful regiment pursues in all probability, and the great difficulty in all cavalry history has been to prevent success leading to ultimate disaster, from the difficulty of rallying in anything like order. With the non-pivot system as long as squadrons or even troops rally, it does not signify in what part of the line they form up. Men and officers get so accustomed to continually changing their place in column and line, that they know they are not ' clubbed ' or in confusion wherever they may be placed, and it gives all ranks great confidence.

APPENDIX B.

TWO LETTERS FROM MAJOR-GENERAL FITZHUGH LEE.

I.

Baltimore, Feb. 27, 1868.

COLONEL,—I have the honour to acknowledge the receipt of yours of 18th January.

Pray accept as an excuse for delay in responding, the fact, that I was not at home when your letter arrived, but that it has followed me about from place to place and only within the past few days, been received.

My time is so limited this morning I can only reply briefly to your questions, with the idea that reaching you earlier, they would be more welcome than more extended response at a later period.

1st you ask ' the best arm for cavalry ?'

I reply, Colt's navy-sized revolver, Sharp's breech-loading carbine, and the French sabre.

' The best method of fighting cavalry at present, whether mounted or dismounted against the other arms ?'

I conceive it depends entirely upon the nature of the country.

'The best saddle for cavalry ?' I think there is no comparison between what is known in this country as the ' M'Clellan Saddle,' and any other.

'Whether the rank entire system is better than the double rank?'

My experience in the old United States army as in the service of the Confederate States is decidedly in favour of the latter. You can *never get ground sufficient to manœuvre large bodies* of cavalry by the single rank system, and in charging by platoon, company or squadron front, the advantages of the single rank can be always obtained by directing the rear rank to hold their horses back a little until the interval is attained.

I have no objection, Sir, to your using what I have so hastily and incompletely written in any way you may deem proper. I regret to have written so briefly, but if you will address me, on reception of this, to Box 301, Alexandria Va., I promise to take time to give you my views upon the use of cavalry and the best means to make it effective in battle.

Yours most truly,
FITZHUGH LEE.
Maj.-General Commanding Cavalry Army N. Va.
during late war.

Lieut.-Colonel G. DENISON,
    Toronto, Canada.

II.

'Richland' Stafford Co. Virginia, April 30, 1868.

COLONEL,—I have the honour to acknowledge the receipt of your letter in which you request my 'opinion on any points connected with the cavalry service as may strike me,' and in reply, the following views are submitted.

In all countries the squadron is the unit of the arm of

cavalry, though in itself containing subdivisions for greater convenience in handling. Mount sixty-four, light, active young men who are good riders, upon supple, well ribbed-up, round-barrelled, short-coupled, spirited though docile horses, not as a general thing over fifteen hands high, and you have the essential conditions of good cavalry. The number, sixty-four, of course, varies always in proportion to the number of men for duty. I only give it as a good average. For rapidity of motion and facility in manœuvring keep the squadrons small and give 'plenty of elbow-room.' In the American service such a unit is composed of two companies, and the whole subdivided equally at each formation into four platoons. A company of cavalry in the regular service is officered with a captain, one first-lieutenant, one second lieutenant, which would give six officers for the squadron, a leader, a file closer, and a commander for each platoon.

I eschew heavy cavalry, the ' cuirassier ' *sans peur*, they can only be employed during actual conflict, and in this country, from its topographical features, opportunities seldom occur for charging with large masses of cavalry, like Murat and Bessières at Eyelau, or Seidlitz at Zorndoff for instance ; so seldom, indeed, that the expense does not justify keeping up such organisations whilst awaiting such opportunities. I participated in every battle fought be - tween the two principal armies in Virginia during the late war between the North and South, and cannot recall a single instance where cavalry *en masse* was employed on the battle-field, save in a few instances against cavalry it-self. Raiding, scouting, reconnoitring, &c., 'heavy men mounted on heavy horses' are unfit for, and hence their

A A

disorganisation and disuse. The dragoon, that admixture of 'foot and horse,' and like all hybrids possessing the qualities of neither to any degree, has also disappeared among us, and now light cavalry alone is recognised. It was found that it too could be made very effective on foot, when occasion required, its light armament affording facility for the rapid transition. Though cavalry ranks as the second *tactical* arm on the field, its duties before and after battle have become very great ; when it can be used during conflict, it must be led with celerity and boldness and even, when called for, *recklessness.*

The average weight of a light dragoon in the English service some years ago (I do not know how it is now) was 10 stone 3 lbs. or 143 lbs., and his height from 5 feet 4½ inches to 5 feet 8 inches. The average weight of his equipments was 103 lbs., which would make the horse carry 246 lbs.—*too much weight.* The equipments in the United States service are much lighter, which would allow the man to be heavier, but the total weight I should prefer to come below 200 lbs.

As a general thing *young* men make the best cavalry (though I do not forget that Cromwell was 44 years old when he first drew a sword, nor deny his great cavalry genius) ; they possess more enthusiasm, cheerfulness, dash, greater fondness for riding, are more careless of life, always eager for enterprise, and will ride more recklessly when occasion demands. To such traits intelligence must be added, for the trooper is so often detached and must think for himself. His duties as vidette, courier, orderly, member of patrol and reconnoitring party, all demand the exercise of it. Cavalry, too, cannot be improvised to the extent infantry can, but requires a long training of man and horse before made effective.

Good horsemanship is the basis of a good organisation. I do not think your schools in Europe pay sufficient attention to riding; at West Point, the military school of this country, requisite particularity I know is not exercised. No officer should be admitted to the cavalry arm of the service who does not become a good horseman, and evince a partiality for all pertaining to the animal. Without the first quality, a desire to lead his troops when moving at a rapid rate, and where obstacles intervene, is apt not to exist; and the absence of the second interferes with a bestowal of attention to the comforts, appetites, and health of his horses. Whilst on duty at West Point (just previous to the breaking out of the late war) as instructor of cavalry, I noticed that in a class where there were two cadets who had never been on horseback in their lives (and there were frequent instances of that kind among young men from the Northern States), one would early assume a good seat, and in time become an excellent rider, whilst the other never could learn; he would go mechanically through the drill, but to his graduating day he always looked awkward, unsafe, and uncomfortable on a horse; still, if he stood high in his other studies and got few demerits, his chances to be put into the cavalry upon graduating, were he disposed to urge them, would be better than any who stood below him in class rank, though higher in the theory and practice of that arm. The defects of the system are manifest. I would recommend, too, the getting rid of all troopers who cannot be taught to ride, either by discharge or transfer to other arms. It will save many sore backs to horses and much useless time and drill in trying to get such up to the proper standard. A proper instructor can tell, after seeing a squad ride for a few days, who are going to become horsemen and who never will. The system in the United States is to recruit men by voluntary enlistment (wherever they can be found) for the mounted corps, certain conditions as to age and health being fulfilled. They are then sent to Carlisle, taught to saddle and unsaddle a horse according to prescribed forms, mount and dismount, with a little insight into the elements of tactics, after which they are drafted to the different regiments as required. You can see the defects of such a system which will permeate through the whole country. Height and weight should be consulted, with the thinning out of bad horsemen after they are found to be so, and more perfect training given them. Above all perfect them in managing a horse at speed (which seems now never to be thought of), first shaking them into good seats by long preliminary trots day after day. How helpless a man feels when riding a horse at full speed for the first time, and how little like using the weapons fastened to him ! Can he take care of himself in the *mêlées* charges so often resolve themselves into ?

I favour the double rank in preference to the rank entire system for many reasons, and among them the following :— more men can be manœuvred on a given piece of ground, particularly in line formations—an important object to achieve, for ground is always scarce for cavalry purposes. The efficiency of a cavalry charge lies in its shock, the rear rank augments that, fills up the gaps and in the *mêlée* that succeeds gives more sabres on hand for service. It also carries confidence to the front rank as such close backers will. Instruction should be given them to rein back a little in the charge though, to prevent riding over their file leaders should they or their horses fall. The principal objection to charging with single rank formation is that after the charge when the usual spreading out takes place, it is scattered too much for its own strength ; another, that all men and horses, however good the cavalry, are not fit to lead. The experience of nations who have tried such a system are not favourable to it, even the Cossacks have abandoned it. Our own in the past war was decidedly against it, after a fair test. Several regiments were manœuvred entirely by the 'rank entire' system until practice proved its inadmissibility. I know that the Duke of Wellington, as well as such experienced cavalry officers of the same epoch as your General Bacon, Lord William Russell, and Lieut.-General Sir Henry Vivian recommended the adoption of the 'rank entire' system, but I doubt whether in practice it attained the expectations they formed of it from theory.

As to the equipment of cavalry, I would arm the trooper with the Sharpe breech-loading carbine and sling, Colt's navy-size revolver, worn in holster on belt around his body, and the light French cavalry sabre. The lance was amply tested in our late war, but did not answer, and was abandoned as an arm for cavalry. For a saddle I prefer above all others what is known in this country as the 'M'Clellan pattern,' being the result of the observations in that particular by General George B. M'Clellan whilst in Europe as one of three officers sent there by Honourable Jefferson Davis (when secretary of war) in April 1855. It is lighter, more durable, stands exposure to weather better, and is more comfortable to man and horse. In the pouches on either side the soldier ought to carry currycomb and brush, two spare horseshoes and necessary nails, a change of under clothing, soap, brush and comb and towel, strapped behind the saddle he carries, rolled up in an oil cloth covering, his overcoat and blanket. The felt pad, so highly recommended by Captain Nolan, 15th Hussars, in his very valuable work on cavalry, which always accompanies his saddle, I cannot recommend. I tried one myself when an officer in cavalry in the United States army previous to the war. It did not answer on long scouts in hot weather. The perspiration absorbed from the horse drying would make it too hard, and as a consequence chafe the animal's back, besides being very hot and uncomfortable to him whilst on the march; I know nothing superior to the common saddle blanket. Valises with the letter of troop upon them and shabraques have been discarded with us, also wallets and saddle holsters, as tending by the weight of their contents to produce that very troublesome and common disease known as 'Fistulous withers.' For a bridle I recommend a light, but strong and well-finished headstall, the bit to buckle on to the two lower rings by straps attached to it, a halter strap to buckle to the ring under the throat, and on the march the other end to be tied to a ring in front of saddle; unbuckle the short straps, take the bit out of the horse's mouth, untie the halter strap from the saddle, and your horse is ready to be secured. The reins of course go with the bit. I prefer only one rein, as less cumbersome and more simple. The bit to be moderately powerful, with the cheeks rather long to give sufficient leverage. Everything depends upon the bitting a horse first receives whether

he is to have a hard or a soft mouth, and great care should
be taken lest you make him restive and sensitive by an
injudicious use of the stiff bit. The Cossack uses nothing
but the simple snaffle, whilst the Turk and Arab use bits
so powerful as to break the jaw of the horse if suddenly and
violently checked. Hence I say it is not so much the bit
you put in a horse's mouth, as the manner in which you
teach him to obey it; for can anyone deny the horsemanship of the Cossack or Arab, and yet what different means
they employ to control their steeds.

For the rest, I remark in conclusion, that to have good
cavalry, you must have it well officered, for it is more
dependent upon the example and bearing of its leaders
than any other arm. General Foy, you know, in his history
of the Peninsular War says :—' Après les qualités néces-
saires au commandant-en-chef, le talent de guerre le plus
sublime est celui du général de cavalerie. Eussiez-vous
' un coup-d'œil plus rapide et un éclat de détermination plus
soudain que le coursier emporté au galop, ce n'est rien si
vous ne joignez la vigueur de la jeunesse, des bons yeux,
une voix retentissante, l'addresse d'un athlète et l'agilité
d'un centaure.' And when we consider that cavalry is the
most difficult and delicate of all arms to handle on the field
of battle, I don't think the General's opinion is so exaggerated.

As to its strength, military authorities put it down from
one-fourth to one-sixth of the infantry in the same army,
though its numbers ought to vary with the nature of the
country and strength of the enemy's cavalry. On the field of
battle it should generally be employed on the flanks of the
army, though ready to be moved to any point favourable
for its action.

Cavalry has been very properly termed ' the eyes, ears, feeler and feeder of an army,' a sentence comprising a great deal. Upon the information gained by it the movements of the whole army are based, and the proper forced recon-noissances with an intelligent secret system, demand the utmost attention on the part of the leader. My own ex-perience taught me to select a small body of men taken from the regiments in which they could be found, who were denominated ' head-quarter scouts.' These men were noted for their daring, intelligence, truthfulness and know-ledge of the country; they hovered in squads of two or three on the flanks, front, rear and within the lines of the enemy, and promptly and accurately reported his every movement. I would not recommend that they be put under any officer, but be ordered to report to the chief of cavalry direct, or when it was more convenient, and the information was very important, to the chief of an army corps, or the commanding general first. Subordinate offi-cers to have nothing to do with them, as only tending to delay the transmission of their intelligence by causing it to come through them. I found that twenty-five resolute men, scattered in the way I have described, could always keep me supplied with much necessary information. They were made to see for themselves and not report what citi-zens might tell them they had seen, were always made to dress in the uniform of their command, and pains were taken to keep them well mounted.

And now I bring this to a close, not wishing longer to delay its transmission, lest you think my promise had not been complied with. If anything I have written should prove of service to you, Colonel, or anyone who is interested in the welfare of your branch of service, I shall be amply compensated.

Most respectfully,
Your obedient Servant,
FITZHUGH LEE.

Lieut.-Colonel GEORGE T. DENISON, Jun.
Commanding Governor-General's Body Guard,
Toronto, Upper Canada.

.

APPENDIX C.

LETTER FROM LIEUT.-GENERAL STEPHEN D. LEE, C.S.A.

Brooksville, Mississippi, United States, February 22, 1868.

COLONEL,—I take pleasure in complying with your request as to the points you ask my experience relative to the cavalry arm of service during the recent war in the United States, and although such information rendered in a letter is brief and imperfect, still if you think it valuable it is at your service.

In my opinion, the great improvement in fire-arms has made an essential change in the handling and using of cavalry, and the charge against infantry or cavalry as formerly, is less frequent and more dangerous. The long range fire-arms now in use, are so effective, that battles are decided quickly, and at longer range than formerly, and the hand-to-hand conflict is not so frequent. Hostile bodies are compelled to approach each other with more caution, and cavalry offering a good and effective mark must select its opportunity for the charge, or it will pay dearly for it.

As to ' the best arms for cavalry,' and ' the best arms for mounted riflemen,' I will treat together, premising with the remark, that nearly all the cavalry used by the Confederate States, and in fact by both sides, was nothing more than mounted riflemen. The sabre was done away with by the

Confederate States cavalry pretty well, and rarely used in action by either party, and in my opinion has lost much of its merit, since the revolver has been brought to such perfection. The proper and best armament for the cavalry man, by which I mean all mounted men, is the light-repeating rifle, and two large-sized six-shooters (revolvers), and a sabre so arranged as to be left with the horse when the cavalry man is dismounted. With this equipment, the cavalry man is always ready for the charge with confidence, and can always be used dismounted, either against cavalry or infantry.

As to the ' comparative merits of the sword, lance, carbine, revolver, and rifle for mounted troops,' I am clearly of opinion that the carbine and lance have ceased to be effective weapons for cavalry, the carbine being replaced by the equally light, and more effective, repeating rifle, and the lance as useless against modern improved weapons. The sword is a good weapon, though but little used during the recent war ; it has lost much of its effectiveness by the improved revolver, with which the cavalry man will make the dashing charge with more confidence. My experience was, that the cavalry man was timid with his sabre in fighting against the revolver, and for the least excuse, will drop the sabre for the revolver, and in many instances is compelled to do so, in actual conflict by irregularities of ground, obstacles, &c. I don't see well how the sword can be dispensed with permanently, as some such weapon is required in case ammunition should be exhausted; but if any weapon is to be dispensed with, I should say the sabre in preference to the rifle or revolvers. These latter two, rifle and revolvers, are indispensable. In every instance under my observation, the revolvers replaced the sabre, with the *morale*, with the trooper, and against the enemy. Again, in the hand-to-hand conflict, which rarely occurs now (owing to the improved fire-arms) the momentum or pluck decides the affair before the eighteen rounds in hand are exhausted, and the momentum with good cavalry is as readily obtained with the revolver as with the sabre, my observation being the sabre is timid against the good revolver. The revolver is the all-important weapon with the cavalry man in motion, and is indispensable in his equipment.

The repeating rifle makes him a mounted rifleman, and is all important since the great improvement in fire-arms as to range and efficiency. And on foot the cavalry man is almost the equal of the infantry soldier, lacking only in metal, and under ordinary circumstances his weapon is just as effective. He does not hesitate to engage infantry as formerly.

As to the best saddle, I am unable to give a correct opinion, as the Confederate States cavalry had to use what saddles they could get, and no good article or variety was furnished by the War Department. The Confederate States trooper considered himself fortunate in getting a M'Clellan tree.

The ' best method of fighting cavalry on foot or horseback ' of course must be determined by the surroundings. The most effective is with the rifle dismounted, and long range guns nearly compel a fight on foot in every instance. In case of any success or ' the morale ' being clearly on your side, the fighting should alway be pushed mounted and with the revolver.

The equipment of the cavalry man with the recent re-

peating rifle and revolvers of modern invention, in my
opinion, has increased his efficiency proportionally more
than either the infantry or artillery arm has been by the
inventions applicable to those arms. It enables the commanding general almost to detach an army corps of infantry
with the celerity of cavalry for an important blow at a
distance, or even on an extended battle-field for a critical
flank. Almost in all ages the cavalry man has held himself superior to the infantry man, but when brought to the
actual test, before unprejudiced judges, has had in almost
every instance to yield to the stolid infantry man, for
whom he always had and still has a deep respect. Now
he has some excuse for his proud assumption, for he is
almost the equal, and the respect of the two arms of service
is mutual; the infantry not having the cavalry in contempt as formerly. A large body of cavalry as now armed
is a match for almost any emergency, and it is an army in
motion, and on a flank its blow is terrible. And against
communications, magazines, &c., its damage disastrous.

I am, Colonel,

Yours respectfully,

S. D. LEE.

APPENDIX D.

LETTER FROM MAJOR-GENERAL T. L. ROSSER, C.S.A.

Baltimore, Md., Jan. 27, 1868.

COLONEL,—Enclosed you will find a few thoughts on the subject of your enquiry of the 18th instant.

I have given you the summary of my convictions without discussing the circumstances which led to them.

Neither the Yankees nor Confederates employed cavalry in the late war, it was all *mounted rifles*. I had one brigade (Ashby's old command), and its history fully sustains the theories of Sydlitz and Nolan as regards the irresistibility of cavalry charges.

Cavalry can sometimes be employed successfully in a *coup de main*, but is not safe to undertake it without mounted rifles. During the late war I rode into the strongly-fortified post of New Creek and captured the garrison, with cavalry, and with the loss of only two men. But when I undertook the same thing at Beverly, I saw I would not succeed on horseback, and dismounted in two hundred yards of the camp, and attacked it as infantry, and thus easily accomplished on foot that which I undoubtedly would have failed in on horseback.

Cavalry was not used on the battle-fields as Ney and

Murat used it under the great Napoleon, and the reason was, *that it was not cavalry!*

I am pleased to serve you and my noble friend General Early.

Very truly yours,

THOS. L. ROSSER,

Major-General, C. S. A.

Colonel GEO. T. DENISON.

The Cavalry Soldier.

No soldier should be taken into the cavalry service *directly*, but into a general camp of instruction, and there exercised in the use of the various arms until his capacity for each be determined, *intellectually* and *physically*. Then no one should be taken into the cavalry who is not possessed of at least ordinary intelligence, a strong constitution, and of more than ordinary muscular power, for in battle his *muscle* and weight of his horse, are to determine results. Hence he should be a good rider and possess a strong arm.

My experience has been, that the majority of men are defective as soldiers in the feet, and if this is the only difficulty they answer just as good a purpose for cavalry service with this defect as without it. Cavalry which is not *thoroughly drilled* and *ably officered* is worthless under any circumstances. These requisites are necessary in every arm, but more so in cavalry than any other; for in battle, a cavalry soldier has his frightened horse to manage and at the same time to use his weapon, at close quarters upon his adversary, whilst infantry and artillery are employed more or less at long range.

In this country, United States, where there is so much

wooded and mountainous country, mounted troops should consist of *cavalry* and *mounted rifles*, in the proportion of two of cavalry to one of *mounted rifles*. The cavalry armed with *sabres* and *pistols*, and *nothing else*. The mounted rifles armed with *breech-loading carbines* and *pistols, without sabres*.

·I regard the lance a fancy arm entirely; does very well on parade, but worthless against disciplined troops. The sabre should be light with sufficient length and strength, and almost if not entirely straight.

The pistol, Colt's heavy revolver, I think the best. '*Spencer's light charge*' carbine, I think, is the best for mounted rifles. The next in order of efficiency is th' *Sharpe's carbine*.

The M'Clellan saddle is by far the best I ever saw f cavalry It is strong, light, and comfortable to man and hor

Cavalry in this country cannot be regarded as a *defensive* arm of service, and should never be detached from the main army without being accompanied by *artillery* and *mounted rifles*. It is worthless except in the charge, and should never be used for any other purpose. The cavalry soldier should never be dismounted to fight if you expect him to ride over masses of infantry, but be educated to the belief *that nothing can withstand a well-executed charae of cavalry*, and should feel perfectly at home on b'.....back. All picketing should be done by mounted rifles, and all escorts and guards for trains and the like should be composed of the same, and the cavalry *always kep! in mass, and used in the charge alone.*

I much prefer the *single rank* formation to the double. It is more easily managed, and nothing like so many accidents occur.

APPENDIX E.

THE SADDLE AND REVOLVER.

THE following remarks on the Saddle and Revolver
·e from the pen of a General officer of high rank
· l great experience, in whom I place the utmost
ance. They deserve to be carefully perused as
ideas of one who has practically tested the
ctness of the views he advocates.

I. *Cavalry Saddle.*

The greatest difficulty with regard to cavalry is to keep
it mounted on a campaign, and to do that, of course, the
first requisite is a supply of good horses, and then there
must be forage to keep them in serviceable condition.
Next to these indispensable requisites is the question of a
prope. "` lle. Experience has shown that more cavalry
men are dismounted by reason of sore backs than all other
causes, and sore backs are almost always produced by defects
in the saddle. Bad saddles destroy more horses than are
killed or disa. led in *action* by *long* odds. This is particularly the case in extensive thinly-settled countries, when
marches or raids have to be made for very long distances.
The saddle injuı .s the horse's back, principally by pressing

B B

unequally on it, by being over-weighted and by galling it
in hot weather.   Of the saddles used by the Confederate
cavalry with the army in Virginia, the M'Clellan saddle
was considered by far the best.   This saddle was obtained
by the Confederates by captures from their enemies.   It
was devised for the cavalry of the United States by
adopting many of the features of the Mexican, Comanche,
and Texan saddles.   This saddle was not padded at all,
but the tree was covered with raw hide, made smooth,
and so shaped as to rest uniformly on the horse's back,
without unequal pressure on either part: at least, such
was the object, though sometimes from faulty make, the
object was not accomplished.   It was found that all padded
saddles injured the horse's back much more than those
without pads.   Though this saddle was lighter than most
others, still one defect of it was. its weight, as the tree
was held together by iron-bands, and for the purposes of
adding to its appearance, more leather was used than necessary.   To give as much ventilation as possible, the saddle
was left open on the seat between the lateral parts of the
tree ; and in this manner not only was ventilation secured,
but direct pressure on the backbone was avoided.   The
saddle was very easy to ride without anything on the
seat, but often a blanket or shawl was thrown across the
seat, and sometimes a loose moveable pad was used.   The
English Hussar saddle was imported into the Confederacy,
and was used by some officers from mere fancy, though
never by any cavalry officers.   The objection to this saddle
was its great weight, and it was found to injure the horse's
back much more than the M'Clellan saddle, the superiority
of the latter being generally conceded.   The Texas cavalry

used what was called the Texas saddle, and preferred that to all others. It combined the best qualities of the Mexican and Comanche saddle. Its essential parts are a wooden tree, with a large horn in front, braced together without the use of iron, and covered nicely with raw hide and iron fixtures or rings for attaching the stirrup-leathers and girths. No buckle was used for any purpose, not even for fastening the girth, or regulating the length of the stirrup-leather, but the girth was fastened by a strap with a peculiar knot, and the stirrup-leather regulated by thongs with holes in the leathers. The girth was made of horse-hair platted, and had a large ring in each end. The saddle when fully rigged, was little more than a bare tree, though it was susceptible of being ornamented with stamped leather to any extent, but this latter was not necessary, and was rather an incumbrance. Under the tree, an ordinary saddle-blanket could be used, but a cloth made of horse-hair, was much preferable, as chafing or scalding of the back was less common with that than any other contrivance. Anything to be carried was readily attached to the saddle before or behind by means of buckskin thongs. The saddle presented rather a curious appearance to one not accustomed to it, but after a horseman became accustomed to it, he would not exchange it for the most costly saddle of any other pattern. The important requisite with this saddle was accuracy of construction, for if not made right, it was worse than nothing. Mounted on his horse, with a saddle made of wood, raw hide, and a very little iron, with a blanket, a canteen, or what was better, a canteen gourd tied to the horse, a rifle, and a revolver, the Texan ranger was the most formidable horseman in the world. He had all the dash and jaunty bearing of the Mexican Caballero, with the intelligence, perseverance, and unyielding spirit of the Caucasian, educated to a frontier life. He had to be killed or disabled before he would be unhorsed, and himself, his horse, and his saddle seemed to be but one being. At a full gallop he could pick up anything from the ground, and you never saw him bobbing up and down like a wood sawyer, but he maintained his seat apparently without the slightest effort.

With the M'Clellan saddle, as well as with the Texas saddle, a wooden stirrup was used with a leather covering in front. This stirrup was a protection for the foot against rain, and a much better protection against cold, being infinitely preferable to any wrapping for the latter purpose. A man who had once used a wooden stirrup, could not be induced to adopt again the metallic one. The Texas saddle was not used in Virginia because it could not be procured. The Texas cavalry had the opportunity of trying both, but they preferred their own.

II.—*Colt's Revolver.*

This arm was invented by Colt prior to the year 1838, and the inventor established a factory in New Jersey. He made efforts to have his revolving breach rifle as well as his pistol introduced into the United States service, but without success, as the weapon was looked upon as a fancy one, not suitable to be placed in the hands of common soldiers. The officers of the army thought it too complicated, and that it would be impossible to get soldiers to keep it in serviceable order. Even the percussion musket had not then been introduced into the service, and the old flint-lock was looked upon as the one most suitable for soldiers. Colt made efforts to introduce his weapon to the notice of the English and French Governments, but without success or encouragement. In the early part of the year 1831, while the United States troops were engaged in the war with the Seminoles of Florida, Colt obtained permission to carry some of his rifles to Florida for experiment, with power to the commanding officer there, to purchase a limited number, if a board of officers should report favourably upon them for that service. A board of officers was appointed, who, after experimenting, reported that the weapon was a very ingenious one, and might under certain circumstances be used efficiently, in defence of positions that were to be held, as for instance, of breaches in fortifications against assault, but that it would not answer for active service in the field. Being foiled in his efforts to introduce his arm into the military service, and compelled to rely on private patronage, Colt's factory in New Jersey proved unprofitable, and the manufactory of the arm was discontinued for a number of years. He had, however, made a number of pistols which got principally into the hands of the Texans, then engaged in a predatory war with the Mexicans and Comanche Indians. These pistols, which were called 'five-shooters,' were valued very much by the Texans, and at the breaking out of the war with Mexico in 1846, the fortunate possessor of one of them would not part with it, unless under absolute necessity. One of them, when it could be purchased, would sell very readily for 200 dollars in gold, and was always good for that amount. A battalion of Texas Rangers (mounted) went into service with the army invading Mexico, and there were a number of them armed with Colt's revolver or 'five-shooters' of the old manufacture. In a very short time, the value of the weapon in a hand-to-hand fight with cavalry, was demonstrated very conclusively, to the satisfaction of the hitherto doubting officers of the United States regular army. A number of personal rencontres between Texan Rangers and Mexican Lancers occurred, in which the great superiority of the 'five-shooters' was demonstrated in such a manner, as to cause a cry for the resumption of the manufacture. As the arm was then almost exclusively in the hands of Texans, it obtained the cognomen of the 'Texas revolver;' other revolvers had been manufactured which were cheaper, and many of them were carried by officers of the army, as they had been previously in use by private persons, especially one which had six barrels and was self-cocking. This proved to be utterly worthless, and was called the 'pepper-box.' During the Mexican war, when the value of his revolver had been conclusively shown by actual use in the war, Colt resumed the manufacture of it, and it became plentiful at the reduced price of 40 dollars by the close of the war. He has since made a large fortune by manufacturing the pistol for the United States Government and for private sale. The size adopted for the cavalry service during the late war in the Confederate States was what is called 'the army pistol.' The United States cavalry was furnished with this, and most of the Confederate cavalry supplied itself with the same arm, mainly by capture from their opponents.

Some change was made in the outside appearance of the pistol, but no improvement has been made in the mechanism since the time the Texans showed its value, and all attempts at improvement have proved failures. A number of revolvers were introduced into the Confederate States during the war, from England as well as France, some of them very beautiful in their appearance and mechanism, but a little experience proved that ' Colt ' was superior to any of them, as well on account of its accuracy, range, and simplicity, as because of the ease with which it was kept serviceable. It did not get out of order as readily as the others, and when out of order it was much more readily repaired.

One reason assigned for the superior force of Colt's pistol as compared with others, was the fact that by having the cap on a tube immediately in rear of the chamber, when exploded, the flame from the cap was driven longitudinally through the powder, causing the instantaneous ignition of the whole charge. It certainly shot with much greater force than any other pistol, having the tube at the side of the lower extremity of the chamber.

I think Colt's pistol, with the tube and cap as at present, will always shoot stronger than any other pistol with the explosive cartridge introduced at the rear, for the reason that with the explosive cartridge there must be some loss of powder by the back action, and because the charge in the latter, as at present used, is not ignited as instantaneously as with Colt's pistol. In this there is no loss by back action, but on the contrary the force of the cock drives the flame from the cap forward and closes the slight interval between the chamber and the barrel.

The charge in the cartridge for this pistol ought to be covered with explosive paper, or material of some kind, so as to leave no fragments behind.

The difficulty about capping the pistol can be greatly lessened, by using a little instrument for capping similar to that used with fowling-pieces, which will render the process a very rapid one, without removing the breach, and by simply turning the chambers at a half-cock. Loading also without taking off the barrel is very easy and rapid when proper cartridges are used.

LONDON: PRINTED BY
SPOTTISWOODE AND CO., NEW-STREET SQUARE
AND PARLIAMENT STREET

THOMAS BOSWORTH'S

RECENT PUBLICATIONS.

CAVALRY: its History and Tactics. By the late Captain
L. E. Nolan, 15th Hussars. Third Edition, post 8vo. half-bound,
with coloured Illustrations, 9s.; or by post, 9s. 6d.

'A well-written and well-digested book, full of interesting facts and valuable
suggestions.'—DAILY NEWS.
'The most masterly and the most attractive book which has been written on
Cavalry. It is an important contribution to military science.'—MORNING POST.
'We know no book—we believe there is none—which will adequately supply the
place of this. To those belonging to this arm of the service, Captain Nolan's book
is indispensable; to members of all arms it may be useful; while, from the rich fund
of interesting anecdote with which it abounds, it will attract and delight the general reader.'—INDIAN MAIL.

THE MUTINY of the BENGAL ARMY: an Historical
Narrative. By ONE WHO HAS SERVED UNDER SIR CHARLES NAPIER.
Seventh Edition, 1 vol. 8vo. cloth, 4s. 6d.; or by post, 4s. 11d.

'A very spirited and instructive sketch of the revolt, which we hope to see completed. It is written by one who knows India well.'—ATHENÆUM.

THE ART of EXTEMPORE SPEAKING: Hints for the
Pulpit, the Senate, and the Bar. By M. BAUTAIN, Vicar-General,
and Professor at the SORBONNE. Fourth Edition, fcp. 8vo. cloth,
3s. 6d.; or by post, 3s. 10d.

'A book of suggestions for men who would practise extempore speaking. . . . .
Eloquent, forcible, full of apposite illustrations.'—ATHENÆUM.
'Written by one who has thoughtfully depicted a large personal experience. We
cordially recommend this unpretending but valuable volume, and press both the
book and the subject on the attention of our readers, as worthy of their most careful
consideration.'—RECORD.

THE OLIVE LEAF: a Pilgrimage to Rome, Jerusalem, and Constantinople in 1867, for the Reunion of the Faithful. By WILLIAM WYNDHAM MALET, Vicar of Ardeley. Crown 8vo. cloth gilt, 6s. nett; or post free, 6s. 6d.

'One of the most singular volumes we have ever come across.'—SATURDAY REVIEW.
'We cordially commend Mr. Malet's interesting volume to our readers.'—CHURCH TIMES.
'There is a freshness about Mr. Malet's descriptions which gives much life to his narrative. He has an eye for the beauties of nature, and without pretence to fine writing he gives graphic sketches which will interest those to whom the special objects for which he undertook his Pilgrimage may not altogether approve themselves.'—CHURCH NEWS.

BOOKS of ACROSTICS.

1. ACROSTICS in PROSE and VERSE. Edited by A. E. H. 18mo. cloth, gilt edges, 2s.; or by post, 2s. 2d.

2. A KEY to the above. 1s.; or by post, 1s. 1d.

3. A SECOND SERIES of ACROSTICS in PROSE and VERSE. Edited by A. E. H. 18mo. cloth, gilt edges, 2s. 6d.; or by post, 2s. 8d.

4. A THIRD SERIES of ACROSTICS in PROSE and VERSE. Edited by A. E. H. 18mo. cloth, gilt edges, 2s. 6d.; or by post, 2s. 8d.

5. EASY DOUBLE ACROSTICS. Edited by A. H. 18mo. cloth, 1s. 6d.; or by post, 1s. 7d.

6. HISTORICAL ACROSTICS. Edited by M. L. B. 18mo. cloth, 1s.; or by post, 1s. 1d.

7. SCRIPTURE ACROSTICS. Edited by A. H. 18mo. cloth, gilt edges, 1s.; or by post, 1s. 2d.

'The passion for Acrostics is not likely to die out for want of gratification. Those who do not find six days in the week sufficient to devote to this engaging work may satisfy at once their taste and their consciences by taking on Sundays to the Scripture Acrostics, edited by A. H.'—GUARDIAN.

THE REVIVAL of the FRENCH EMPERORSHIP ANTICIPATED from the NECESSITY of PROPHECY. By the late Rev. G. S. FABER, B.D. Sixth Edition, fcp. 8vo. 1s.; or by post, 1s. 1d.

'We recommend this book to the attention of our readers. It is candid and ingenuous.'—CHRISTIAN OBSERVER.

ORGAN HARMONIES for the GREGORIAN PSALM
TONES, giving Eight Varied Harmonies to each Tone and End-
ing. By ARTHUR H. BROWN. Royal 8vo. sewed, 3s. 6d. post free.
' Almost a dictionary of Gregorian Accompaniment.'—CHURCH CHOIRMASTER AND
ORGANIST.

CARMEN RUSTICANUM : an Essay on the Condition of
the Peasantry, considered in connection with—Memory as the
Mould of Character; Hope as the Companion of Improvement;
and Self-Love as the Mainspring of Human Exertion; with Inci-
dental Reflections. By ARISTYLLUS HAZEL. Fcp. 8vo. cloth, 3s. 6d.;
or by post, 3s. 8d.

THE EVANGEL of JESUS ACCORDING to JOHN: a
Literal Rhythmic Version from the most Ancient Texts. By C.D.
BRERETON, Rector of Framingham Earl and Bixley, Norfolk.
Small 4to. cloth, 3s.; or by post, 3s. 4d.

Also, by the same Author,

VERSES and LECTURES. Second Edition, enlarged.
Crown 8vo. cloth, gilt edges, 7s. 6d.; or by post, 8s.

SPEECHES in PARLIAMENT and MISCELLANEOUS
WRITINGS of the late HENRY DRUMMOND, Esq., M.P.
Edited by LORD LOVAINE, M.P. 2 vols. 8vo. cloth, 12s.; or by
post, 13s. 2d.

' The speeches, dating from Mr. Drummond's return to Parliamentary life in
1847, are brilliant, original, and entirely unaffected by ordinary prejudices and
conventionalities. In many instances they must have been beside the purpose of
the debate; but they contain more striking aphorisms, more pregnant epigrams,
more pointed statements of abstract truth, than the collective eloquence of a dozen
ministers and leaders of opposition. It might be expected that so acute and original
a mind would provide for itself a suitable mode of expression; and Mr. Drummond's
language is remarkable for its idiomatic felicity and force.'—SATURDAY REVIEW.

LECTURES, chiefly on Subjects relating to the Use and
Management of Literary and Scientific and Mechanics' Institutes.
By H. WHITEHEAD, M.A., Curate of Clapham; T. C. WHITEHEAD,
M.A., Incumbent of Gawcott, Bucks; and W. DRIVER. Fcp. 8vo.
cloth, price 3s.; or by post, 3s. 3d.

' A volume of sound and shrewd practical lectures containing the solid experience
as well as the acute thought of educated and practical men, chiefly on the management of book societies, literary institutions, and associations with kindred objects.'
NATIONAL REVIEW.

SOME MEMORIALS of RENÉE of FRANCE, DUCHESS
of FERRARA.   Second Edition, 1 vol. crown 8vo. cloth, with Portrait and Frontispiece, 5s.; or by post, 5s. 6d.

'The Author here submits to the public an interesting memoir of the Princess Renée, Duchess of Ferrara, and youngest daughter of Louis XII. of France. The work is admirably conceived and executed, at once securing the sympathies of the reader in behalf of this highly-gifted but strangely unfortunate scion of royalty. The reader will find much information and considerable amusement from the perusal of this well-digested and elegantly-written volume.'—LEADER.

'We cannot conclude this brief abstract of the leading events of her chequered life, without expressing our sense of the service which the author of the present memoir has rendered to the cause of religious biography.'—THE PRESS.

WHO'S WHO; or, The Three Brothers: a Tale for the
Day.   By W. P. MANN, Author of 'From the Cradle to the Grave,' &c.   Fcp. 8vo. cloth, 3s. 6d. nett; or by post, 3s. 9d.

HANDBOOK of the GEOGRAPHY and STATISTICS of
the CHURCH.   By J. E. T. WILTSCH.   Translated from the German by JOHN LEITCH.   With a Preface by the Rev. F. D. MAURICE, M.A.   2 vols. small 8vo. cloth, 18s.; or by post, 19s.

'Wiltsch's volume is one of vast research and industry. Without pretending to have read it through (which would be nearly as absurd as giving out that we had perused Forcellini's Latin or Dr. Johnson's English Lexicon), we have referred to it for explanation of several geographical and statistical difficulties, and we find it both ample and correct.'—CRITIC.

A HUNDRED SHORT TALES for CHILDREN.   From
the German of C. VON SCHMID.   By the Rev. F. B. WELLS, M.A., Rector of Woodchurch, Kent.   Third Edition, 18mo. cloth, 1s.; or by post, 1s. 2d.

'Incidents, accidents, natural phenomena, thrown into the form of little narratives designed to impress lessons upon children, at the same time that interest is excited by the tale.'—SPECTATOR.

'This is about as pretty a book, in whatever sense we may speak of it, as could be placed in the hands of children; and we highly recommend it to parents, teachers, and all who have the care of them, as being an excellent help in developing their moral character.'—LITERARY GAZETTE.

'A book with a hundred tales for little children, short, spirited, and pithy, about birds, beasts, fishes, fruits, vegetables, eatables, drinkables, jewels, clothes, watches, clocks, brothers, sisters, fathers, mothers, and every other imaginable noun-substantive, is too welcome a family guest not to be much in demand. Very justly, therefore, have Schmid's 'Tales for Children' reached a third edition. It is a common school-book in Bavaria, and English parents will be glad to know that it is worth getting.'—GUARDIAN.

THOMAS BOSWORTH, 215 Regent Street.

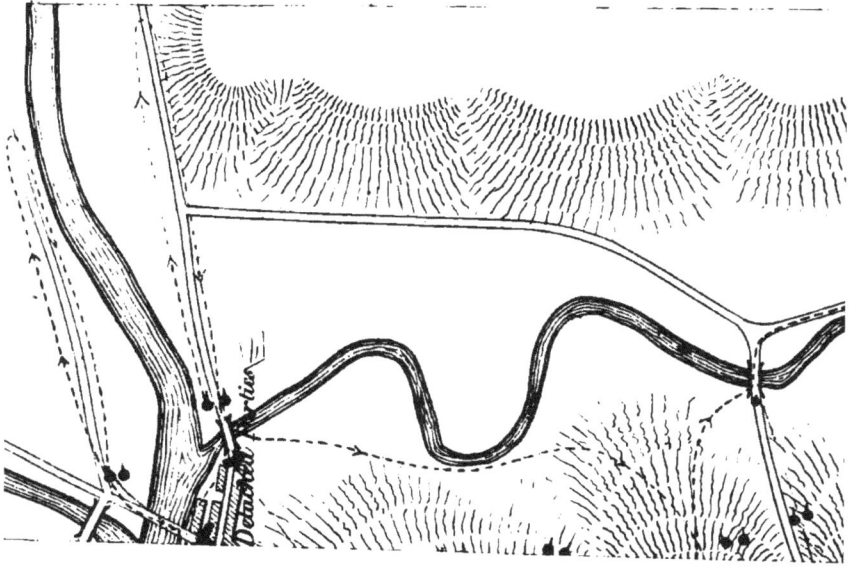

www.ingramcontent.com/pod-product-compliance
Lightning Source LLC
Chambersburg PA
CBHW032317280326
41932CB00009B/840